MIGRATING PHYSICIANS
DOCTORAS & DOCTORES
CON ALAS

MIGRATING PHYSICIANS DOCTORAS & DOCTORES CON ALAS

THE STORY OF 15 PHYSICIANS THAT MIGRATED

Book Coordinators:
Sandra Lopez-Leon MD PhD
Ilan Shapiro MD
Talia Wegman MD PhD
Preface: Dr. Julio Frenk MD PhD

Library of Congress Control Number: 2022902940
ISBN: Hardcover   978-1-5065-3985-0
                         Softcover   978-1-5065-3987-4
                         eBook   978-1-5065-3986-7

Print information available on the last page.

Rev. date: 03/11/2022

To order additional copies of this book, please contact:
Palibrio
1663 Liberty Drive
Suite 200
Bloomington, IN 47403
Toll Free from the U.S.A 877.407.5847
Toll Free from Mexico 01.800.288.2243
Toll Free from Spain 900.866.949
From other International locations +1.812.671.9757
Fax: 01.812.355.1576
orders@palibrio.com
838057

INDEX

INDEX BY AUTHORS

Preface

Julio Frenk[1]

The number of migrants in the world has grown dramatically in recent years. In 2000, there were 173 million migrants in the world. By 2017, the number had increased to 257 million. Migrants are persons who leave their country mostly in search of work and better living conditions, who are running away from political and military conflicts, or who are victims of disasters. There are also those who migrate for emotional reasons or are drawn to different professional environments because they find them more promising.

These factors have affected doctors as well. The number of emigrating doctors has grown significantly in recent decades. The countries with the most foreign physicians in the world are the United States, the United Kingdom, Germany, and Australia. In Australia they make up astonishing 32% of all the doctors in the country.

Until recently, the overwhelming majority of those physicians emigrated from India, China, Pakistan, the Philippines, and Iran, but the number

---

[1] Current President of the University of Miami and Minister of Health in Mexico (2000-2006)

of those coming from European and African countries has increased considerably.

Due to the recent increase in the migration of health workers, the World Health Organization and the Organization for Economic Cooperation and Development, among others, have carried out several studies on this topic. We now know not only how many doctors are migrating and the countries they are emigrating from and immigrating to, but also many of their demographic characteristics, the type of professional training they received, and the level of their integration in their adoptive countries. These studies indicate that emigrating physicians have contributed significantly to improving the scope and availability of health services in the countries to which they migrate and to meeting the growing demands for health care.

The personal stories of these doctors, however, are not so readily available. We know very little about the individual reasons that prompted them to leave their country, the specific obstacles they faced in the migration process, or the problems they had when adapting to a new society and a different work environment. We know even less about how they benefited from this change and which rewards they reaped from such enriching experiences. Since I am a migrant doctor as well, I am extremely interested in exploring these territories. I was born in Mexico City, where I also studied medicine; now I work at the University of Miami. I also come from a family of migrant doctors. My grandfather, a German physician, moved to Mexico with his wife and two children, fleeing Nazi persecution. My father, who was born in Hamburg, studied medicine at the *Universidad Nacional Autónoma de México* and practiced in his adoptive country as a pediatric endocrinologist all his life.

Doctores con Alas is meant to fill part of the void of personal stories about this fascinating subject. It tells the story of fifteen doctors, mostly

Mexican, who left their country for various reasons, to practice their profession in different corners of the world. Throughout this book, they all answer the same ten questions. I dare say, at the risk of being refuted by an anthropologist, that this is a genuine ethnographic study, since it allows us to examine the actions and interactions of a certain group through a series of questions that give rise to authentic interviews. *Migrating Physicians* also has the advantage that it is the doctors themselves who, plainly and openheartedly, narrate their migratory adventure.

It is also interesting to know the different ways in which these fifteen physicians faced similar situations: entering medical school; making the decision to emigrate, most of them to receive specialization or residency training; facing tedious and never-ending immigration and school revalidation procedures; adapting to a new culture; tackling the challenges of a competitive and sometimes aggressive work environment; and, finally, accepting the need to visit their country of origin to reconnect with family, old friends, and the landscapes, customs, and food of their youth. It's striking how much they all miss Mexican food!

This book covers a wide professional and geographic spectrum. There are surgeons, internists, psychiatrists, and medical researchers telling their stories. These fifteen doctors have also migrated to different countries and, therefore, have faced very different situations. While someone migrates to Ethiopia as a reconstructive surgeon and is received with open arms, another one enters a residency program in the United States where he suffers such mistreatment that he starts to second-guess his professional career and migratory choices.

Migrating Physicians can be of interest to people of all ages: from the children and grandchildren of doctors who came to Mexico from afar and helped build the main health care institutions in our country; to doctors in training, many of whom will study abroad and end up experiencing situations very similar to those described in this extraordinary text. These stories will also be extraordinarily useful for practicing doctors, who will be able to learn about the challenges of professional practice in other countries.

Perhaps the main message of these fifteen stories is that the challenges that migration brings —both personally and professionally— help us think outside the box and beyond conventional frameworks. And by operating outside of what's familiar to us, our self-confidence increases, our adaptability grows, and our perspectives widen in wonderfully unusual ways. Only then can we think of flying again, as these *Migrating Physicians* did in their adoptive countries.

Introduction

Interview with doctors Sandra López-León and Talia Wegman-Ostrosky, coordinators of the book

What is the book Migrating Physicians about?

Migrating Physicians is the autobiographical story of fifteen doctors, mostly Mexican, who emigrated to other countries. They write about their experiences in the United States, Europe, the Middle East, and Africa. The book addresses what it means to be a migrant and, more specifically, what it's like to migrate as a doctor.

How is the book structured?

Each chapter narrates a topic related to the life, experiences, and training of this group of physicians, and in each chapter, it's also possible to read about each of the physicians' experiences related to the same topic.

The book has two indexes; one general, which presents each of the topics addressed by the physicians, and another one that specifically refers to the authors, which indicates the pages where it's possible to find each doctor's contributions. The reader can follow the book by subject, country, or author.

This book was written during the COVID-19 pandemic. Do the physicians comment anything about it?

We present a whole chapter that explains how each doctor is experiencing the pandemic in their new country, away from family and friends.

Where did the idea for Migrating Physicians come from?

The idea arose in a social media group for Mexican physicians who are also mothers, who lived abroad and connected online. In 2019, we published the book *Doctoras con Alas. 26 Historias que abren horizonte* and, in 2021, *Doctores con alas. 12 Historias de médicos migrantes.* The books have been well received and we were invited to present them at embassies, consulates, universities, and various other forums.

We also opened the Facebook page *@Doctorasconalas*, where we continually post information about what it means to migrate, and where physicians can turn to, to find answers to their questions. *Doctor@s con alas* became a movement where every doctor who migrates becomes a doctor with wings.

In this new version, we decided to translate stories from both books into English. We want this movement to become global and intergenerational.

For whom is the book intended?

This book is very valuable for those who have already migrated, because they can identify with various aspects, which will help them grasp and make sense of certain things.

It's essential for those who plan to emigrate, because each doctor provides, in a practical way, an explanation of the procedures necessary to practice the profession and live in that country. The physicians also talk about their experience adapting to their new country and they paint a literary picture of what their new lives look like.

The book can be very interesting for anyone who wants to read something that broadens their horizons and allows them to see life from another perspective.

You mentioned that the **Doctor@s** *con* **alas** *movement is intergenerational. What do you mean by that?*

We're keeping in mind three generations of physicians who migrate: the past, the present, and the future. The first is made up of physicians who immigrated to Mexico two or three generations ago. They established the foundations of medicine in Mexico as we know them today, and created hospitals, medical centers, and charities. They were men and women who arrived without speaking the language, and who started with nothing. They revalidated their studies and did social service in the poorest regions of Mexico. Several of these physicians were our own relatives or friends, and essential in our training as physicians. We carry them in our hearts, and they serve as an example for us to follow.

We are also thinking of the future generations of physicians. Globalization and communication have made it possible for them to have the world at their fingertips. This book provides them with practical information and presents them with the challenges of migrating. The most important message we want to relay is that they are not alone. All generations are connected.

What is the difference between migrating as a doctor and migrating when practicing another profession?

The physicians who migrate have a vocation of service and commitment to humanity; they seek to avoid suffering, pain, and death. The physicians that migrate seek to help their new community, while still maintaining a bond with their country of origin. So, the physicians that migrate have a new and enriching vision of medicine; and while adapting, they also add a multicultural perspective to medicine.

Why emigrate?

There are thousands of reasons why people leave their countries of origin and there even is scientific evidence for a genetic predisposition, which is linked to the survival of the species. There's a gene, a dopamine receptor, that's associated with both migrating and seeking new experiences. All the physicians who emigrate encounter adventure, new experiences, and strong emotions, but the main reason we do so is because we seek a better life for ourselves and our families.

What do the physicians in this book have in common?

All the physicians in this book left their countries of origin in pursuit of the best places with opportunities for professional development; places that are also safer and more stable. They all emigrated by choice after having studied medicine and thought it would be easier than it actually ended up being. They all came to the conclusion that, despite the difficulties, emigrating was worth it.

Why wasn't it easy?

You will have to read the book to find the answer to that question.

However, some factors can be attributed to the Ulysses syndrome, or emigrant syndrome, since every migrant —in one way or another— goes through some of the dissociative or anxious processes associated with the syndrome. We as migrants part with our loved ones, mourn for every close person and memory we left behind, and experience profound hopelessness when things don't go as planned. We also suffer from fear of the unknown.

It's important to know that it's normal to go through a stage of denial, as well as to feel anger, anxiety, sadness, melancholy, and even symptoms of depression. Emigrating is not easy; it changes your life in a moment. These feelings can also return at any time in our lives. For example, when we visit our countries of origin, or when our loved ones fall ill or die.

It's also difficult because we arrive in a country where we're suddenly a nobody, we have no history, and we're right back to square one. Sometimes, we are not fully recognized as physicians and often, we don't even understand the language. Many of us experience an existential or identity crisis. We all stumble, we all question ourselves, we all despair; it is all completely normal.

What recommendations do you have to overcome those moments?

We recommend reaching out to other people who have already gone through the same situations or by reading about the experiences of those who emigrated in the same circumstances. But above all, we urge you to be aware of your feelings. Meditate on the reasons that led you to emigrate or the reasons why you want to do so. Make a list of pros and cons and sort out your priorities. If you identify them, you will fight for them. Keep in mind that choosing any one option means giving up another. One must know what one wants and what one is leaving behind.

In the most difficult moments, it's our duty to keep our inner fire burning bright, to remember the reasons why we studied medicine in the first place, and to fill ourselves with strength.

In circumstances like these, we question our vocation, priorities, and the reason for our existence. But remember, you're not alone. We've all been there. We want to remind you that "the one who succeeds once, has overcome a thousand failures."

To emigrate is to start again, change, transform, and reinvent oneself. Most of the people who have emigrated agree that from the day they left their countries, nothing was ever the same again. One changes profoundly but maintains one's identity. When emigrating, one is filled with enthusiasm, hope, and freedom. You feel like you can fly and make your dreams come true. To emigrate is to build a future without limits and brimming with opportunity. It helps us grow, learn about other cultures, and make friends who will become family.

We've been asked for advice time and again, and we agree that this is the most important: emigrate. Go live in another country, even if only for a few years. The experience is extremely enriching. It makes you grow in all imaginable aspects. It's difficult, but worth it. All these challenges strengthen us, help us value what we have, force us to re-evaluate our priorities, and make us question our purpose in life.

One day, we will realize that we are stronger, more patient, more human, that we are more resilient, and we feel fulfilled and satisfied with our lives. We start creating our new world from nothing. We begin to integrate, to free ourselves, and to create ourselves.

We hope you enjoy these fifteen stories, thank you for flying with us.

1

This is how my story begins

Patricia Bautista Rivera
(United States)

In a book about migrants, my story begins with a migrant. An internal migrant, who escaped poverty and physical abuse in search of a better future. She traded her hometown for a city with better opportunities, as many other migrants have done, not only in Mexico but around the world.

Her life wasn't easy, but she made it. She found a job and the love of her life. Unfortunately, he didn't feel the same way. Soon she became a mother. My mother. I was born in Mexico City, in a medical center she was immensely proud of, since the medical care she received when I was born was financed in part by her own work. She's an intelligent woman who's very aware that the only way to move forward and progress is through study and constant effort. Despite only barely knowing to read and write, she helped me learn those skills. She always encouraged me and my siblings (I have a younger sister and brother) to do our best, and frequently reminded us that going to school is a privilege, and knowledge is the key that opens doors to better opportunities.

I grew up under the wing of this hardworking woman, who through daily example taught us to earn an honest living. She's also proof that there are no barriers too high to overcome or too strong to break down; that, although the road might be challenging, she once told me, "If you fall down, you get up. If you fall down again, you get up again, and if you fall down again and you no longer have the strength to get on your feet, I will help you up." She also taught me to be generous because, although we had to tighten our belts from time to time because there wasn't food to spare, it was always possible to share what we had with someone in need. Her generosity fills my soul with gratitude. I don't know how many times during college she knocked on my door at three or four in the morning to tell me, "*Mi hijita*, you asked me to wake you up so that you could finish studying." I learned from her to always be grateful for each and every blessing I receive.

I grew up surrounded by a great number of people, the neighbors of the building in which I lived, who filled my days with incredible experiences (some great and some not so good), and who also allowed me to discover and work on developing empathy and a desire to be of service to others and to help anybody around me who needed it.

This wish to help others has prevailed throughout my life and so, when my mother suggested I study medicine, it led me to say yes. When I was a little girl, if someone asked, "What do you want to be when you grow up?", my response usually surprised them. Perhaps because, in an environment where most of the girls around me thought of being secretaries or housewives, it was odd that I wanted to be a plastic surgeon. I wanted to be a doctor.

Patricia Bautista Rivera (Continues on page 35)

Edmundo Erazo

(THE NETHERLANDS)

I'm Mexican; I was born in Chihuahua, an internist. I live in the Netherlands. The beginning of my history with medicine has three key moments: when I was fourteen years old, when I was a medical student and, finally, when I was doing my internal medicine residency in Mexico City.

My interest in medicine started at an early age. Since I was little, I remember that I wanted to be a doctor. At the age of fourteen, I was involved in a car accident in New Mexico, in the United States, and, therefore, I suffered a skull fracture and other serious injuries that forced me to stay in the hospital for three weeks. It was there that I had the first significant contact with my future profession. I experienced being a "patient" first-hand. I realized the importance that doctors, nurses, and the rest of the health personnel had in my care, improvement, and physical state and how they were relevant for my state of mind and general well-being. This left an imprint on me and inspired me to follow that path. It was there, in that hospital, that I concluded that I wanted to study medicine.

As I progressed and entered medical school, I realized, in addition to the interest that medical knowledge generated in me, that what I enjoyed the most was talking to people, listening to their stories, and accompanying them when they were at their most vulnerable.

During my internship and social service, I noticed that research was another area I also loved about medicine. That led me to do my social service in research at the Salvador Zubirán National Institute of Medical Sciences and Nutrition.

After finishing my internal medicine residency and living many experiences that shaped me, I decided that I wanted to live and study in another country. So, I looked for a program abroad and applied for a scholarship.

Edmundo Erazo (Continues on page 38)

Sandra López-León

(ISRAEL, THE NETHERLANDS, SPAIN, UNITED STATES)

I was born into a family that considered education and mental health a priority, as my mother had a Ph.D. in psychology and my father had studied medicine, psychiatry, and had a Ph.D. in bioethics. I grew up in a multicultural environment because I attended the American School in Mexico City (ASF), and my grandfather was very active in the Spanish community.

For as long as I can remember, I knew I wanted to study medicine, and from a very young age, I was also certain that I wanted to live in other countries. There is research that shows that people with the "novelty seeking" personality trait exhibit gene variants that increase their desire to emigrate. This resulted in human beings populating the world, thus allowing the survival of our species. There is also research that shows that studying medicine is hereditary. I am sure that I have both genetic predispositions: my grandfather emigrated by boat to Mexico from León, Spain, carrying only one suitcase. My father, who studied medicine in Mexico, went to Canada to do his medical internship and, after he got married, he went to the United States for his psychiatry residency. My two brothers emigrated as well and moved to the United States after having finished medical school.

4

The first time I moved to another country was during my medical internship. I went to Hadassah Hospital in Jerusalem. There I realized how much I loved research, and decided I wanted to do a Ph.D. I am very passionate about psychiatric genetics, as I have always been interested in the mind. In those days, the first sequencing of the human genome had just been published and, in a romantic and poetic way, I found it fascinating to be able to make the unconscious tangible. When I returned to Mexico to do the obligatory community service, I had the opportunity to work with Dr. Guido Belsasso in his psychiatric clinic, and to visit the Instituto Nacional de Psiquiatría Ramón de la Fuente Muñiz, where Dr. Humberto Nicolini had a psychiatric genetics laboratory. My time there only confirmed how much I loved this field. A year later, I graduated from medical school, married a Dutchman, and went to live in the Netherlands.

Sandra López-León (Continues on page 39)

Rafael G. Magaña
(ENGLAND, UNITED STATES)

I was born in Chihuahua, Mexico, a state I know very little since my father was a military doctor and frequently changed regiments. Since I can remember, we continually moved to different parts of the country.

In 1977, we travelled to London, where my father specialized in neurosurgery. We spent several years in England, where he was transferred frequently: from London to Stoke on Trent, from there to Wakefield, and then to Swansea, in Wales.

When my father finished his specialty, we returned to Mexico City. I was already a teenager, and it was especially difficult for me to adapt, due to the clash of cultures I experienced. Time passed, but I remember the influence that English culture had on me and how much I absorbed from the Mexican one.

Since I was little, I had a penchant for the arts. I was especially interested in cinema and special effects, and I wanted to dedicate myself to that field, although I also came to consider plastic surgery since several of my relatives are surgeons. An uncle of mine was a renowned plastic surgeon in Mexico and a very close family friend was as well. My family always thought that I had an aptitude for it, and they frequently reminded me of that. Later, in high school, I went from taking an interest in the specialty to seriously considering it as a career.

However, I always had a great passion for creating things with my hands. In high school, I began going to the department of maxillofacial prosthetics at UNAM and learned the basics of prosthesis manufacturing. I manufactured from acrylic eyes, to ears, noses, and dental prostheses, among other artificial pieces. This led me to pursue a career in Hollywood, where I took a special effects course at Joe Blasco's Make Up School in Los Angeles. My plan was to continue this passion and work on movies but, shortly after finishing the special effects course, I got into medical school, and decided to temporarily abandon the idea of making movies. And so, my academic path began.

Rafael G. Magaña (Continues on page 42)

Nissin Nahmias

(UNITED STATES)

I was born on May 28th, 1974, in Mexico City, a place whose mere mention fills me with emotion. Mexico is a wonderful country where anyone's dreams can come true and where a person of humble origin can become the best version of themselves if they set their minds to it.

Thanks to the immense diversity of landscapes, cultures, gastronomies, and identities, growing up in Mexico shapes you forever.

I'm the eldest of Alberto and Anita's two children. My parents are wonderful beings of impeccable values, endowed with unparallel people skills, and generous by nature. They gave me all their love, supported me, and raised me with principles, morals, affection, and religion. Thanks to them, I managed to forge an identity and become the person I am today.

I'm incredibly thankful for them, not only for having brought me into the world, but for teaching me everything, from learning how to walk and eat, to showing me how to love and improve myself, how to be insightful, set goals and never leave them unfinished, to always see them through.

I come from an upper-middle-class family that had their home in Las Alteñas, in Lomas Verdes, municipality of Naucalpán, in the State of Mexico.

I'll never forget the beautiful childhood I spent in the neighborhood gardens, alongside my dear friends, nor the old days, when I attended the Thomas Jefferson school, finished primary education, and met many classmates and friends, some of whom I still have contact with.

Growing up in Mexico was incredible. My parents made sure I had a very happy childhood. They took me fishing, swimming, and hiking, and they were part of the Bosque de Echegaray Lions Club, so they taught me to be altruistic.

My dad presided said organization and, under his direction, multiple fundraising events were held. I remember that, on one occasion, we sold tickets to a bullfight with the purpose of raising funds to change the mattresses in a nursing home. The people who lived there had no resources and their relatives had already forgotten about most of them.

When my dad found out about this situation, he took on the task of changing the mattresses, and also organized several parties to cheer up the people in the nursing home. He taught us that one should always give the best of oneself and that, whenever you set your mind to something, you'll achieve your goal with God's help.

My parents worked in the trading business, as did my grandparents, who had a jewelry store in downtown Mexico City. Sometimes, when I close my eyes, I can still listen to its sounds, its street vendors, its trucks, and the noise of people hurrying down the avenues. Whenever I picture that in my mind, I smile and thank God for the opportunities he's given me.

I remember that, on weekends, my brother and I would go to work with my parents: we cleaned the shelves and cabinets, we mopped the floors, we learned to engrave rings and medals and sold them to earn a little money. Sometimes, my brother and I took over our parents' work on the weekends, so that they could have a well-deserved rest.

However, my father always told us to study, because "one person slaving away is enough in this family"; he worked from Monday to Monday, and he wanted us to work from Monday to Friday, as those with a career and a profession did.

I attended junior high and high school at the Colegio Hebreo Sefaradí A.C. However, I wanted to follow in my father's altruistic footsteps, and, when I was around 17, I decided to join the Mexican Red Cross as a paramedic. To be part of that institution, you have to invest time and money, since you must buy your own uniform and medical supplies.

I remember the training and the shifts. We had to be there at seven in the morning, perfectly uniformed and, on vacation, we used to spend two to three weeks on the road, treating traffic accident victims, with the sole purpose of saving human lives.

It was thanks to that experience that, years later, I decided to become a doctor. Back then, my family's friends begged me to give up that idea and to work in the trading business instead. They said becoming a doctor is very difficult at the beginning: you must study countless hours and have no additional source of income. What's more, what you earn is not proportional to the hours you put in. It's not until years later, once you've already acquired prestige and made a name for yourself, that you can reap the rewards of your efforts. These friends would tell me I'd be better off helping my parents get ahead. I didn't listen to them and decided that I would at least try and see how far I could go, because I was convinced there was a better version of me capable of saving human lives.

I must say that, before studying at the Universidad Anáhuac, I tried applying for public university on several occasions, but the UNAM admissions system does not allow students from private schools to enter easily, so I was rejected.

The two years of private classes I took in order to prepare went out the window. Despite having all the knowledge to pass the admission exam, the system never allowed me to enter said university.

Finally, with the support of my parents, I enrolled in medical school at the Universidad Anáhuac del Norte. That was certainly one of the best moments of my life. That first year, I enjoyed every day to the fullest. However, it was also around that time that my parents lost all their estate.

We went through a rough patch, the kind that builds character and toughens you up. We went from being used to having everything, to experiencing economic deprivation. At home, however, we had love to spare, and my family's support helped me not to give up on my dream. My brother was also always there for me in all the ways he could; his affection and friendship are one of my greatest treasures, and I'm lucky to have such a wonderful person to turn to.

I also remember that my uncle Benjamin was a great source of strength to me, and to this day I appreciate his words of encouragement and advice. He's a gynecologist and gave me a job as his assistant. I had no experience whatsoever, but he patiently taught me everything. He was an excellent teacher and I think it's thanks to him that I'm a good teacher as well.

Thanks to the help of God and to my efforts —I got really good grades in my first year— the university gave me a scholarship that allowed me to finish my degree without being too much of a financial burden for my parents. Since the scholarship didn't include re-enrollment, my parents went to great lengths to pay for it and keep me in med school.

I went to the university on countless occasions with only a piece of fruit, a subway ticket, and 20 pesos in my pockets. I remember that many of my colleagues helped me in many ways: they'd give me rides, invite me over for lunch... in brief, they showed me their friendship in a myriad of forms, and, for that, I'll be eternally grateful.

During my time in medical school, I had the opportunity to leave the country to take part of an undergraduate internship. I was selected to go to Miami, and I had to find the resources to leave for six months. In Miami, I lived with some cousins, bought a second-hand car, and did everything necessary to get ahead.

I also met people from all over the world who broadened my horizons. I was very impressed with the way they worked, particularly the surgeons, and, since I loved the idea of living in the United States, I returned to Mexico determined to do my residency there.

I graduated with honors in a ceremony that was filled with absolute happiness and joy, both for me and for my family. My parents were immensely proud I had finished my degree, and I was grateful for everything they had done to get me there. In a few years, I went from being a street vendor in downtown Mexico City to being a doctor with dreams and aspirations.

Nissin Nahmias (Continues on page 46)

Susana Ramírez Romero
(SPAIN)

My name is Susana. I'm Mexican and the mother of two wonderful children, and I am a dermatologist. I was born in the city of Puebla, and I was the first granddaughter to both families, the oldest of four children and the only girl. I was the spoiled one but also the one to set an example for my siblings and over 25 cousins.

I ran away from home when I was three years old in an act of rebellion and, although I think of myself as shy, I've always had the courage to follow my dreams.

When I think of my ancestors, I come to the conclusion that I'm probably a carrier of the genetic variant associated to novelty seeking and therefore migration that Dr. Sandra LL mentions. My maternal great-grandfather traveled from Germany to Mexico in the 1920s and, although my grandmother did not emigrate to any country, because at the time it

11

was unthinkable, she always emphasized that her greatest dream was to go backpacking around the world. She did it her own way: she was an alpinist, conquered several hilltops and visited many countries.

Perhaps that's why, since I was a teenager, I dreamed of traveling to different countries as a missionary. In fact, one of the reasons why I studied medicine was because I wanted to go to Africa; I thought that, as a physician, my presence there could be much more useful. While I was preparing to become a doctor, I started visiting some indigenous communities in Mexico; sometimes educating children on health issues and, later, trying to solve medical problems in distant villages, where rarely any doctor arrived.

I've been passionate about medicine ever since I was a little kid. I remember that I used to take my dolls to the operating room to perform surgeries on them if they ripped or became unsewn. That drive led me to study a specialty in pediatrics, then a specialty in dermatology and later a master's degree in Clinical Research. Without realizing it and because I only had eyes for my studies, I got a little off the missionary path, especially when I married and got pregnant. However, wherever I am, I always enjoy the privilege of being able to help others through the knowledge I've acquired.

Susana Ramírez Romero (Continues on page 50)

Luis Rodrigo Reynoso
(ETHIOPIA)

I have wanted to sit down and write about my life for years, but I just had not given myself that opportunity and today, the universe and circumstances - the result of an unknown and feared virus allow me to do so. Thank you for this magnificent cathartical experience.

My story began 38 trips around the sun ago; I was born in a city called Aguascalientes, 1,845 meters above sea level. I am the second of the offspring of the renowned lawyer Don Pancho Pistolas and the much-loved Doña Emita Copetes. Like many of my medical colleagues, I inherited the profession in the genes and in particular from my paternal grandfather, who, running away from the Cristero War, decided to settle in the state capital Aguascalientes, where he passionately carried out his profession as an "old school" general surgeon, one of those who, by necessity and dedication, would go into any anatomical cavity without fear.

He never got to know that his genes make my skin shiver with excitement every time I use the scalpel to transform a body, as he died of complications after being run over when I was just ten years old. Sometime after, when my grandmother was on her deathbed, I could not help but send him a message; I looked into my grandmother's peaceful brown eyes and said, "Please, Grandma, when you see my grandfather tell him I am staying here to continuing his legacy. I do not know what the hell was going through my mind; I was supposed to give her some words of encouragement, but I swear I could feel that this was going to be the last time we would see each other.

And then, I did my studies in general medicine among three stiff corpses. Panchito was our favorite. If Panchito could speak, he would tell you about the chips and candies that we as students smuggled into the amphitheatre to cope with the long hours of anatomical study, regardless of the intense smell of formaldehyde. He would tell you about the time when we examined the cavities of an amputated female pelvis, driven by curiosity and by, the desire to explore; and he would tell you about the nervous laughter that we exploded into at the surrealism of what we were experiencing.

Studying came easy to me – I mean, without having to much effort into it, I always stood out in my class – so I framed the acceptance letter I received from the Benemérita Universidad Autónoma de Aguascalientes. It was to my great surprise when I received my first partial anatomy exam's results: I had barely managed to pass! I had only seen that grade on other people's academic records.

It took me a bit to understand that I had to put in triple the effort if I really wanted to continue in that career. I had to juggle my hyperactivity with my passion and with the effort it takes to be a doctor; I finished my general practitioner degree and then continued with a bigger obstacle called the National Exam for Medical Residency Applicants (at that time, it was said that among 45,000 applicants, only one in ten managed to pass).

So, I finally migrated to the capital of roast beef or so-called *carne asada*. The North of Mexico gave me the most sobering, humbling, and impressive experiences of my life, and I was able to successfully complete my specialty in general surgery and laparoscopy.

I must admit that I miss the adrenaline, the blue codes, the patients arriving by helicopter, their hearts beating in my hands, the surgeries in which I ended up drenched in blood, and the smell that lingered in my nose for days.

But I must also be grateful that I did not have to see so much suffering, because I saw plenty of it! Drug shortages, late diagnoses, cancer, car accidents, lawsuits, and worst of all, bureaucracy!

At that time, I ended up disagreeing with the entire health system. I bribed the hospital staff with tacos and cakes, so the patients were transferred to us to the OR.

At that time, we survived a hurricane; my caffeine addiction began, I tried "special brownies", and I gave my heart away countless times and made great and dear friends.

During the second half of my major, I came across what has been the most terrifying experience of my life so far: a home invasion and an assault that lasted an hour and a half but felt like an eternity.

In those moments I feared for my life, they immobilized me physically and mentally. I hid my fear, negotiated like in the movies and finally came out well off; either way, this was a traumatic experience for me. As I write this, I feel like I am healing a little more.

That was a turning point for me, and it changed my outlook on life. I believed that there could be nothing worse, but this was just beginning. Sometime later, I would have to diagnose my best friend with lung cancer. After a thoracoscopy, I had to explain in detail the possible surgical scenarios, the alternatives. Then, I disguised the discouraging prognoses for him: his lungs seemed to be covered by a coral texture. But I made him see that the three months of life expectancy that the medical literature indicated, did not have to be true. So, it was! Life gave us many more months, so many that I have already lost count, and I treasure every bitter moment that we lived together. Every lesson I learned came accompanied by a big shake, by tears, laughter, and dark humour. After all those tears, I always saw a little more light.

I finished the first specialty and received the best professional praise from one of the strictest teachers. A couple of days before my departure he told me:" So, are you going to continue with plastic surgery? What a waste of a general surgeon and laparoscopist!"

As if I were playing the board game "Touristo", I continued my journey in my own country; I went to the Bajío, to Guadalajara, to the city of the mariachi, the "drowned tortas" and the most beautiful eyes that I had ever known. It was there, while celebrating my admission to one of the reconstructive and aesthetic plastic surgery institutes in the country, that I met the woman who, until now, has accompanied me in each of my adventures, always so loyal and passionate. Her name is Anahí, – a Guaraní warrior and witch; she possesses a unique and unmatchable beauty. First, we thought about each other often, and communicated by telepathy, then through texts on social media, and now, every step we take, we take it together. Thus, since the beginning of my training as a Reconstructive and Aesthetic Plastic Surgeon, we have accompanied each other, feeding, encouraging, and comforting each other. With her communication skills, emotional intelligence, and love, she manages to counterbalance my impulses. But do not think for a moment she's so sane, some of you have already made your guesses: "What the heck is she doing by my side?" Exactly ... She is always seeking to heal something, and I thank her infinitely for that...

During the last semester of the subspecialty, I attended an international congress focused on cleft lip and palate. I was ecstatic listening to stories of war heroes with post-traumatic syndromes and learning about inspirational organizations and individuals when suddenly four slender African men (that is, as I, they were under 1.70 meters) and with thin complexion (similar as me, since they did not reach 60 kilos) began to speak.

> *"Hello, we are from Ethiopia. The Operation Smile program has just been in our country to carry out the first cleft lip and palate surgical campaign and we are deeply grateful. We do not have plastic surgeons and now they have taught us a little about the management of these patients. Thanks for everything".*

-"We don't have plastic surgeons!"

Luis Rodrigo Reynoso (Continues on page 52)

Alejandra Rodríguez Romero
(UNITED STATES)

I was born on May 11, 1984, in Hermosillo, Sonora. I'm the proud daughter of Dr. Marco Rodríguez Zamudio and Dr. Elvira Romero Borja. I attended elementary school, middle school, and high school in the same institution, where I was lucky to make wonderful friends that, after 31 years, are still part of my life. During my school years, I remember getting annoyed with my parents sometimes because, when I got sick, I was not allowed to miss school as my classmates did; they would give me a painkiller, or some other medication depending on the situation, and send me off to class. After years of listening to my parents talk about medications, when my friends got sick, I would tell them what they had to take to get better and I sort of became their family doctor (even though they would end up asking my mom or their doctor). I remember listening to my parents talk about their interesting medical cases during the meals as if it were yesterday. I don't know if at some point when I was very young, I found them weird or boring, I just remember enjoying the conversations.

Over the years, I had the opportunity to attend many of my parents' medical consultations. All these interactions, along with the medical environment at home, caused a true interest and an unparalleled love for medicine to grow in me. The passion and dedication with which they treated their patients made me the doctor and person I am today. Knowing exactly what I wanted to do with my professional life, I applied to medical school at the Autonomous University of Guadalajara in 2002. In August of the same year, I packed my bags and started a new stage of my life away from home. I finished my four years of medical school in Guadalajara and began my internship in my hometown, at the General Hospital of the state of Sonora. Nothing in this life had prepared me for that year. I have no words, only feelings to describe it and, to be honest, sometimes when I remember it, it feels like it was just a dream. My mom still recalls that, some nights when I got home from my 36-hour shifts, I would fall asleep over the food she had kindly served me.

It was an intense period of learning, sleepless nights, though times, endless shifts, and the constant thought of whether medicine was really for me. And as the Mexican saying goes, nothing lasts 100 years and, luckily, this only lasted 12 months. Immediately after my internship, I started my social service in Matape, Sonora, a community about an hour away from Hermosillo, with approximately 650 inhabitants. It was a breath of fresh air in every single way. I very much enjoyed giving consultations to the population, implementing fumigation, vaccination, family planning, and obesity campaigns, among many others. This stage also lasted only 12 months, but as opposed to the internship, I wish it would've lasted more so I could contribute to that community a bit longer. The next thing on the list was to enter the medical residency; but, by that time, I was already engaged to my American boyfriend, and we had already started the paperwork so I could move to the United States. I want to mention that, in my plans prior to meeting him, there was never any desire to emigrate. I honestly saw myself working for the same institution where my parents worked until I retired, just as they did. Had I known that that was not the path my life was going to take, my story would've been very different.

Alejandra Rodríguez Romero (Continues on page 57)

Jack Rubinstein

(UNITED STATES)

> "I must study politics and war, that our sons may have liberty to study
> mathematics and philosophy... in order to give their children a right to study
> painting, poetry, music, architecture, statuary, tapestry and porcelain."
> —John Adams

My story begins with my name and the unpronounceable Anglo-Saxon "j", which in Spanish is pronounced like a harsh "h", leading to a lifetime of being called either a "hack" or a "yak", but rarely by my given name. Coupled with my foreign surname, I think I was destined to grow wings and fly from my homeland. I grew up in Mexico City when it was still considered a Federal District. I'm the grandson of immigrants who fled persecution in Europe, and the son of the first generation of Jewish Mexicans who settled down in the city center. Upon arrival in Mexico my family and my community got their act together pretty quickly and by the mid-20th century, they already had businesses, associations, and synagogues that mirrored their different origins and philosophies.

The Mexican-Jewish community was noted for its resilience and organization, and soon became the envy of other Jewish communities around the world. For nearly a century, it has managed to maintain international sports associations, community services —which offer from food distribution and medical services to funeral services— and high-level schools that have produced world-renowned politicians, doctors, and journalists. However, this protection provided by the community —necessary given the hardships that other Jewish communities have endured in exile— led to a certain degree of estrangement between it and the rest of the country.

I grew up in this environment, supported in every way by my family and the community, which at the same time limited my interactions with the outside world. This changed when I entered medical school, where my personal and intellectual horizons were opened and, to a certain degree, overflowed. Having first-hand knowledge of the great contradictions between excessive wealth and extreme poverty made me open my eyes to the serious difficulties that my country has experienced and continues to face. Filled with the idealism that characterizes youth, I considered that these problems had a solution. I even considered that some of them could even be easily solved but, as we will see in the next chapters, reality quickly outweighed my idealism.

Going back to the beginning of my history in Mexico and my development as a doctor, the quote that John Adams wrote more than 200 years ago is highly relevant. My grandfather fought in World War II so that my father could make his business prosper. Their efforts gave me the chance to study what I wanted and go to university. I was always fascinated by mathematics, science and philosophy, and their application in medicine was an irresistible combination for me. I was initially interested in pediatrics because my dad's best friend was a respected pediatrician, but this idea changed radically long before I was faced with my first dirty diaper or the call from a nervous mom at three in the morning. I remember the day I fell in love with cardiology in greater detail than the day I met my wife. The last rays of the sun still left enough light to illuminate the room; I was sitting by the window, and I felt their warmth on my right arm. My physiology teacher —whom I still consider my mentor today— gave us an EKG to study. It was no more than a photocopy of a patient with sinus bradycardia, boring and benign by all measures, but for me it was an invitation to spend the rest of my life exploring science, mathematics, and philosophy through the most fascinating organ of the body.

Jack Rubinstein (Continues on page 58)

Alberto Saltiel

(Israel)

Everybody has a story, and this is how mine begins. I was born in Mexico City on March 17th, 1986, into an upper-middle-class Jewish family. I'm the younger of two siblings. My parents, both born in Mexico, are the children of immigrants, also called second-generation Mexicans. On my father's side, my grandfather Alberto (RIP) was born in Mexico City, but his parents came from Thessaloniki (Greece), and Izmir (Turkey). My grandmother Thelma was born in the United States; her parents had emigrated from Russia to Philadelphia, Pennsylvania. As for my mother's side, my grandfather Moisés (RIP) emigrated from Kiev, Ukraine, to Mexico City at the age of four; and my grandmother Flora was born in Tampico, Tamaulipas, to Russian parents.

I studied at the American School in Mexico City from kindergarten through high school. During those years, I participated in multiple extracurricular activities such as baseball, soccer, capoeira, boxing, swimming, and American football, among others. In addition, I was a member of the Jewish Scouts of Mexico for approximately 16 years, where I reached the highest management level of the organization. I was a directive member of Gamp Coaj (a pre-hospital medical Jewish support group), as well as a volunteer of the group of paramedics of the municipality of Huixquilucán, in Mexico.

As a child, and to date, I've always been a very curious, restless person, constantly wanting to know more. That restlessness, which I now see as a virtue, was misunderstood for many years, and entailed consequences that, for the most part, weren't positive. When I was just a boy, I was diagnosed with attention deficit disorder; that label has accompanied me throughout my life and because of it, many people have tried to set limits on what I could achieve.

I remember very well the day I decided I wanted to be a doctor. People say that studying medicine is, in the end, a matter of vocation or calling. Well, for me, that vocation began at the age of seven, in the first grade, and I never strayed from its path. I remember sitting in science class, skimming through a book that explained, in a kid-friendly language and with many diagrams, how the heart worked. Suddenly, I turned to my team partner and said, "I'm going to be a heart doctor!", to which he replied, "And I will be your partner." From that moment, my life followed that dream, which allowed me to get to where I am now. Little did I know how difficult this path would be, but I was convinced that I would make it. As an ADD child, I always felt questioned. So much so that, when I was in my final year of high school, my tutor did not allow me to attend the college fair with the argument that I could never get into university, much less become a doctor. However, that didn't stop me. On the contrary, it strengthened me. For years, my only goal was not to get the degree, but to show the world that had had such little faith in me, that I could do it.

And so, I started to reach my goal. I studied medicine at the Anáhuac University in Mexico City. I did the rotational undergraduate internship in Mexico and in Israel, my social service in research at the Anáhuac Public Health Institute and, in 2011, I got my medical degree. During the first years of training, I still wanted to be a cardiologist but, as I continued through my studies and learned about different disciplines, I fell in love with surgery and, in particular, with vascular surgery. In 2013, I decided to move to Israel to do a specialization and, thus, start a new chapter in my story.

Alberto Saltiel (Continues on page 61)

Luana Sandoval Castillo
(SPAIN, DENMARK)

Just like Juana, but with an L: Luana. My father boasted of his popularity among the girls and, because his name is Luis Antonio, some called him Luis, and some called him Toño. My mom put an end to that and decided that it was neither Luis nor Toño, it would be Luan and, when I was born, I was named Luana which, according to my dad means "love star", an unverified yet conveniently credible fact, in my opinion.

My father grew up in the north of what's currently known as Mexico City. He was the son of a mother who became an orphan at a very young age. My grandmother cooked and cleaned for some Mexican-Jewish family and, after getting married, she became a housewife, making the most out of her cooking skills. My grandfather, originally a bricklayer, became a policeman as the years went by and, wanting to improve his status, he was promoted to the rank of Major. He was present in the Mexican Movement of 1968 in Tlatelolco, around the same time that his children, strangely and at his father's request, were detained in Autlán. My father, the second son in his family who, at the time, was considered abnormal for being left-handed and forced to write as right-handed, developed ambidextrous abilities ranging from cognitive mathematics to musical skills. he was a man drawn to freedom and as he was touring his Mexico lindo while working as an accountant, he ended up living in a hotel (hotel California) in Oaxaca in the late 1970s.

My mother was a woman from a town of less than 800 inhabitants, where one third of them were probably my family and another third, family's family. She was the proud daughter of *Don* Silvio and *Doña* Con. *Don* Silvio was the son of both the Revolution and a single mother, and became a farmer, merchant and even town judge. *Doña*

Con, on the other hand, did everything pretty young: she got married, had 14 children, and died at 53 from cervical cancer. My mother, third child and first-born girl, had to pave the way for those who came after her, which led her to pursue her studies and move from Labor Vieja to Morelia and finally end up in what used to be known as the Federal District. Worker, entrepreneur, and head nurse, she was involved in teaching from early stimulation and pediatric–psychiatric nursing to drug addiction prevention at the Juvenile Integration Center. As I write this, I remember her coming home with her uniform impregnated by a mix of cigarettes and psychotropic drugs. She finally landed in Oaxaca at the end of the seventies to do her teaching internship and help renew the old syllabus that was lost in a fire, for which she had to live in the same hotel my father was staying at.

For as long as I can remember, my mother says that, when I was a child, she explained to me how the heart worked and, as soon as I got the chance, I gave my first lecture on the subject to a cab driver who turned to my mother with awe, saying that I should study medicine. Well, he would be right. Although my mother tried her best to convince me that it would not be a career for me because it was too long and challenging, too demanding and because I'd be a woman in a man's world, the effect was the exact opposite. I think it was exactly each of the things she said combined with an intangible "you can't!", what strengthened my decision to study medicine. A confrontation with the exquisite and bureaucratic healthcare system after a sprained ankle in a basketball game also played a huge role. Sadly, it made me see that, in my Mexico, what matters are your contacts and friends in the hospital or how much you're able to pay, rather than the seriousness of a diagnosis. However, thanks to each of those things, today I am where I want to be.

Luana Sandoval Castillo (Continues on page 63)

Ilan Shapiro

(UNITED STATES)

Stemming from different parts of the world, a combination of carpenters, butchers and tailors came together in Veracruz, Pachuca, and Mexico City. They moved to a country full of magic and new, exotic flavors, very different from those they knew.

Because they had diverse backgrounds and spoke different languages, Mexico unified them. This first generation, generation zero, came from humid, dark, and snowy places, so finding a warm place —which welcomed them with open arms— represented a break, a relief and, for the first time in years, a chance to be reborn. Many of their relatives had been killed during World War II, and others had moved to other parts of the world, such as Canada and the United States, driven by the same desire to find somewhere with brand new opportunities to start over.

Most of my grandparents were born in Mexico. Among them, they spoke Russian, Polish, Yiddish, and Spanish. The cultural differences slowly disappeared, but their stories have made me ask myself many times if I'd had the same strength to emigrate to a completely different continent without understanding the culture of the place that today I call home.

That led, in the 80s in Mexico City, to a desperate but expected cry that was heard after more than 40 weeks of production and a dozen hours. I went from a place where I was provided with food, warmth, and sustenance to a place with lots of light, sounds and sensations that I had never experienced before. Like me, the following generations fused languages, flavors and aromas with identities that added spice to the culture that makes up my being.

My grandparents and grandmothers (*Zides* and *Bobes*) taught me the importance of appreciating differences, adding opportunities, subtracting problems, and multiplying blessings for everyone because, no matter where you come from, health is your biggest treasure.

Ilan Shapiro (Continues on page 66)

René Sotelo
(UNITED STATES)

Unsupported like the colors in Master Cruz Diez's work

I've always had trouble remembering birthdays and anniversaries. Dates that encompass an event worth commemorating because of its special meaning. I admire those people whose minds run like a Swiss clock, aware of date and time, and always ready to celebrate one more year of engagement, or marriage, or a date of particular significance to their relationship. I must confess I find it epic. Not because I don't care or am unwilling to celebrate it, it just simply slips my mind. I find myself absorbed in my daily routine where, as a doctor, meticulousness is key—and how. My patient, their affliction, their treatment, and their life as a whole take possession of my mind, my breath, and a huge part of who I am. Then again, it makes sense since medicine means everything to me.

As a safeguard, I buy gifts, I hide them and keep them at hand to give to my wife or children, or anyone I'm especially fond of. They remain hidden until something or someone reminds me that a special day has arrived, and then the present is revealed.

I know the affection I feel and the way of saying "I care about you... I love you" are included in finding that spot where the gift will remain anonymous, dormant, until its moment arrives to come forward and steal the show. There's a sort of tacit seduction to it, a way of shouting out "You matter to me. A lot. You're special". It's mainly due to the stubbornness of my memory and my belief that one should seize the day beyond dates and time constraints that, when I buy a present, I want to give it immediately, without waiting another second. That's my way not only to ingratiate myself with that person or celebrate a date of special transcendence, but to come out of a commemoration with renewed forces. It's my way of sharing a meaningful moment with the people that matter most to me and honoring those who deserve recognition on this special occasion. At the end of the day, it's all about our loved ones, the people in our lives who we applaud, cheer for, and cherish.

Monday the 3rd, 2015, however, is a day I could never forget. It could not pass me by, even though I've never been good with dates. As a matter of fact, when I got married, I did it before the scheduled date because a few relatives happened to be in Caracas at the time and I wanted to celebrate it with them. The date engraved in our wedding rings is different than the one it should have been. However, escaping from what this specific day of August means to me is simply impossible. That day was one for the books, for myself and my family. It marked a before and after in my life, my wife's and my three kids'. That Monday, a new horizon loomed for me and my loved ones. I couldn't see it at the time, but there it was: a new opportunity tattooed on my skin. Colorless, embossed, three-dimensional and capable of burning through the coldest winter.

And there I was, right in the middle of Carlos Cruz-Diez's iconic masterpiece, that genius of Venezuelan kineticism who immortalized Venezuela in his piece: *Cromointerferencia de color aditivo*. Standing on the 2,860 square meters of this work of art that takes up the walls and floors of the Maiquetía Simón Bolívar International Airport–my country's main entry and exit point– time stood still. I opened my arms towards the immensity of an uncertain future and, at that moment, the only thing I could do was hang on to my story, the urological authority that René Sotelo had been in Venezuela. I thought of my past and present at the Minimally Invasive Urology Center in Caracas, (CIMI) founded by my father and doctor Oswaldo Karam. The latter, who also founded the Medical Institute of La Floresta, had taken me under his wing and put his faith is me. He believed in the changes I insisted had to be made in order to keep up with the up-and-coming medicine, one characterized by innovation, rigor and daring. I thought of the chapter in my life I had written with his help, along with hundreds of anecdotes and stories of all the patients I connected with through medicine. I thought of my family's sacrifice, all the hours of laughter, tears and love I didn't share with them, forever kept in my wife and my children's narratives. I thought of affection put on hold, paused; of my wife whispering over the phone that the kids had a fever, of their life stories videotaped and sent to me and which I used as inspiration while prepping up in Japan, or Brazil or the States. Hours and hours dedicated to my professional development, to ensuring my children a future, to building a name for myself and gaining recognition as a doctor. All I did for my kids, for how much I love them, for their education, for my patients, for how much I adore medicine. All of it was trapped there, in a net that would be thrown into the ocean and develop its range over the years but that I was far from identifying at the time, a net that makes up my life's greatest truths: how passionate I am for medicine, how much I love the life stories I write along my patients, how much pleasure I take in what I do.

The salty flavor and wetness of my tears–and the baffled and astonished looks on my children's eyes and those who had dropped us off at the airport– were what brought me back down to earth. The Medical Board of California had recognized the merits of my medical career path after 72 years in which the only previous license had been granted to a Japanese physician, and that just six years earlier. This door was opening for me, and it was decisive to achieve my residency and a license to practice medicine in Los Angeles—without having studied in the United States—as part of the staff of the University of Southern California. The product of years of effort and sacrifice with the support of my family began to fade away and become imperceptible in my mind. The only thing that seemed real was the comfort of walking across the halls of the Medical Institute of La Floresta in Caracas, the closeness of my Venezuelan fellows, the mutual respect I had developed with my patients, the pleasure and joy of a hug or a cup of coffee with one of the people staying at the recently inaugurated rehabilitation wing of the medical institute, which was on the rise and becoming the epitome of medical recovery. All of it had taken over my thoughts. Before my gaze, melancholy and uncertainty stood Cruz-Diez's work, a piece of art that had already transcended him. Its colors began to fade, attenuate, turn to whites, grays and blacks despite the strength and immortality of his technique. The only thing beating on my chest was my love for Venezuela, my deep passion for the bond created with my roots, and the satisfaction I had felt as a doctor while attending births in the small villages of my country (Río Chico or Cúpira, where tending to laboring women and receiving the affection of the patients would forever depict the meaning of medicine for me). That which emerges from making room for the connection with the stories of those who are called PATIENTS in capital letters, because later they will become everlasting FRIENDS, maybe even FAMILY.

Right then and there, my story as a migrant doctor was starting to come to life, perhaps emulating my father's, a Mexican who settled in Venezuela and married my mother, from Mérida, whom he met in a guesthouse in Caracas and married six months later. A new story began there, on the kinetic mosaic of someone who was already part of mine, the master Carlos Cruz-Diez, but my feelings and melancholy for Venezuela clouded any possibility of success, joy, or clear thoughts. In August 2015, a new story was beginning. Bringing color to the new pages of my life would be my responsibility, it would be the result of the acknowledgment I once achieved, the product of believing and looking to the horizon and succeeding in the face of doubt, and the desire to believe that the future would bring new wonders to discover and embrace.

New pages ready to be colored were struggling to break through. However, the recognition of succeeding in the die that had been cast ten months before to make room for my experience in front of the Medical Board of the University of Southern California and the state of California; the ties and support of my great friend and teacher Dr. Inderbir Gill, who opened the door to what would be my new story; the recognition by the Academy before my description of the robot-assisted simple prostatectomy... All of it barely appeared, glimmered, but there it was, unsupported, like master Cruz-Diez's colors.

René Sotelo (Continues on page 67)

Karla Uribe
(UNITED STATES)

My story begins in early 1978. My mother had a preterm delivery after twenty-nine weeks gestation, in a public hospital in Guadalajara. According to the doctors, my chances of survival were practically nil and, if I did make it, my quality of life would not be good, so they decided not to offer me any postnatal care. My dad, however, who was doing his medical social service at the time, insisted that I be put in intensive care and, as a favor for being a colleague, the doctors agreed. Despite the lack of knowledge and technology of the time, it took only six weeks before, against all odds, I was able to go home.

Despite the circumstances of my birth, the sequels I suffered were mild. According to the textbooks, I have infantile cerebral palsy, but thanks to my mom's care and my dad's teachings, I believe I just have a different style of walking.

As I mentioned before, my dad is a doctor, so the passion for medicine is in my genes. After graduating, my dad set up his medical practice in an underserved community with very limited health services. That's where I spent my childhood. My house and my dad's practice were right next to each other and even connected by a door. In the beginning, my mother had to work to support the family financially, so I was under my father's care during my early years. Every time a patient came in, I would sit in the back of the chair in his office (he would sit on the edge) and listen to the consultation. The patients, who were also our neighbors, watched me grow up and I bonded with them before I could even walk.

It's difficult to define the exact moment when I decided to become a doctor, because for me it was always something natural; it was part of my daily life. Although that's how I was raised, I showed interest from a very early age. When I was six years old, my father taught me the technique to open a package of gauze without contaminating it, and to identify the various types of sutures. At twelve, I attended my first surgery. Experiencing firsthand that closeness with people from such a young age filled me with joy and satisfaction. I have always admired the way my father treats and respects his patients. He is an excellent professional and my greatest teacher. That's why, when I finished high school, I made what for me was a natural decision and enrolled in the School of Medicine at the National Autonomous University of Mexico.

Throughout my studies, every time I took a new subject, I wanted to choose that specialty. I fell in love with everything. Then, one day, during a shift at the General Hospital of Mexico, when I was a third-year student, I saw a resident dissecting a temporal bone. He saw that I was so blown away that he gave me a set of ear ossicles as a gift. I decided then and there that I would become an otolaryngologist. To this day I still think I could not have chosen a better specialty.

My life began with a challenge, but life is a challenge as well. I feel extremely fortunate and grateful to be part of this world.

Karla Uribe (Continues on page 72)

Jeannette Uribe
(UNITED STATES)

I stem from a traditional but diverse family. So diverse, in fact, that when I was born my dad asked: "What happened to my daughter?" And how could he not? My older brother was blond with green eyes; five years later, my second brother was born, another blond boy with blue eyes ("This can't be happening to me", I thought) and, finally, my little sister was born ("A brunette with dark brown hair like me, oh, what a relief!").

Regardless of our skin color, we were all raised by the best parents we could have asked for. My dad didn't teach me human medicine, but he taught me how to farm, build, raise livestock, and manage my money. My mom, on the other hand, showed me how to spend it, but she also taught me valuable things like how to pray, and how to help others. She did instruct me in medicine, only it wasn't evidence-based, but rather herbalism-centered. To both of them I owe what I am now, and I'll always be thankful for all the sacrifices they made in order to give me and my siblings a better life. As my dad says: work hard so you can offer your children what I couldn't give you.

Ever since I was a little girl, I knew I wanted to be a doctor. I had no role model, but I had a dream. In high school, I studied to become a nurse technician and, by the age of 14, I was already handling instruments in my first surgery: a cesarean section with Dr. Perez. I still remember that moment and the feeling that came with it. It lasts to this day: when I'm in the operating room, I feel that time stands still, and I experience immense pleasure. When I was 15 years old, I went to take my psychometric exam to be accepted into medical school. The doctor told me that, in order to get in, I had to finish high school first. A few months later, I was already his student at the Faculty of Medicine of the beautiful city of Pachuca, *La bella airosa* ("The windy beauty"), whose facilities resemble a tropical paradise. I don't know if it was the city's chill or the fact that I was alone, without friends or family at the age of 16, but everything felt overwhelmingly new.

By that time, I had already met the man of my life. He was working in the United States, and we only saw each other during holidays or weekends. He was the best thing that ever happened to me; my boyfriend at the beginning of university and husband by the time I finished it. He became my partner in crime and an unconditional source of support, not only throughout medical school, but also during my specialty in Gynecology and Obstetrics in Mexico and in the United States. He's an excellent husband and father to our two children. "Wherever you go, I will go", he told me, and he kept his word. We moved from *La bella airosa* to Aguascalientes ("The good people's city"); from Leon, in Guanajuato, to the Huasteca Hidalguense region; from Florida to Michigan (with a stopover in Georgia) and now we're living a new adventure in New York City.

Jeannette Uribe (Continues on page 75)

2

How and why I got here

Patricia Bautista Rivera

(UNITED STATES)

When I entered middle school —a turning point in my life—, I found myself in the youngest group of my grade, and better yet, the kids that got the best grade point averages in elementary school. I found the people with whom I could share my dream of becoming a doctor and from whom I did not receive a surprised face or a sarcastic smile in return.

When I finished middle school, I had the great opportunity and the blessing of entering the high school system of the Universidad Nacional Autónoma de México (UNAM). I was accepted into the College of Sciences and Humanities (CCH) system and went to the Vallejo campus. Almost at the end of my third year at the CCH, I applied to medical school: one of my biggest dreams was to enter the School of Medicine at the Ciudad Universitaria (CU).

Praise God! I got into my dream school and the adventure began. Studying medicine is a gigantic challenge. It's even bigger when economic limitations, like the ones I unfortunately had, stand in your way. One of the most important memories of the beginning of my degree was the worry of not having enough money to buy books, uniforms, or supplies. But what I lacked in resources, I had in determination: I was determined to become a doctor and I knew that the only way to do it was to study hard and with dedication. However, I didn't take into account that the country's economy was going to worsen and that what little my mother could earn would be reduced, thus jeopardizing my chances to continue studying.

I knew that, in order to continue, I had to find a source of income. So, in a moment of desperation, I sought out my physiology professor, a brilliant and dedicated researcher who taught me a lot and asked him for help. He advised me to enroll in the Physiology Laboratory Instructor's course, and I was accepted. When I finished the course, the university hired me, and I started working at the UNAM School of Medicine and became a university academic. That, thank God, definitely improved our situation. Better yet, it allowed me to continue studying. I did my internship at the Hospital General de Zona 1A, Los Venados, where I learned a lot and had many positive experiences. I was awarded the prize for the best intern of the year. My social service was in the town of Ticumán, in the state of Morelos. There, I learned to treat scorpion bites, to deliver babies all on my own, to take care of a community, and many other things.

Six years into my degree, I realized I no longer wanted to be a plastic surgeon. I finally decided that the area of greatest interest to me was (and still is) pediatrics. I applied to the National Institute of Pediatrics (INP), a place of excellence in patient treatment and teaching.

And I was accepted! Yes, I was accepted at the INP and yet another adventure began, a new stage of learning. The first year (R1) was a deadly on-call year, with an A-B rotation: I was on call every other day, with a modified schedule on weekends. My, that first year was hard! On the internal medicine rotation, there was a really smart third year resident (R3) who was kind of quarrelsome: he would argue with anyone if, for any reason, his patients were not getting the treatment they deserved. His genuine love and interest for his patients were evident.

In the second year, as an R2, there were two rotations with patients with oncologic conditions: hematology and oncology. If you rotated in one department, you didn't have to rotate in the other. My first rotation was hematology but, over the course of the year, the chief resident decided that I had to rotate in oncology, despite my protests. The oncology resident (R4) was very nice and highly skilled at performing procedures (IVs, lumbar puncture, arterial sampling). He was the one we turned to for the most difficult cases.

This R4 is the same R3 I mentioned previously, who showed up everywhere at the hospital —to check on his oncology patients, according to him— with chocolates for me. He asked me out on several occasions, and we began dating. At that time, he had invited to spend some time at the bone marrow transplant unit at a hospital in Kentucky (KY), where he made a great impression because of his intelligence and dedication.

After dating for a year, we got married. When we returned from our honeymoon, there was a letter waiting for him with an invitation to do a fellowship in bone marrow transplant in KY, which he accepted.

I finished my specialty in pediatrics and was accepted for further training in pediatric allergy. I was halfway through the year when we received word that the paperwork to apply for the visa was almost done. So, I finished the first year of the subspecialty and, in March, we moved to Kentucky so my husband could continue his training for 2 years and I traveled alongside him. That's how I got here.

Patricia Bautista Rivera (Continues on page 77)

Edmundo Erazo

(THE NETHERLANDS)

While a medical student, I visited Germany and decided to do a postgraduate degree in Europe. The infrastructure for doing clinical research and the quality of life seemed attractive to me. Another reason why I wanted to study abroad was that the people I've admired the most and from whom I've learned the most —not only in medicine but in life— studied abroad, either in Europe or elsewhere. That experience was an essential part of developing their professional career and personal judgment.

So, during my last year of residency, I sought out a master's program in clinical research. Some of the factors I considered were the academic quality: language, cultural diversity, and a high level of research. That led me to the Netherlands, a small country compared to Mexico, but with great cultural diversity, especially in Rotterdam —where I arrived— which is home to people of 120 different nationalities.

In the Netherlands, most people speak English, so the language outside the hospital and university was not a barrier in my day-to-day life. I applied to the Erasmus Medical Center, one of the largest and most recognized academic centres in Europe. After meeting the requirements for admission, you had to demonstrate financial means. Studying at a university in the Netherlands without being European is expensive, so I applied for a scholarship to study abroad for two years. I am grateful to Grupo Ángeles for granting me the Olegario Vázquez Raña scholarship in 2017. I was able to do a master's degree at the Erasmus Medical Center. Furthermore, I thank my mentors in the internal medicine course, especially Dr Alejandro Díaz Borjón, who became not only my mentor but also my friend.

Edmundo Erazo (Continues on page 80)

Sandra López-León
(Israel, the Netherlands, Spain, United States)

There are various reasons why people migrate. I have moved to live in another country four times, and each one had a different reason behind it. I went to Israel in search of adventure, to the Netherlands to follow love, to Spain to live close to my family, and to the United States because there was a greater opportunity for professional growth and a better education for my children.

Many people have asked me, of the five countries I have lived in, which one I think is the best. I can tell you that there is no worse or better place, all of them have their negative and positive aspects. What one should do is focus on the positive things. At a certain moment, a country may be perfect for one's priorities, but the needs and priorities change throughout life. Regardless, I recommend everyone to go and live outside of their homeland, even if it is for a short time. It is amazing to realize how much of a capacity to grow, learn, understand, and live we possess, once we make that jump. It opens our eyes, broadens our horizons, and changes our perspective.

I went to Israel to live there for a year. When you only go somewhere for a year, it sort of feels like an extended vacation. During that year I witnessed, learned, and experienced very different things. I traveled all over Israel, Palestine, Turkey, Egypt, and Jordan. I rappelled on the Sudanese border, hiked on the Lebanese one, went scuba diving in the Red Sea, hiked in the desert, traveled by horse, donkey, and camel. I learned a little Hebrew and a few words in Arabic. I studied the Old Testament and Kabbalah. I learned to cook and dance in Latin bars. I even wrote a book about several of my adventures, called *Toma mi mano y vuela conmigo* (Take my hand and fly with me). What surprised me the most was that I had gone to Israel to choose my profession. In the last rotation of my internship, I chose psychiatry, but since my Hebrew was not good enough for me to communicate with psychiatric patients, I was sent to do research in psychiatric genetics. That was when I decided I wanted to be a researcher.

In my fourth year of medical school, I fell in love with a Dutchman, so, when I graduated, I moved to the Netherlands. During my first few months there, I focused on looking for places where I could get my Ph.D. I found that the Erasmus University in Rotterdam had an excellent epidemiology department and that they kept databases with psychiatric and genetic information. After plenty of reading, I realized that I needed knowledge in epidemiology, statistics, and bioinformatics to do my research.

I started my master's degree one year after arriving in the Netherlands. My first child was born the following year. During the seven years we lived there, I studied a master's, a doctorate in science (DSc) and a Ph.D. in Genetic Epidemiology, and focused on locating genes related to personality, ADHD, manic-depressive illness, and depression. My Ph.D. thesis was called *Genetic Determinants of Depression*. Since then, I have dedicated myself to identifying genes related to memory, migraine, anxiety, mood, attention, sleep, and substance-use disorders.

The third time I emigrated I went to Barcelona. We moved there because of my husband's job, plus my parents told me that they would also move to Spain if I lived there. Soon after I settled in Barcelona, my adventurous parents left Mexico and moved to Spain as well.

Living in Barcelona was amazing. The city is incredibly beautiful. It has unbeatable food, sea, mountains, music, love, and passion. In Barcelona we forged strong friendships, and during our time there, my middle son and my daughter were born. In the Netherlands I had attended many classes on the importance of networking; how to socialize, meet and open to all kinds of people and, above all, to provide help whenever I had the chance. I also went to many job opportunity conferences, where they told us about all the options available in hospitals, universities, non-governmental organizations (NGOs), clinical research organizations (CROs), service providers, consultancies, and the industry. In one of those classes, I was told to keep all the business cards I was given.

When I arrived in Barcelona, I looked through my cards and found someone who lived there: he was a guy I had met during a pharmacoepidemiology course in the Netherlands. I called him and asked for guidance. He encouraged me to apply for the pharmaceutical industry and gave me the contact email of the right person. I sent my CV, the following week I was interviewed, and, within a month, I was hired.

After living seven years in Barcelona, my job gave me the opportunity to emigrate to the United States, more specifically to New York, close to where my two brothers lived. I got the chance to work mainly in the fields I am most passionate about: neuroscience and genetics. I am currently developing new monoclonal drugs and gene therapies to treat neurological illnesses such as migraine, Alzheimer's, multiple sclerosis, and other monogenic diseases. As they saw that all their children and grandchildren were going to live nearby, my parents were quick to pack their bags and emigrate as well. As my five-year-old son used to say: "Leaving is as simple as closing the door and hopping on the plane".

Sandra López-León (Continues on page 82)

Rafael G. Magaña
(England, United States)

In 1998, I was in my first year of general surgery in Mexico City. I remember it was one of my most difficult years, because the ISSSTE (Mexican Civil Service Social Security and Services Institute), where I received surgical training, didn't fit my aspirations. To be more accurate, I felt I wasn't gaining the surgical technical expertise I knew I needed to achieve my goals. At the same time, I experienced a culture shock: in Mexico, there's a hierarchical system within the general surgery residency. I recall a stupid habit: the attached physician would only exchange information with third or fourth grade residents (R3 or R4, referring to the year of graduate residency), because of the simple fact that, in the program, us rookies were considered almost subhuman.

In addition to that, I was not mature or flexible enough at the time to tolerate what I perceived as abuse. In the residency, there were unreasonable punishments, some even illegal, on the grounds that this was the best way to learn.

One night on duty, fed up with my superiors' arbitrariness, I remember thinking that I no longer tolerated the atmosphere of the residency. I thought about quitting altogether and doing something else that would make me happy. Youthful, immature sentiments.

After a few ups and downs that lasted months, I decided not to give up. However, if I was going to continue on this path, I would not do it in a system that I considered inefficient (referring only to the program I was in); rather, it would be in a place with more academic postgraduate structure. I contemplated doing my residency in England or the United States. I went for the second option.

One afternoon, I visited my dear friend Sandra López-León to ask for her advice on the USMLE (United States Medical Licensing Examination) exams that are required to apply to residencies and, eventually, to work in the United States. I was very fortunate to have her valuable advice, since her two brothers had already gone through the same process.

With the love and financial support of my parents, I decided to accept the challenge. I flew to New York to take a course for the USMLE, Steps one, two, and three. I got on the plane with mixed emotions. On the one hand, I was excited, on the other, concerned, and full of doubt, since I had no excuse for not doing what I set out to. I was terrified of making a fool of myself and failing at my residency. I had no clue what I was getting into.

I arrived in Manhattan looking for an apartment to start my course as soon as possible. This was quite a challenge: the living spaces were tiny and astronomically expensive, but with persistence and luck I found a small studio apartment. I completed several courses at Arc Ventures, the now-defunct USMLE study center. During that year, I took the USMLE Steps one and two, and the TOEFL; requirements for the Educational Commission for Foreign Medical Graduates (ECFMG) certificate.

I submitted over 100 applications to preliminary and categorical general surgery programs. I never got back from any of them. I decided to call both general surgery and internal medicine programs in the hope I'd match. I managed to get two interviews in general medicine, one of them thanks to a friend, and another for general surgery.

Two things happened that, in hindsight, worked in my favor. Never underestimate tenacity, faith (in my case non-religious) and, above all, luck.

Fortune comes when you least expect it. I thought that, if it was necessary, I'd do internal medicine, and then general and plastic surgery. After the Match, I stayed in internal medicine at the Bronx Lebanon Hospital, but there was a small problem: I managed to get a preliminary general surgery position outside of the Match, the National Residency Matching Program (NRMP). This position was for only one year of general surgery after which they could simply decide not to hire me for the next. It's like a year in which they have an extra intern, but without guaranteeing them progress in the program, much less graduating as a general surgeon. I didn't give it much thought, and, with a bit of fear and uncertainty, I took the position in general surgery. It's worth mentioning that I had problems with the Match system and that they were not exactly pleased with me in the internal medicine program at Bronx Lebanon Hospital. Fortunately, there were no major consequences. I preferred to have an unstable position than doing something I didn't really want to do.

Initially, the program director in general surgery did not offer me the position. When I went to the interview, I came out feeling sad, discouraged, and scolded. Burton L. Herz, the director, barely looked at my letters of recommendation and résumés and, without much empathy, suggested that I should apply for family medicine. He also told me I'd never be able to complete a general surgery residency in the United States. Without giving him the satisfaction of a reaction and with the certainty that the doors were closed in that academic program, I thanked him for his sincerity and expressed how deeply disappointing his words were.

I stood up, shook his hand, and without making a big deal out of it, left his office. Ten days later, I received a call from Donna, the program coordinator, with a message from the doctor. He offered me a contract for a preliminary year. They renewed my contract annually and, during my years of residency, I moved from R1 to R2 and so on. In the fourth year, the program expanded, and I was offered a categorical position if I repeated the last year. I agreed, and, six years later, the same doctor who assured me I'd never be a general surgeon handed me my graduation diploma.

Applying for plastic surgery was even more daunting than my initial attempts for residency. Since I was in the fourth year of general surgery, I applied annually for plastic surgery. My interviews through the Match were null, and the ones that I obtained with the help of recommendations did not yield any results. My plan was to just keep applying and finishing academic years.

I did two years of intensive care and burn surgery at New York Hospital, and, finally, I started getting interviews for plastic surgery. However, all of them were unsuccessful. After NYH, I moved to Salt Lake City, Utah, to specialize in craniofacial surgery at the Intermountain Healthcare System and the Children's Hospital.

To this day, I've never gone through such a tough and intense academic year. Finally, during that time, I was able to obtain a plastic surgery position in Augusta, Georgia, at the Medical College of Georgia (MCG). The whole process (application, acceptance, and initiation) takes about a year. In other words, in 2008 I was accepted to start the 2009 program.

This left me with a year I used to do a specialty in oncoplastic breast surgery in New York.

I remember that plastic surgery residency very fondly; it was one of the most pleasant experiences of my life. Augusta really lacked charm, but the friendships and academic environment were exceptional. When I finished residency, I decided to enter private practice and returned to New York with renewed hopes.

I currently reside in Greenwich, Connecticut, where I do cosmetic and reconstructive surgery at a private practice.

Rafael G. Magaña (Continues on page 84)

Nissin Nahmias
(United States)

Once I decided to do my residency in the United States, the next step was to apply for the different programs available. That's done through a system in which one applies, and the places that are interested reply with interview offers. I applied to neurosurgery and general surgery.

I got interviewed for around a dozen hospitals. This made my family happy, but it also caused them great concern regarding how expensive it was to pay for twelve trips abroad; evidently without God's help, I could not have succeeded.

After much struggle, I found a place for a preliminary year in general surgery in Philadelphia, Pennsylvania. Since my goal at that time was to do a neurosurgery residency, I prepared to leave Mexico and start a new life in the United States. I want to clarify that I was not selected right off the bat. I fought hard —both financially and emotionally— to

46

obtain that preliminary position. Also, once I started residency, I was no longer the standout student who had graduated with honors; I was now one of the foreigners who wanted to survive in the American system, which gives nationals priority over foreigners.

The surgical residency system in America is tough. I'm sure it's that way anywhere, but for me it was particularly intense as a foreigner. In that program, there were also several people with a really negative attitude who had all kinds of prejudices against Mexicans: in general, they thought that Mexico was a town full of charros and donkeys, and they'd think of Speedy González each time they looked at us. All of this led me to think about quitting on several occasions.

I remember returning to my apartment after a long day of enduring countless taunts and insults at work from my colleagues and the general practitioners. I came home wanting to cry, alone, and in silence. Fortunately, I had the support of my friends. My friend Pedro helped me a great deal, and I also met Julián Guitrón, another Mexican I spent great moments with.

When my mother called me and asked me how things were going, she'd always encourage me, remind me how proud she and my dad were of me, and cheer me on. That gave me strength to continue.

Those six months were very hard. I had to adapt both to the internship and to life in a new country, but I also had to learn to adapt to the American system: training in Mexico gives priority to field work, to performing surgeries and procedures. In the United States, however, before even making an incision, you need to have a pile of knowledge (especially when it comes to the patient's history). I also tried my best to make the people I worked with like me, since, as a foreigner, they were not very willing to teach me.

At one point, I had to choose between continuing my clinical career or doing a year of research. I opted for the first option and focused on general surgery. At the end of the first year, I was proclaimed the intern who had progressed the most and they offered a categorical position for the entire program, which I happily accepted. Again, God gave me the opportunity. I knew it wouldn't be easy, but I also knew I had all the tools to succeed.

I remember how I earned my categorical position. One day, I was getting off work after a 72 hour-long shift at the hospital. I was on my way to the parking lot when I ran into a transplant surgeon who said, "Come, join me for a cigarette." We were behind the hospital, at the emergency entrance and all I could think of was how exhausted I was and how my couch was waiting for me at home. He was my mentor, and he told me that I had done a very good job and that he was very proud of my work.

At that moment, an ambulance arrived. The doctor had to go urgently to Delaware to collect some organs and asked me to go with him. I, who didn't know how to say no, tagged along. My couch would have to wait for me a little longer. That day, we made the trip from Philadelphia to Delaware and back with the organs. We performed a kidney transplant and finished around three in the morning. After that operation, it no longer made sense for me to go home: the residents begin at five in the morning. I just washed my face and kept working; I had to update the list of patients to start the day.

During the fourth year of general surgery, I had many conflicts with my fellow residents without ever understanding why they happened in the first place. I was early for work, but the residents under my command were late and paid no attention. When I spoke to the resident chief, he would scold me and assign me more work. Eventually, I spoke to the program director, and, to my surprise, he mentioned that he was very unhappy with me, that he didn't understand what was going on and why the other residents were always complaining that I wasn't doing my job.

For a time, I actually thought I was going crazy. Thanks to fate, I discovered what was going on: in that hospital, there were people who wanted to undermine me, and they started spreading lies about me. But again, my dedication and work spoke for themselves. Everything settled down and I got my boss to admit that everything that was said about me wasn't true, and that I was an excellent employee. It was a difficult time, but I had to do the right thing: I faced my boss and explained the situation to him; he was able to corroborate it, and never doubted my word again.

I graduated in 2008 as a general surgeon. I remember that, when my family from Mexico came to the ceremony, all my classmates were very surprised. They thought that short, brown-skinned charros were going to arrive riding on donkeys. When they caught a glimpse of them, they couldn't believe that my parents, my brother, his wife, and my cousins were Mexican. That taught me not to stereotype.

Later, I specialized in bariatric and minimally invasive surgery. I trained in the state of Virginia, at Virginia Commonwealth University, one of the largest academic centers in the United States, where I was fortunate to learn from some of the pioneers in the field of weight control surgery in the world.

By this time, I also passed the bar exam, was fully recognized as a surgeon, and prepared for my first job: an internship in the state of Connecticut.

Nissin Nahmias (Continues on page 88)

Susana Ramírez Romero

(Spain)

The adventure of emigrating from Mexico to Spain began in 2009. I was living in Mexico City, married, with a one-year-old, in the last year of my subspecialty, finishing my master's degree in clinical research and I was also pregnant. It might seem like a bit much; but at the age of 32, I could handle that and more. I thought that, by the end of that year, I'd be able to focus solely on work and being a mother. I had achieved many goals but still had many dreams to accomplish.

Next on the list was moving to a quieter city, where the children could play and grow up without haste or rush. We wanted a small garden and Mexico City, besides being chaotic, was too expensive to have the house of our dreams; and so, we considered moving to a smaller town.

With that in mind, my then husband received a job offer from Barcelona. The subject came up in the middle of an Emergency Medicine congress with a Catalonian doctor. When it became a real proposal, we didn't hesitate: we decided to move, only further away.

He started the process to revalidate his medical degree in Spain and, after several months, it was homologated. We started the paperwork without knowing if my second child would be born in Mexico or in Spain.

With the work contract in our hands and our hearts full of enthusiasm, we went to the Spanish embassy, where my husband was given his visa in a few days and was told that mine and the children's visas would be ready in a month at the latest. We decided it was better for him to travel first because our second child was about to be born, and it'd be more comfortable for me to arrive already having a place to live.

We sold furniture, books, and other knick-knacks that one accumulates, and, in August, my then husband flew to Catalonia. He arrived at the home of an elderly couple, who became our "angels", because they only knew him by hearsay and still put him up in their house free of charge, helped him with the city registration and were his guarantors so he could rent the apartment. My children call them their "Spanish grandparents." We will be eternally grateful for everything they did for us.

Once the hot month of August was over, I moved to my parents' house. Autumn arrived, the leaves began to fall, but my visa and the children's visas were nowhere to be seen: three months had already gone by. It took forever; the most distressing thing was not knowing if we'd get them. My husband even contemplated the possibility of returning, but I thought that, after all the changes and everything we'd sold, we couldn't just give up.

During that time, we only communicated via Skype and so my husband watched the baby go from eight pounds to thirteen and then to seventeen. He did it from afar, without being able to touch, smell or kiss him. The oldest, only two years old, at first talked to his dad all the time but, as the days went by and he saw that we were still separated, my son was very angry and gave him the silent treatment. I was still breastfeeding, and my emotions were running high, so this situation of involuntary separation hurt me deeply.

November came around and we still had no answer. Since I'm not exactly patient, I decided to buy plane tickets for the three of us and enter as tourists; and, once there, wait for the consulate's response in Barcelona. Once the visa was issued, we'd have to return to Mexico, pick it up and enter Spain again as residents, which implied an unplanned expense but, so what? Some time together was long overdue.

After a long twelve-hour flight, carrying six suitcases, two children, a blanket, and a few stuffed animals, I arrived in Barcelona on a cloudy November afternoon alongside my brother, who helped me during the trip. My two-year-old son ran to his dad's open arms, and both immediately burst into tears. He cried and cried as much as he could, hugging his daddy without letting him go, so he wouldn't have to be apart from him ever again...

Susana Ramírez Romero (Continues on page 90)

Luis Rodrigo Reynoso
(ETHIOPIA)

I must admit that while I was in Ethiopia, I wondered many times how and why I got there. Even now, every time new life lessons and perspectives come up, I wonder about it. I must admit that I asked myself that same question over and over while I was in Ethiopia; and I keep doing it every time new life lessons and perspectives come up.

Leaving aside the spiritual and metaphorical aspects, I will try to remember certain events that were signs for me.

In the previous chapter, I mentioned that at a conference I heard the speech of four Ethiopian doctors. Wooow! Immediately afterwards, I Googled "Ethiopia" (in English). My brain started to synapse, I got excited and started making plans: How do I get there? What do I need? What language is spoken over there? Are there really no plastic surgeons in Ethiopia? Naaaah! it must be a joke! How can I get there?

The first thing that occurred to me was to get the phone number of the NGO founder. I wrote him a text message to let him know my deepest wishes; I am paraphrasing below:.

"I am interested in being part of your cleft lip and palate project in Ethiopia. I was recently in training at the headquarters of your foundation, and the speech I heard there motivated and inspired me. I think that if they do not have plastic surgeons there, I would be willing to train myself, to start from scratch, as an errand boy, an office worker or whatever. I would love to be the one who follows up the patients being operated on in that country, and whom, tomorrow, could oversee these procedures. I am six months away from finishing my specialty in cosmetic and reconstructive plastic surgery and I would like to dedicate my life to this project. I ask you to guide me so that I can help you continue your mission and make my dream come true".

I anxiously waited for my device to notify me that the message had already been read, but a few days passed, and I received no news. I checked, checked again and nothing. I am very intense, so I decided to dial him on the phone, but he did not answer either. A few days later I received an answer: "Hello. Thanks for your interest. Contact my assistant so she can guide you through the process".

I am not lying to you: my message was impregnated with all my wishes, so the answer seemed insipid. But I was not demotivated, I contacted his assistant and what do you think? A few days later I received his reply:

"Thanks. At the moment we only require donations. For you to belong to the group of plastic surgeons and attend any of our conferences, it is necessary to go through a certification process; we would have to open your file once we call you to participate ».

—*Ok, thank you.*

At that moment I was furious. I spat out curses that came from my guts, but I said, if it is not that way, then another will be.

At that time, my wedding was about five months away, so my parents had decided that we would take a trip to Las Vegas to enjoy ourselves as a family. There in the "Sin City" I took a taxi. After the usual greetings and courtesy phrases - "Good afternoon, how have you been? Busy shift? -- suddenly, impulsively, and for no apparent reason, I asked the taxi driver: "Are you from Ethiopia?"

Surprised, he replied: "You have been there or why do you ask?"

I could not believe it! What happened then, I remember as an explosion in my head: I told him about my failed plan. He got excited! I got excited! He told me that he himself could put me in touch with his cousin, a nephrologist who worked in Addis Ababa (the capital of Ethiopia), he asked me to give him my contact information. He motivated me to look for more options and keep knocking on doors ...

As we said goodbye, he said: "My people will thank you, there are many people who need you!" Oh geez! That meeting was so unexpected, but I still had to wait for the taxi driver's cousin to contact me to see if he would accomplish anything.

Around that time, another event happened that somehow led me to Ethiopia. I belonged to a Facebook group called International Plastic Surgery Network in which we participated residents and plastic surgeons from all over the world. In that group I found a post that said: "We welcome Anteneh Gebru, Ethiopia's first plastic surgeon!" I immediately contacted him through social networks, and we began an intense correspondence.

In one of Anteheh's messages. He told me:

"In Ethiopia there are six plastic surgeons who have taken courses for three or six months abroad and practice reconstructive surgery. But there are no courses in Ethiopia yet. In fact, I want to be the first plastic surgeon to graduate from my university. I am trying, despite the low possibility of obtaining books. I do have money to continue studying; I am an orphan: my parents died of AIDS, and with great efforts I have been able to continue this career".

I swear to you, reading this was hallucinating to me. I saw it as virgin territory with great academic, surgical, and humanitarian opportunities. "I have to live and perform surgery in Ethiopia!"

Then everything started to flow. There is little or no information in English on the internet; and I did not know Amharic, which is the language spoken in Ethiopia. This language descends from a Semitic language, and I could not even read its writing which seemed to be made up of ancient hieroglyphs, so I needed an interpreter to contact people.

I will have to learn, I told myself. Unfortunately, I could not find books or forums where I could study it. "We'll have to wait to get in touch with her," I told myself. At the moment, Anteneh taught me a few words whenever he could connect, because as he explained to me in Ethiopia, social networks are restricted.

A couple of months passed during which they continued to refuse my admission to the Addis Ababa University Hospital. But I kept making plans. "I just need a room with a bathroom and food, my future wife and I will take care of the rest," that's how each letter he sent asking for an opportunity ended. Finally, someone answered my call. I received an email from Tewodros, a surgeon who had specialized in the United States.

I answered his email very excited and, suddenly, we were already talking on the phone.

"You come to me at the right time. I was just looking for someone who could help me, he told me. "We are about to open a small clinic and we are going to need one more surgeon. I think the planets are aligning for both of us".

I could not believe it! I am not exaggerating when I say I was almost peeing myself with excitement. In addition, Tewodros (Ted) told me that he loved to paint, write, and have deep talks, those that change the world. I was excited beyond belief.

«Doc, you will say. We are on, and I say us, because in March I am getting married. I would like to take a couple of weeks for the honeymoon, but my intention is that in April we will already be with you" I said.

In the background you could hear the children playing, the songs of the birds and the noise of that city that seemed enigmatic to me, and which I did not dare to google so as not to spoil the experience I was about to live.

"We are going to need some documents to carry out the pertinent procedures, I tell myself. "I have some friends who can help us speed things up. I will be writing to you these days, to let you know what documents we need".

It was three in the morning, and I perfectly remember that, after hanging up, I entered the room where Anahí slept to discover that all that time she had been awake, listening to the conversation.

–*Anahí, we are going to live in Ethiopia!*

Luis Rodrigo Reynoso (Continues on page 91)

Alejandra Rodríguez Romero
(United States)

In my last month of medical school, just weeks before graduation and the beginning of my internship, I met Chris, an American boy who came to Guadalajara for the wedding of a mutual friend. The wedding, however, was canceled a few days before the scheduled date and, because Chris had bought his tickets well in advance and could not change them, he decided to make the trip anyway. It was his first time visiting Mexico, and he was excited to see the country.

My friend asked me to help her with Chris because my English was very good, and he didn't speak a word of Spanish. Even though we were in the middle of a stressful week, full of exams and projects, I decided to give her a hand. A few days later, we picked him up at the airport and I had dusted off my English to show him the beautiful city of Guadalajara and its surroundings. After spending a few very pleasant days, feelings of friendship and love began to emerge. When it was time for him to return to the United States, sadness overcame us both, and we exchanged phone numbers and social media profiles so we could keep in touch. In the following weeks, we talked daily and due to the great connection and friendship we created, I decided to invite him to my graduation, to which he gladly accepted. That day he also met my parents, and even though at first things were a little awkward because of the language barrier, the conversations took off after a few hours.

The next two years we maintained a long-distance relationship. The city and town where I did my internship and social service are about 5 hours away from Tucson, where he lived, and he visited me twice a month. Knowing clearly that we wanted to formalize the relationship, we began to do a little research on the necessary steps to be able to get married and allow me legal entry to the United States. We decided to start the Alien Fiancé(e) process, which consists of submitting the application while the fiancé(e) is still in his/her country. Documents are requested to prove that the relationship is bona fide and, approximately 6 to 9 months later, the interview date arrives, which in this case was in Ciudad Juárez. During that time, I finished my social service and we started to plan the wedding. I had mixed feelings. On the one hand, I felt a great satisfaction for having finished medical school, which had been my lifelong dream, and I was excited to have found a person to share the rest of my life with. On the other hand, I was weighed down by a feeling of uncertainty, as I would have to cross many barriers to be able to practice my profession in this new country.

The interview date finally arrived. In it, they review previously performed medical studies and evidence regarding the case, and one must also speak to an immigration agent. After so much paperwork and time, my application was accepted, granting me entry to the United States. And that's how, with anxiety, fears, but, above all, a lot of hope and excitement, I began my story in this country on January 9, 2009.

Alejandra Rodríguez Romero (Continues on page 94)

Jack Rubinstein
(United States)

> "When the end of the world comes, I want to be in Cincinnati because it's always 20 years behind the times."
> -Mark Twain

The *here*, right now and for over ten years, has been Cincinnati, Ohio, known by those who live on the U.S. coasts as "flyover country" (for being part of the states that are flown over and largely ignored while traveling between the coasts' main cities). For my Mexican family, Cincinnati is the place close to Chicago and the city where the grandchildren, cousins and brothers live. For my doctor friends, it's the place where cows graze outside hospitals. Professionally, talking about the *here* is more complicated. I'm primarily a clinical cardiologist, focused on echocardiography and patients with cardiovascular disease. However, I'm also a researcher, writer, teacher, and mentor.

During my medical training in Mexico, I realized that it was going to be difficult —if not impossible— to develop my clinical and professional interests within the Mexican healthcare system where, sadly, we say that *la priva mata todo*, meaning that private practice takes precedence over just about everything. That includes the patient's needs or medical research, which is rarely supported at early stages and never paid expeditiously; rather, researchers must go through an arduous process and begin to receive support after the research has been conducted. Instead of supporting early-stage investigators, the national funding mechanism most commonly supports those who have demonstrated success in their professional field. In short, the system does not provide significant financial support for research nor service to the general population.

I didn't give up right away, though. For over a year, I worked for the government of Mexico City but, clearly, the healthcare system was a vaster and hugely more complex beast than I could've ever imagined; it was impossible to change it without monumental reorganization at the national level. Bearing this in mind, I looked for a place that was more aligned with my professional interests. As we will see in the next chapter, the American system for practicing medicine as a foreign medical graduate (FMG) is relatively straightforward to explain, but extraordinarily difficult navigate. For those looking to train in the United States as clinicians, the path is summed up in exams and interviews. On the other hand, those who seek an academic path within the medical system must pass the same exams and interviews while trying to make a name for themselves as researchers, teachers, or writers. My reason for choosing Cincinnati had to do with the need to find a place where I could work as a clinician and, at the same time, have the freedom to explore my other academic interests.

When looking for a place to settle after almost two decades of training, there are always conflicting thoughts and values, and difficult decisions to make. Is it better to look for a large and cosmopolitan city, but with smaller spaces to live? Or should you focus on earning the most money to make up for years of precarious payments as a resident? Could it be that the most important thing is the reputation of the institution? Or the weather? Or the quality of the schools? Or the closeness to your family? These and other factors must be considered and, for my professional goals, the Queen City (as Cincinnati calls itself) was perfect. Thanks to this city and the mentors who recruited and protected me, I am now a well-established physician and scientist.

Finally, no decision or city is ideal, and even if one analyzes all the variables, there will always be an element of luck. For me, luck was finding the prototype of tranquility and kindness of the Midwest of the United States, coupled with a responsible and proactive state and local government that has managed to generate a city with a high quality of life where my wife and I have managed to raise our family. The city might be a bit behind the times — although not the 20 years Mark Twain talks about—: pajamas are still appropriate attire at most supermarkets, I do run into an occasional cow or deer on my way to work, and absolutely no one can mix us up with Chicago. But, for my life —at this moment and for more than ten years— these peculiarities have not been negative, but rather ideal for my personal and professional development.

Jack Rubinstein (Continues on page 96)

Alberto Saltiel

(ISRAEL)

Throughout life, we come across situations in which we must make important decisions which will help us achieve the goals we set for ourselves. Each stage of our lives will be influenced by these decisions, and, in due course, we'll see their consequences.

Growing up as members of the Jewish Community in Mexico, we feel a strong bond with the State of Israel. I went to Israel for the first time when I graduated high school. I had the opportunity to live there for six months in a kibbutz (a mainly agricultural socialist community). During this period, I learned more about the culture, the idiosyncrasy, and the country's way of life. After that trip, I went back each time I had the chance to, knowing that we (as Jews) will always have Israel as an option. However, I never imagined that one day, I'd end up living there.

During medical school, whenever I thought about my future, I always saw myself working as a specialist in Mexico. I had thought about taking the National Medical Residency Exam, entering a prestigious general surgery program, and then doing a subspecialty in vascular surgery. Little did I know how much my plans would change. During the undergraduate medical internship, as part of the university program, I had the opportunity to do rotations abroad. At that time, I travelled to the city of Be'er Sheva, in Israel, where I did rotations as an intern in general surgery, internal medicine, and pediatrics at the Soroka University Hospital. During my stay, I not only learned about medical issues in different specialties, but I also became acquainted with how the health system works in Israel, the technological benefits for patients, and the care provided in hospitals. Being that the healthcare system is subsidized by the country, every citizen has access to high-level medical care at a very low cost.

When I returned to Mexico to finish the internship, I knew the time had come to make the decision that would change my life. Since Israel is a country constantly threatened by terrorist acts and where many citizens are affected and in need of urgent attention, the technology there is extremely advanced. So, after learning about the healthcare system and the local lifestyle, I decided that Israel would be an excellent place to specialize. But was I choosing correctly?

It's funny, sometimes we're forced into making decisions without anticipating how they will affect our future and, although they don't seem to be related to each other, they are always linked somehow. I was about to start the social service, still a year away from finishing my medical degree, and I was already thinking about the future. I knew I wanted to be a specialist, I knew what that specialty would be and where I wanted to do it, but I still didn't know how to get there.

Without a doubt, the decision to leave Mexico was mainly professional, but I can't deny that there's a certain personal component. In Mexico, you traditionally leave your parents' house to go study or because you're getting married. I always considered myself a very independent person and, as such, I felt the need to face the world and make my own luck. With that in mind and knowing that Israel would be a great place to specialize, there was nothing left but to make the decision. Throughout the subsequent months, I managed to gather enough information to give me a general idea of the necessary process to move to Israel and continue my professional training.

Alberto Saltiel **(Continues on page 99)**

Luana Sandoval Castillo

(Spain, Denmark)

Mexico, 2004. A trip made at random because my roommate couldn't stand to see me cry anymore. Her brother had told me: "It's not you, it's me", while his change of heart was already obvious. So, with a blank ticket and a world map, I pointed with my eyes closed to the south of the world and that's where my story began.

Argentina, 2004. With a broken heart in my suitcase and willing to renew myself, I poured myself into writing. A Colombian woman, a German man, and a Brazilian girl came into my life. We tangoed in the streets and banged casseroles and pots with the mothers in Plaza de Mayo: we established unbreakable bonds that passed the test of time. Before Facebook, we explored from Hi5 to ICQ, but it was time to cross the ocean and forget about the online world. By then, the German was already living in England and the Colombian in Barcelona, so Europe would become our meeting point.

London, 2005. Halfway through my medical internship and with the intention of working abroad, I was visiting hospitals around the world; pieces of a puzzle that directed my way to unthinkable places. Hand in hand with the German, I traveled through part of England and took advantage of the "short distances" and cheap airlines to visit the Colombian in Barcelona.

Barcelona, 2005. New seas and sunrises of a different color. Sunbathing in Barceloneta, I discovered a building by the sea that happened to be a hospital: the Hospital del Mar. I went straight to Human Resources, asking for the cardiology department. "Next door on the right, second floor." When I opened that door, my destiny changed.

"Let's celebrate", said the Colombian and, between red wine and some tapas, she asked me for the German's number in England because her sister was coming from Colombia and wanted to save on accommodation. While I was writing down the address and information, she showed me pictures of her family. Staring at the spectacular curves of her sister, I said:

-I better watch out.

-Don't worry, the German is in love with you.

And I said to the German:

-You better watch out.

-Don't worry, I'm in love with you...

They got married in Barcelona in 2006. In a backpack on my shoulder, I carried memories of my Mexico, but yet another broken heart. After a long journey in validations, homologations, and ministries, I was already submerged in shifts and congresses, meeting new friends and welcoming old ones.

My Brazilian friend, who was now living in New Zealand with an Argentinean, came to comfort me and warm my heart. She stayed only one day, but it was a day full of long and deep conversations accompanied by good wine. The next morning, she set out to find her own destiny in Alicante.

November, 2007. The Brazilian woman was returning home, but this time she did not come alone. He offered her to go first into the elevator so she could take her suitcase upstairs. Meanwhile, he was already climbing the stairs and almost knocking on the door. When I looked through the peephole, a tall, blond-haired, blue-eyed guy stood on the other side. My heart skipped a beat, and I couldn't help but open the door: a Dane. We immediately got along, but twenty-four hours later I had a flight to the place where my memories were born. Despite my invitation, he already had plans with a girl north of Barcelona.

London, November 7th, 2007. A call surprises me at Victoria Station saying "Do you mind if I catch up with you? I don't want to be without you." We spent unforgettable days, but my life was now in Barcelona and his in Calpe, Alicante.

Paris, June 2007. We were enjoying the jazz week in the streets of Paris, with a glass of wine in hand, while mixing jazz with summer.

-This is the perfect moment- I told him.

He suddenly had a generalized hyperemia and dropped to the ground. He got down on his knees to ask me if I wanted to share my life with him. No ring.

Flashback: Canada, 2004. A trip with my best friend, who knows for a fact that weddings and children are not for me, but I confessed that, if some crazy man wants to give me a ring someday, it will have to be in a high place.

Plane BCN-MEX, August, 2007. Again hyperemic, he throws himself on the ground and, this time, he takes out a ring. He has definitely chosen a high place. Two weddings later in two different countries and after many stories in our shared home in Catalonia, he has a new goal: to be a dad!

September, 2013. Having finished my residency, I did an external rotation in Copenhagen and fell in love: I discovered my own Denmark without him. I ask him to come back and spend this time together, but he's happy in Barcelona. He has the sun and the beach.

May, 2014. Having been successful in everything I set out to do, I was running out of excuses for not having children. Soon there would be three of us. An excessive rise in unemployment and wanting to offer her not to be a foreigner in her own country brings us to our home in Copenhagen.

Luana Sandoval Castillo (Continues on page 102)

Ilan Shapiro
(United States)

Stemming from different parts of the world, a combination of carpenters, butchers and tailors came together in Veracruz, Pachuca, and Mexico City. They moved to a country full of magic and new, exotic flavors, very different from those they knew.

Because they had diverse backgrounds and spoke different languages, Mexico unified them. This first generation, generation zero, came from humid, dark, and snowy places, so finding a warm place —which welcomed them with open arms— represented a break, a relief and, for the first time in years, a chance to be reborn. Many of their relatives had been killed during World War II, and others had moved to other parts of the world, such as Canada and the United States, driven by the same desire to find somewhere with brand new opportunities to start over.

Most of my grandparents were born in Mexico. Among them, they spoke Russian, Polish, Yiddish, and Spanish. The cultural differences slowly disappeared, but their stories have made me ask myself many times if I'd had the same strength to emigrate to a completely different continent without understanding the culture of the place that today I call home.

That led, in the 80s in Mexico City, to a desperate but expected cry that was heard after more than 40 weeks of production and a dozen hours. I went from a place where I was provided with food, warmth, and sustenance to a place with lots of light, sounds and sensations that I had never experienced before. Like me, the following generations fused languages, flavors and aromas with identities that added spice to the culture that makes up my being.

My grandparents and grandmothers (*Zides* and *Bobes*) taught me the importance of appreciating differences, adding opportunities, subtracting problems, and multiplying blessings for everyone because, no matter where you come from, health is your biggest treasure.

Ilan Shapiro (Continues on page 106)

René Sotelo
(United States)

A Barbecue in Long Island... Things are coming together

The story of my change of residence from Caracas, Venezuela, to Los Angeles, in the United States, begins with a barbecue in Long Island, in the state of New York. It was July 2014, and I had been invited to the home of Dr. Arthur Smith —founder of the Endourological Society and originally from South Africa—for a barbecue, which we Venezuelans like to call a *parrillada*. Medical events such as congresses, seminars and conferences are always an excellent opportunity to learn and share knowledge, which is, I must confess, along with medicine, another of my passions: teaching. These academic spaces, in addition to multiplying what has been learned over the years and which gives so much satisfaction to share, are, without a doubt, a great way to see old friends, talk about trends, strengthen ties, meet so many familiar faces again and create brand new memories.

That afternoon's barbecue, however, was key in bringing many different aspects together. For the first time, the possibility of working in the United States hovered before me and, even though I didn't assimilate it at the time, what for me seemed like a simple conversation would change the course of my life, my family's and my profession.

Dr. Smith, as an immigrant to the United States himself, was fully aware of the possibilities that existed in the country to give entry to foreign talent; he knew it was attainable and not only understood it in detail from his own experience, but he was also familiar with the different ways to offer jobs to colleagues from other countries. In his experience, the United States was a land of opportunities, and he was convinced that it would be for me as well. It was he who presented the option of moving to me and with whom I first discussed the subject. He firmly laid down the proposal and told me that they would be willing to explore the possibility of me working in the country.

I found the conversation appealing, no doubt, but it didn't evolve from there. I did not give it much thought. The reality was that leaving my country was not something I had considered until that moment. I ran a private practice, managed the Minimally Invasive Urology Center I had founded with Dr. Oswaldo Karan, had recently inaugurated an additional location to attend more patients—in a prestigious clinic in the southeast of Caracas—, and I was also in charge of the rehabilitation wing of the medical institute, where I provided my patients with an integral recovery experience. Everything was running smoothly. My days were spent between medical consultations, operations and once or twice a month I would take a break to travel, give lectures, and perform surgeries as a guest professor in different countries. I'd spend time with my family, and, on the weekends, we'd go to Margarita Island, that pearl of the Caribbean I love so much. Starting Friday afternoons, my trips were my break, my rest, my peace, my home. Piedras Blancas, in the town of La Guardia, in Margarita, was that haven where I reconciled with life. Everything fit into place, came together, and worked. The alternative of starting all over again and leaving everything behind was unthinkable. But as I said: that barbecue would turn my life upside down. Arthur was opening a door that would lead me to a new world.

Steve Jobs once said in a speech that, if we look back, we can see turning points in our lives necessary to make way for others, and that, only when they come together, do we understand and make sense of why things happened. Nothing could be truer. The barbecue in Long Island was just that, a point that would lead to another.

In order to make sense of that journey and be able to explain about how I got here, I must talk about Dr. Andrew Novick, a legend in urology, renowned for his contribution to kidney research and renal reconstructive surgery. He was chairman of the Glickman Urological and Kidney Institute at the Cleveland Clinic until his untimely death at the age of 60.

In my eagerness to learn and better myself, I became interested from a very young age in the organization of events in Venezuela. I was always looking for ways to participate and to be an active part of everything related to urology in my country. Among the eminent guests invited to those congresses, the name of Dr. Novick stood out; he, together with Dr. Inderbir Gill, visited Venezuela. On one of these trips, Dr. Novick suggested I should visit the Cleveland Clinic and train there. And I obviously accepted the offer. I visited the Cleveland Clinic many times for medical training and became friends with Dr. Novick. I would go to see him perform open partial nephrectomies. A few years later, he even offered me a job as part of the staff of the new Cleveland Clinic that would branch out into the Middle East. As soon as he started the project, he was already recruiting people. He appointed me part of the international board of the institution, which I visited many times as a member. That was fifteen or twenty years ago.

In that series of trips, I trained with Dr. Inderbir Gill, who introduced me to the basics of laparoscopic surgery. I had already seen other doctors operate laparoscopically, but I must say Dr. Gill performed it in a friendlier way. It was on those trips back and forth to the United States to see Dr. Novick, Dr. Gill and their team operate, that my friendship with Dr. Inderbir Gill, *jigri dost*, which in Hindi means "boon companion", was born. Undoubtedly, another turning point along the way. He was a wonderful friend, great mentor, and someone whose teachings I will always be thankful for.

It was Indi Gill who —a week after the barbecue in Long Island at Dr. Smith's house— surprisingly called me to say he had heard the news and that, if I was considering going to the United States, I should evaluate the possibility of going to USC and joining his team as chairman of the Department of Urology of Keck Medicine at USC. My surprise was twofold: first, because I didn't know how the news had traveled from Long Island to Los Angeles in just one week and second, because, in just seven days, the opportunity to work in the United States had presented itself twice.

Up until that day, my meetings with Arthur in his Long Island residence had been mostly interesting conversations, the kind that take place after congresses to go beyond the medical topics and share personal stories. But then, a life option that I had never considered and didn't know could exist for me as a doctor trained in Venezuela, rose up. Gill's call upped the pace I thought about everything. It represented a turning point in my day-to-day life. I would lie awake at night dwelling on it.

What Gill was proposing was serious business, as I would embark on a whole process before the Medical Board of California, the institution that evaluates whether a person truly possessed extraordinary abilities to practice medicine in the state of California without having graduated as a physician in the United States. If that permission were granted, I could then file an application for the O-1 visa. Thus, a journey of uncertainty and venturing was born.

I confess that, although I was considering it, it was something I still thought was a long way off. It was happening but, to tell you the truth, I was a bit skeptic. After all, it was a tough bridge to cross: the last license of that kind had been granted by the state of California 72 years ago to a Japanese physician. It would be difficult, but that remote possibility was getting closer and closer, it was looming more and more to change my outlook, my life and my family's.

At the same time, the situation in Venezuela was becoming more and more critical. Due to the insecurity that plagues the country, my daughters, teenagers preparing for college, were increasingly demanding the possibility of living their youth, being able to walk on the streets without feeling unsafe, taking part in the activities normal young people do. That contrasted immensely with the restrictions I had set to protect them. And suddenly, the chance of quieting down the thoughts that would rob me of sleep became clear to me. The loose ends were starting to tie up and things were coming together.

René Sotelo (Continues on page 108)

Karla Uribe

(United States)

If twenty years ago someone had told me that at some point in my life I would be living in the United States, married, with two children, with another nationality, but most importantly, that I would stop practicing medicine, I would have thought they were talking about someone else. That was an unthinkable, absurd, and completely impossible idea. Now, that old phrase that says "if you want to make God laugh, tell him about your plans" comes to my mind, because, without a doubt, destiny had something different in store for me.

I was 19 years old when I met the person for whom, ten years later, I did what I never thought I'd be willing to do: leave my comfort zone, my secure and carefully thought-out life. I could not have fathomed I'd find myself here, in another country, dedicating my daily efforts to build a common goal and to walk hand in hand with him through this adventure called life.

At the encouragement of one of my aunts, who lives in Utah, I applied for two universities in the United States. She thought it would be a good idea for me to spend a summer learning English and my parents and I set about the task of meeting the necessary requirements: letters to prove financial statements, health certificates, etc. Before we knew it, Weber State University had accepted me as a student in the English as a Second Language program. And just like that, fresh out of my first year of medical school, I suddenly found myself at the airport on my way to Salt Lake City.

My aunt greeted warmly and with arms wide open. The original plan was for me to study at the university and return home to spend the rest of my time with her and her family. To get to school I had to use public transportation, and I was used to a life of conveniences in which buses, or the subway played no role. I am not very well oriented, plus I have the sequels of cerebral palsy, so walking long distances can be challenging for me. For these reasons, and with my parents' approval, I decided to go live in the university's dormitories.

One day, after class, in the dormitory elevator, I met my husband. It all started there, simply, and with a casual conversation. I can say with absolute certainty that I believe in love at first sight, that at nineteen I met the man I wanted to share my life with, and that I knew it from the very first moment. The summer, however, came to an end, and each of us had to go our separate ways. When I was back home, we talked on the phone a few times, but after a while we lost track of each other completely.

I returned to Mexico, finished my degree, and graduated in Ciudad Universitaria (National Autonomous University of Mexico), an accomplishment I will always be extremely proud of. When the time came to apply for the National Examination for Medical Residency Applicants (known in Spanish as ENARM), the possibility of the Steps crossed my mind, but I thought I really had no need. Having a father who's a doctor in Mexico, gave me a bit of a head start. I applied and on the first try I was accepted for otolaryngology.

One lazy day, ten years after the elevator encounter and when I was starting my last year of residency, that guy popped into my mind, the one from Utah. A Google search gave me a link to a people finder, and I paid ten dollars to get his different addresses, which he'd changed throughout the years. I guess curiosity does have a price, and that's the one I had to pay.

Instantly, a list of about twenty addresses appeared in my email. The dilemma now was deciding what to do with that information. I typed a letter on the computer, printed it out five times, picked addresses at random and sent them off. I had nothing to lose. I figured that, if he wrote me back, he would send me a picture of him with his wife, two kids and a dog. After all, ten years had already gone by, and I was always "just about to finish" my studies.

Six weeks later, I got a reply. Luckily, one of the letters arrived at an address he had moved from two weeks earlier and they were able to forward the letter to his new home. I received an email titled "Hello" that made my heart skip a beat. It didn't say much. Long story short, he enlisted in the Army and had just finished his service. We set up a date via Messenger. After about three lines of chatting, all was said and done:

- Hi, did you get married?

- No, did you? - I replied.

- I didn't either.

What happened next was obvious: we wanted to be together, that was not up for discussion. The only drawback was that we lived in different countries.

He was always willing to go live in Mexico, but the truth is that working as a physician in the States is substantially better paid. So, we decided that I would be the one to move. I just had to pass the Steps and that would be it! How little did I know what lay ahead of me! And so, ten years after meeting in that elevator as I carried two suitcases full of clothes and hopes, our adventure began: all because two people fell in love.

Karla Uribe (Continues on page 110)

Jeannette Uribe
(United States)

I was in my second year of residency in Obstetrics and Gynecology (OB/GYN) when I had an appointment in Ciudad Juárez (Chihuahua) to get the famous Green Card, a process that my husband had started five years earlier. Until that moment, I had not given much thought to the idea of emigrating, so I decided to finish my specialty in Mexico. During my last year of residency, we started making plans to get pregnant. The only reason we waited was that, at that time, the residency system had an absurd and unethical rule that made you repeat the whole year in case of pregnancy. It's curious and surprising how the recruitment process for medical graduates is carried out. Unless they have an outside opportunity to work in a private clinic, a contact, or friends in high places, most of the hundreds of graduates from all over the country must choose from the spots available a couple of days after the graduation ceremony. It's amazing how your future is decided in a matter of seconds. You have no idea which jobs are going to be offered, what the work environment will be like, and there are even places that don't show up on Google Maps. However, there I was: 3 months pregnant and with a husband who was patiently waiting outside, hoping I would be offered a position near my home or in one of the cities I already knew. But, as life would have it, that wasn't the case. When my turn came, my mind was spinning. I got up, approached the person in charge and said, "Thank you very much, but I'm not accepting any of these offers". I left the place and told my husband: "We're moving to the United States".

I said goodbye to my family, and went off to Florida, where we stayed with my husband's relatives and, two weeks later, we were in Georgia, living with my sister-in-law and expecting our first child. I'll always be grateful for their help and support. I can't imagine coming to a different country, to a different language and culture, without your family's support.

There were several factors that led me to make the decision to emigrate. I thought about my son's future, his safety, my professional growth, and the fact that I could legally enter the country without having to apply for a visa. However, a big part of my decision was influenced by my older brother, who had also emigrated to the United States at the age of 14. My brother is a person who likes to think and dream big. In his perspective, I had studied so hard for many years and given so much to people, that it was time for my efforts to be recognized. My brother had no idea that medicine simply works different, and my parents didn't know it either, much less my husband, or even myself. No one knew how bumpy a road it is to achieve the dream of practicing medicine in the United States.

When my baby was two months old, we moved from Georgia to Michigan, where my brother, the one who encouraged me to start this journey, lived with his wife. His unconditional support was a blessing to me and my family. And so, another year went by with drastic transitions and important decisions. I went from being an OB/GYN resident to a full-time housewife and first-time mom. We left my *México lindo* to live in a country with a different culture and language, in a state whose weather was unlike anything I'd experienced before and starting from scratch. I thought this milestone would mark a before and after in my life. I was wrong. The challenges were only beginning to come my way.

Jeannette Uribe (Continues on page 111)

3

Formalities' difficulties. Paperwork, paperwork, and more paperwork

Patricia Bautista Rivera

(UNITED STATES)

We traveled to Kentucky when the paperwork was ready. The staff from the university that had hired my husband had applied for the visa and sent us the necessary documents to do the paperwork at the U.S. Embassy in Mexico, where we had no issues in getting things done. My husband was granted a J-1 visa. The spouses of those who receive a J-1 visa must prove legal marriage, so they and their children can be granted the J-2 visa, which doesn't allow them to work. However, you can apply for authorization to do so. When we arrived, we were able to obtain a social security number and the paperwork was easier, but it became more complicated after the events of September 11, 2001.

Our initial plan was to live in the U.S. for two years and then return to Mexico. I got a rotation with two groups of allergists with whom I continued to learn allergy and English. At the beginning of our second year in the States, we welcomed a baby girl and, almost 5 years later, a baby boy.

When my husband finished his training (after 6 and a half years instead of the 2 that were initially planned), we decided to return to live in Mexico City to put the knowledge we had acquired into practice in the service of our country. He got a job at the National Cancer Institute, and, in the afternoons, he saw patients in private practice. The readjustment to the city was not easy, but it filled us with immense joy to know that we would be close to our families and, better yet, that our children would know them and have the opportunity to grow up near them.

After a couple of years of living in Mexico City, my husband received a job offer in Kentucky. Due to the insecurity of our city and the possibility of a better income, we returned to live in the U.S. This time, he was granted an H1-B visa. For this visa it's necessary to have a contract with an employer that functions as a visa sponsor, and it's valid for three years. Dependents get the H4 visa, which also requires a special permit for its recipients to work.

Regarding the revalidation of my studies in medicine and pediatrics, it was very sad to discover that specialty studies are not recognized. To revalidate a degree in medicine, you need to pass the same exams that U.S. medical students take: Step 1, basic knowledge, Step 2, clinical knowledge (CK) and clinical skills (CS), and Step 3, general medical knowledge.

I took the exams a long time ago, back in the time when there was no online registration. A pamphlet had to be requested by phone from the

ECFMG, with instructions for accreditation of university studies and registering to take the exams. Studying was rather complicated because, between taking care of a two-year-old girl and running a household, I had little time available. However, I devoted myself to it, studied, and took the exams.

My husband was notified by the university that the exams with which he'd been accepted at the beginning of his training were no longer valid, so he had to take the USMLE exams as well. We took one of the exams together, and we both passed.

After some time living here, the medical group that hired my husband recommended that we start the process to apply for permanent residency (Green Card). We hired a lawyer who did the paperwork and we obtained it without any problem. Entering and leaving the country became much easier.

After five years of permanent residency, you can apply for citizenship. In our case, it took a bit longer: it was hard for us to accept becoming citizens of another country. When we understood that the obligations were the same, we accepted for the permanent residency, but not the rights, such as the right to vote, we decided to start the process. It was an emotional ceremony, in which the judge who performed the oath reminded us that we did not renounce our country of origin nor its people.

We believe it's important to be able to participate in the election of those who lead and make decisions that affect the place where we live. We also recognize that, by accepting citizenship, we not only accept the privileges, but also the obligations that come with it.

Patricia Bautista Rivera (Continues on page 113)

Edmundo Erazo

(THE NETHERLANDS)

After figuring out where I wanted to go and how I'd get there, the paperwork came along. Some technical difficulties can be foreseen, and others cannot. In my case, I must admit that it was a relatively straightforward process. The first thing I needed was a letter of acceptance. For that, I had to apply to the program, write a letter of motivation, send certified copies of my diplomas and qualifications, and an English language test. Once I was accepted, I had to wait for the Erasmus Medical Center to start the process to be granted a visa. That was very helpful because they've already notified your case when you go to the embassy, and the process is already on its way. As in many other residency procedures, you hand over your passport, and they grant you a temporary visa; with that, I could start my studies without returning to my country. Then, they gave me a residence permit to stay in the country until I finished my master's.

The procedures that have to be done while in the country are relevant: getting a cell phone number, a bank account, and a lease. You must obtain a residence number for all that, but one of the requirements is to have an address, and, sometimes, landlords don't rent to foreigners without the residence number. Maybe someone rents you an apartment, but the address is not authorized to process a registration number, so you end up stuck in a challenging vicious circle. My advice is to ask the international office about companies that rent to foreigners; that helps. If you travel on a work contract, you can usually ask your employer to find a temporary lease.

One of the most curious things that I found is that, to rent a place, they ask you for an account statement from a national bank, but you cannot process the bank account if you don't have a residence registration number or a lease contract, so, again, you're faced with a possible but tricky process.

In my case, I found a landlord who accepted the grant acceptance letter as an income equivalent, and I luckily could register my address at the town hall. As a graduate student, nobody will solve this kind of problem in advance, so you should be one step ahead. This experience changes once you're hired, and you've finished studying. In my case, when I had a formal work contract in the country, everything got easier.

After finishing my master's degree, they offered me a job in clinical research, so I had to start a new process to change my immigration status from student to employee. In these cases, most of the procedures are carried out by the company or the university; however, in the Netherlands, you must personally register with the city hall for your address and tax payment details to be updated.

It helps a lot to use social networks or websites to contact other fellows Mexicans already living in the country. I even found furniture, appliances, and electronic devices for my apartment through these sites. I found a Mexican going back home and got a deal on what she was buying and selling. It made my life much easier because she also told me where to find foods that Mexicans cannot live without, such as sauces. Anyway, in my experience, this helped a lot. Of course, you should make sure you're safe when contacting strangers on the internet, but, in general, we Mexicans support each other enormously when we're abroad.

As for the academic procedures, everything will depend on what you want to do. If you're going to practice medicine, you'll have to obtain the BIG register. My advice is to start learning the language as soon as possible, as this will be vital to get that certification. Officially, it would be best if you had a B2 to obtain the papers. Realistically, you'll probably need a C1, a level where you can express yourself fluently and understand complex texts and implicit meanings. To work in the Dutch healthcare system, you must also take the AKV test on medical knowledge and skills (General Knowledge and Skills Test) and the BI-skills test, which proves your medical knowledge is the same as the Dutch.

These procedures take three to four years, and the average cost ranges from three to five thousand euros, but this can vary depending on the regulation.

Edmundo Erazo (Continues on page 116)

Sandra López-León

(Israel, the Netherlands, Spain, United States)

The process of revalidating medical education credentials in other countries is complex, time-consuming, bureaucratic, and costly. In addition, one generally must pass very difficult exams or restudy the basic years of medicine.

As soon as I graduated, I started to revalidate my degree in the Netherlands and in Spain. It takes several months to get all the documents they ask for. They all required an apostille and, in the case of the Netherlands, they all had to be translated into Dutch. You must also translate the syllabus of the year you graduated, because they change over the years. At the same time, I started to find out what I could study with the education I already had. The Dutch and Spanish Ministries of Education took more than six months to get back to me.

If I wanted to do a medical residency in the Netherlands, I had to speak perfect Dutch and study three more years of medicine. Furthermore, if I went to live in another country in the future, such as the United States or Canada, they would not revalidate my specialty. The Spanish Ministry replied that I had to take an exam for the basic cycles, but I would have to move to Spain to do my medical residency. I also found out that one could study for a master's and a Ph.D. without having to revalidate degrees and, in addition to that, if I got a Ph.D., it would be valid worldwide.

Since I found just the program I wanted, I decided to do an MSc, DSc and then a Ph.D. That took me about eight years. Meanwhile, I also had two children. I can say that choosing to do a Ph.D. is one of the best decisions I've made in my life. Besides the fact that I am very passionate about my work, it is completely compatible with having a family; I have even been able to move from one country to another and get jobs everywhere.

In addition, I revalidated my medical degree in Spain since it was only a matter of taking an exam. I studied for six months every day for one hour and took my exam at the University of Barcelona. It sounds easy, but it requires a lot of paperwork and bureaucracy. On top of that, they didn't ask me any of the questions they told me to study for. All the material was in Catalan, so at least I learned more of the language. I passed without much difficulty because most of what they asked me, was about genetics, field I already had a Ph.D. in. Once I revalidated my degree, I was able to register with the Official College of Physicians of Barcelona.

Revalidation varies over time. The laws change and it also depends on when you studied medicine. For example, my brothers (who received their medical degree from the same University as me) had their medical studies in Spain revalidated automatically, without having to take an exam. Everything fluctuates and depends on the context, so

I recommend you investigate your case and not to rely solely on the experience of others.

Sandra López-León (Continues on page 118)

Rafael G. Magaña
(ENGLAND, UNITED STATES)

When, as a student, a psychologist confirmed that my aptitude test was oriented towards manual and intellectual activities, I felt validated. I knew I'd made the right choice regarding my vocation and my professional path.

At the same time, I felt —and still feel— disdain for jobs that involve any kind of paperwork. Plus, I tend to procrastinate, as many people from my generation do.

I had never felt more overwhelmed than when I applied for a student visa in the United States to take the courses that were my gateway to the USMLE exams. These courses allowed me to be in the country legally until I obtained a surgical residency position.

Every time I finished one, I signed up for another, and then another, and so on. But there came a time when I was running out of courses, and I still didn't have residency offers. I felt like the world was closing in on me.

The intervals between one course and another and immigration approval were times of great stress, because I didn't know if my student visa would be renewed. I had to get used to stress and come to terms with the situation, because my goal was to get a permanent visa.

After several courses and exams, I finally obtained the preliminary residency and was luckily granted the H-1 visa. This visa allows you to apply for permanent residence in the future, on the condition that a hospital sponsors it. The alternative was the J-1 visa (for academic exchange) which, after six years, forced me to return to my country for a minimum of two years, although there are some exceptions to that condition.

I enjoyed each year but, at the same time, I was worried that I wouldn't be able to continue with the program. However, every year, my H-1 visa was renewed.

The program was part of an outdated educational system, where a pyramidal format and the survival of the fittest prevailed. No one had any guarantee they'd complete the training; it was necessary to perform well in the annual exams to be promoted to the following year, and you also needed to get good evaluations from each attached physician.

Each year, in the graduation ceremony, the hopes and expectations of some colleagues shifted and, for a few of them, it represented the end of their career in surgery; many others changed courses. Of all the residents that started the program, only about two graduated.

Luckily for me, every year I got more and more optimistic. During the fourth year of residency, the program was expanded to three chief residents, which meant there was one more position in each subsequent year. That was the opportunity I was waiting for to repeat the fourth year of residency, not as a preliminary resident, but as a categorical one. I didn't think twice and accepted the offer.

After finishing the general surgery program in New Rochelle, NY, I went to the New York Hospital to continue my training with the hopes of specializing in surgery for burn patients. I was also interested in the opportunity to practice plastic surgery and, thus, gain experiences overlapping specialties.

Starting the program, however, required a whole lot of documents. That's when I learned that program coordinators can be important allies that can help you out in the future.

While I awaited the long sought-after Green Card, and as my H-1 was about to expire, I went through a rough patch in terms of continuity in work and graduate studies.

NY Hospital, in particular, is quite strict and loves bureaucracy. Nonetheless, with the help of the coordinator and the program director, I managed to continue treating burn patients without interruption. It must be said that it's highly possible that a letter from Hillary Clinton, who was senator at the time, expedited my process.

I was at NY Hospital for two years, during which I applied and finally received invitations to residency programs in plastic surgery.

After being interviewed for various programs, I started a craniofacial specialty. Each state has its own licensing requirements, and, in Utah, the process was time consuming and complex. I also had to overcome these same difficulties at the Children's Hospital and Intermountain Health Care.

This was the only state where the state licensing department of education asked me personally why I was applying for a medical license there. After explaining it to them, they were very cordial and asked me for about two million documents. I also had to take courses on prescriptions for controlled substances in the state and other associated workshops.

A never-ending flow of documents… Yes, that's a big component of the degree and any specialty of medicine. When I finished the program in Utah, I had already applied, been interviewed, and been accepted into the Georgia MCG plastic surgery program.

The year I was free, I did a specialty in oncoplastic breast reconstruction in New York. But, again, I had to apply for the New York medical license. It was already July 2008, and, for some reason and despite my multiple calls trying to speed up the process at the department of education, my state license hadn't arrived. Luckily, it came just in time, and I began a year of academic experience in which I learned and enjoyed a lot.

During that year, I filled out all the necessary documents for the Georgia license, which was the state I'd do my plastic surgery residency in.

Between the documents required for the state license, the educational program, and the hospitals —especially the ones for the Veterans Affairs (VA) Hospital— I think I filled out the equivalent in words of a Tolstoy novel. I've never had to fill out so many papers or give so many explanations, particularly to the VA, because it's a government institution.

My apologies to the readers. This chapter seems like a constant rant, but filling out that much paperwork was harder than the long on-call night shifts.

Finally, let me tell you about my experience when it comes to housing. Sometimes it's easy to find a place, but that isn't always the case. For example, in New York, the hospital provided me with very affordable housing, but elsewhere it was different. My advice is to contact your predecessor in the program and ask them to give you a few tips. The program coordinators are also very helpful.

Rafael G. Magaña (Continues on page 121)

Nissin Nahmias

(UNITED STATES)

It should be mentioned that there are several procedures that must be carried out to go to the United States and do a medical residency. It's essential to find a way to bear all the expenses that this represents: traveling for the interviews; the cost of the visa, the revalidation of the titles and the exams, and the Steps, until everything's done.

These procedures are divided into three sections:

1. Getting the visa.
2. Revalidating your degree.
3. Passing the exams and getting the ECFMG certificate.

1. Getting the visa

To get the visa, you have to understand that, depending on your situation and the institution you'll be part of, you can apply for different types. The most common is the student exchange visa (or J-1) which, as its name implies, forces you to return to your country of origin at the end of your training. Thank God, I'm Mexican, and only a three-hour flight away from home. I remember two colleagues, one Iranian and the other Pakistani, who had a really tough time returning to their countries. There are some exceptions that allow you to stay in the country with this type of visa, such as when there's an extraordinary need for doctors, or when you're offered a position in an area of the country that lacks specific physicians. Another option, a bit more complicated for the institution, is the H-1B or temporary worker visa. The H-1B has the advantage that, if you have relatives or are marrying a U.S. citizen, you don't need to return to your country of origin, and you're allowed to apply for the Green Card. Among other procedures, I had to get a letter saying I'd be acting in Mexico's best interest if I trained in the United States.

2. Revalidating your degree

The revalidation process entails that most of the work be done in Mexico: getting apostille stamps, translations, and so on.

3. Passing the exams and getting the ECFMG certificate

It's essential to pass the USMLE Step 1, and Step 2 exams, as well as the CSA (Clinical Skills Assessment). Without these requirements, the candidates are not even considered, especially if they're foreigners.

After all this, comes the Match process, where, broadly speaking, a candidate looks for an institution to do their residency in; they're the ones who select the candidates, not the other way around. I remember these processes require great emotional strength and integrity because, when you're not selected right off the bat, you must look for which institutions failed to obtain candidates and which new positions were opened; and then you must give yourself the task of making calls, sending emails, and finding out how to get in. Obviously, many foreigners are rejected, because the institutions give preference to nationals; and foreigners always occupy the last spots. It took me a lot of hard work to get to where I am today.

At the last minute, and at the last second, with God's help and thanks to the support of my family and friends, I got a spot.

Nissin Nahmias (Continues on page 122)

Susana Ramírez Romero
(SPAIN)

Bureaucracy is horrendous anywhere in the world, but in Spain it takes the cake. When it comes to my experience, migrating involves an amount of paperwork and red tape that seems nearly endless.

In Spain, you can apply for two types of visas: student and tourist. The duration of the first one will depend on the study program, and the second one lasts three months. Residency is the temporary permit that allows you to live and work and must be renewed every four years on average.

You can apply for nationality after having lived in the country for two years, so that's what we did. You must pass an absurd test on Spanish politics, gastronomy or culture and hand in several documents confirming your employment status. We applied at the same time, but everyone's files took surprisingly different paths, giving the impression that we were applying for different processes. Information that was requested for one child was not required for the other, such which school they attended. We submitted the paperwork in 2013, and the first to get the appointment to take the oath to receive the nationality was my eldest son in February 2018. In my case, the nationality was denied to me at the end of the same year, even though Spanish is my mother tongue, I worked in healthcare and, of course, paid taxes. I filed an appeal, which was supposed to be answered within two years. The last time I asked about the process, they only answered that, due to COVID-19 issues, the reply could take two more years to arrive. In my case, having the nationality is not a game changer, so I've let it take its course. Apparently, however, some files remain frozen, and I'll probably have to resort to lawyers.

The homologation and validation of studies, on the other hand, are an absolute nightmare than can last a decade. It's sad to admit that the people who work in these offices see you as just another number in a file and the faster they get it out of the way, the better. A refusal will always involve less effort than a thorough analysis. Some people at these desks also have the misconception that migrants are a burden when many countries have grown thanks to their work and determination.

Susana Ramírez Romero (Continues on page 123)

Luis Rodrigo Reynoso

(ETHIOPIA)

Before traveling to Ethiopia to take the position as a surgeon, the hardest challenge about it came to be: the paperwork. I had to confront the bureaucracy and not let the infinity of no's that I was going to receive affect me. I believe that in that process is where your mettle is put to the test, and you begin to become an expert on the subject. I have had the opportunity to live in other countries, and I can say that filling out all the forms and documents is always a pain in the bones ... It is not only because of the ignorance of the procedures, but because of the little empathy that the people who oversee these procedures have.

Apparently in Ethiopia the paperwork was not so strict but, of course, official translations had to be made of each of the documents to be sent, with their respective notarial signatures. They almost asked us for the bishop's blessing. There was no choice, I filled out each of the documents with my best handwriting, as clean and tidy as possible, and trying to be friendly. This was what my obsessive-compulsive disorder demanded, and this was how it should be done.

The entry ticket to Ethiopia depended on my responses to those formats, so we were extremely careful. What if a couple more copies if we could send better photos ...? I hate the stiffness of official photos; I do not understand why we are not allowed to smile on those photos.

I remember that when I finally completed the entire file (which checked and reviewed four times), I asked Anahí to take it to the most reliable courier office. That day I had left home, as usual, at six in the morning and had left my fiancée a note with the details to make the shipment. My day passed between surgeries as usual, and every so often I would check my messages. Suddenly I got a message from Anahí.

> "Luis, are you sure the address is correct? In your note there is no street name, nor a number. It seems to me that important data is missing, if not, how is this going to be delivered?"

"Dr Tewodros near Gerji, in front of Unity College, next to the Korean Hospital. Addis Ababa, Ethiopia".

All the data were correct, there was no other reference, there was no street name or number. The address was more than complete: "There is nothing missing from that address", I told her. "Just with that you can find out more or less where we are going."

So, I sent all the documents: university degrees, course certificates, TOEFL, letter of intent, vaccination card, application to the Ethiopian government to work as a surgeon and the letter of commitment from Tewodros to award me a US $ 700 scholarship to keep us in said country.

I had no idea what the lifestyle was like in Ethiopia, much less the state of the economy, but Ted had told me that the scholarship was enough for Anahí and I to get by without problems. In addition, he would oversee preparing the clinic so that we could live there when we arrived, but this would be temporary, and with the intention that in the future we could rent our own place.

Time passed and we received no news. They only told us that the procedure was in process. Two, three months passed and nothing, there was only uncertainty. Dr Ted wrote to me recommending not to buy the flights yet, since the clinic would not be ready for another two or three months. Finally, he told me that if I wanted to, buy the tickets, and enter the country as a tourist. Later we could fix the whole immigration issue, work permits, licenses and so on.

-Enough said!

My answer then was more or less this: "Doc, if everything goes according to plan, we will be arriving at Addis Ababa airport on April 11, 2018. Is there anything you consider important or necessary to bring? Is anything on this side of the world that we could bring you?"

Ted asked me to bring all kinds of sutures, since the few that they had, had been obtained on the black market, since his government does not allow imports. He travelled to the United States twice a year and it was when he took the opportunity to stock up on material.

I managed to gather more than a thousand sutures of different types, with expiration, without expiration. With packaging details, cautery pencils, electrocautery plates, my favorite needle holder, fine scissors, precision tweezers, microsurgery magnifiers, surgical suits ... I also packed some rain boots (in Ethiopia it rains for three months in a row, and the start of the rainy season coincided with our arrival), a tequila to thank Ted for his welcome gesture, and some Mexican culinary products such as mole, flour to make tortillas, pickled jalapeño peppers and the occasional spicy treat that I knew my wife would miss.

We were ready to start the new adventure, but there was another detail: Mustafa! Perhaps animal lovers can understand that our intention was to take our cat with us. We had already been warned that there was neither litter nor food for cats in Ethiopia. At first that did not matter to us: we would find something for him to eat, and a little corner for his cat litter... that was enough. However, meeting the requirements for our cat to travel became tedious and excessively expensive, so we decided to postpone his trip until we saw how everything flowed. We had a round ticket, with a return date in six months. Maybe at that time, we could bring him with us.

Luis Rodrigo Reynoso (Continues on page 125)

Alejandra Rodríguez Romero
(UNITED STATES)

I entered the country on an Alien Fiancé(e) visa, which is applied for by filing form I-129F. U.S. citizens or residents who intend to marry a foreigner and bring them to the United States are eligible to apply for this visa. The immigration process, in my case, was relatively simple and quick. The complicated part was the revalidation of my degree through the Educational Commission For Foreign Medical Graduates (ECFMG), an organization in charge of certifying foreign doctors. In order to do that, you must pass 3 exams called Steps. In Step 1, knowledge of basic subjects is tested and in 2CK, knowledge of medical specialties is evaluated. These exams are both theoretical. Then comes the 2CS, a practical exam where 10 scenarios are created with fictitious patients to assess clinical skills. After what seemed like an eternity of studying and multiple hurdles along the way, I passed all 3 exams and earned my certification.

Next on the list was to get hands-on experience through hospital rotations. This required a lot of money and effort, since I had to travel to several places in the country, but I knew it was necessary and, with the support of my family, I began the adventure of being part of the medical system in the United States. Since I already had letters of recommendation, I started with the application for the medical residency, which is regulated by the National Resident Matching Program (NRMP). It's a complex process, where the candidate has the option of applying to all the hospitals in the country that offer the specialty of choice. The application consists of creating a profile with information that includes clinical experience, both in the country of origin and in the United States, volunteer work, and a written statement of why the specialty was chosen. Letters of recommendation issued by physicians with whom the rotations were performed are attached (it's advisable to have done rotations in at least 3 different hospitals to gain experience and letters of recommendation).

The call for applications begins in September of each year and ends with the selection of new residents in March. A physician graduated from an American university only needs to apply to about 10-15 programs to be selected. A foreign physician, on the other hand, needs approximately 80 programs to increase his or her chances of being considered. Each hospital or program has its specifications, such as the number of years after graduation, minimum Steps scores, and whether the program accepts foreign doctors. The major limitation for me, and for a large number of foreign physicians, was that it had been more than 3 years since we graduated.

As I mentioned in the first chapter, had I known this would be my future, I would have studied for the Steps during my career and not upon completion, thus gaining valuable time. Out of approximately 4000 applications per hospital, about 100 candidates are selected and called for an interview. The results of the selection are published online in March, whether one was selected and where. If you are not selected, you must repeat the same process the following year, making sure you have gained new experience and new letters of recommendation.

Alejandra Rodríguez Romero (Continues on page 129)

Jack Rubinstein
(UNITED STATES)

"You know where that little word comes from? "Bureau" from the French *bureau*, which means desk, and "cracy", from the Greek *kratos,* which means power. In other words, what you people exercise is desk power".
—Cantinflas' speech on bureaucracy in the film *The Minister and I.*

Bureaucracy's bad reputation precedes it all over the world, and particularly in developing countries like Mexico, where we have all faced difficulties in carrying out government procedures that are controlled and often blocked by bureaucrats. I gave it an honest try, but the Mexican system that I left twenty years ago was not a system that I could deal with, and that led me to search for new options.

American bureaucracy also has a bad reputation, but the system required to practice medicine in the United States is relatively straightforward and, at the same time, extraordinarily difficult. Let's start with the USMLE (United States Medical Licensing Exam), which are the required exams for all medical students, American and foreign medical graduated (FMGs), who want to participate in a residency or practice medicine within the United States. In the 1990's there were only two steps for this examination, the basic (Step 1) and the clinical (Step 2). Today, however, there are four tests in total (though it appears that COVID-19 will force the number back down to three). The year I applied for residency was the first year that all four steps were required. The first change was a split of Step 2 (which consists of a written exam and a simulated clinical exam), and initially only affected FMGs, but now applies to all. Finally, Step 3 can be taken after starting residency, but before you can practice medicine.

The total cost of these exams amounts to around five thousand dollars, plus the cost of books and training courses, which are indispensable. For the FMGs, the courses and books are a must, not only because of the content of the subject matter, but also because of the differences in training and studying between the Mexican and American systems where, from a very young age, students are prepared for standardized exams. There's even the term "test taking skills", which refers to the ability to obtain better results in the exams, not necessarily by having the knowledge of the subject matter, but by learning (and training) the required skills. In my experience, I've learned that the more prep books and specific courses I take prior to an exam, the better my results will be. However, despite the time and money I invested, I'm still far from an expert in taking exams.

Once you have passed the initial exams, you have a lifetime of tests ahead of you that will allow you to obtain and maintain medical certifications in your chosen specialty and subspecialties. This process begins when you finish the residency and is repeated at least once more upon finishing the subspecialty. In fact, until a few years ago, the exam was repeated every ten years until one retired. All these requirements led to a broad discussion among the medical community that questioned the difficulty of the exam, the excessive expenses, and the emotional exhaustion it represented. As a result of these controversies, the examiners (who function in a semi-regulatory manner) are attempting to decrease the frequency of subsequent tests and make them less intense. Sadly, most of these changes have yet to be approved, and those who have already started the USMLE process have no choice but to take the exams (with very few exceptions).

Regarding the USMLE, a concern that comes up in almost every conversation has to do with scores. What's considered a good score? The answer is not easy, and it depends, to a large extent, on the specialty one is applying for. My recommendation for FMGs is to take the courses, buy and memorize the books, and do as many exercises as possible, but I also advise not to let too much time pass between medical school and the exams. A silver lining is the fact that all USMLE paperwork and information can be found on the same website. By the same token, all necessary requirements to apply for residencies and subspecialties can be found on another specific website.

In this part of the process, you will have the opportunity to enrich your academic history with pertinent details and distinguish yourself with letters of recommendation and publications that demonstrate your analytical skills and the quality of your work beyond the USMLE results. In my case, my interest in research substantially improved my application since my USMLE scores did not stand out on their own. After taking the exams and filling out the forms online, comes the fun part: the interview. Once the applications are reviewed, the directors send out the invitations for the interviews.

These interviews are like blind dates, and everyone has opinions on how to excel at them. After having gone through countless interviews, and having been judge and party on various occasions, I offer the following suggestions:

Attire: Wear a dark blue suit and a plain shirt (male and female). If you feel the need to stand out, stick to one item: flashy socks, a society pin, or maybe an eye-catching haircut. Regardless, bear in mind that this is not the time to wear some designer's new collection.

Homework: You must have "done your homework" before arriving for the interview. No excuses. Find out the city's soccer team, the program director's scientific or clinical interest and the administrative assistant's name. Similar to a blind date, the more information you have, the better the results.

Prepare canned responses: In the United States, students are instructed to prepare canned responses: previously prepared answers to typical questions ("Why do you like this specialty?", "What has been your most complicated patient?") and questions related to your record ("Why did you get a bad grade?", "What did you do during a sabbatical year?"). Practicing these responses and polishing them before the interview is just as important as presenting them as bright and "fresh" ideas, just as if they were a special dish in a Michelin-starred restaurant.

Jack Rubinstein (Continues on page 130)

Alberto Saltiel
(ISRAEL)

Every time I spoke with an Israeli about the immigration process, revalidation of studies, state exams and application to residencies, I was told it would take months of paperwork and eternal red tape, but my answer was always the same, "I'm from Mexico. There's no country with more bureaucracy than mine..." Boy, was I wrong.

As a foreigner, there are two possibilities to specialize in Israel: the first option is becoming a "foreign resident" and the second is as an Israeli citizen. Of course, in both cases, all academic documents must be translated into Hebrew, including degree, identity card, academic records, etc., and everything must be apostilled. That translation is only valid if approved by a notary recognized by the State of Israel.

Foreign residents

This option is aimed at anyone who wants to come to Israel to do a specialty knowing that, upon completion, they must return to their country of origin. There are several limitations for residents of this category; however, it entails many appealing benefits. For that reason, there's a respectable percentage of the country's medical population considered foreign residents. To enter this program, one simply applies directly to the selected specialty and waits for the program director's response. As a foreign resident, there's no need (up to the time this chapter was written) to take a revalidation or national exam. However, a foreign resident is recognized as a doctor solely and exclusively by the host hospital, not in Israel as a whole. Inside the hospital, they have the same benefits and rights as any other resident, but outside the hospital, they cannot practice medicine. In other words, they don't have the possibility of prescribing anything to patients outside that institution.

Another limitation as a foreign resident is the issue of basic salary and overtime. These hours include shifts, working hours outside the established ones and, in the case of surgeons, surgeries that are carried out outside the morning schedule. Historically, foreign residents — unlike citizen residents— lack a basic salary, and only receive overtime as monetary compensation. There are some hospitals where they're given a salary similar to that of Israeli residents, although lower, because the tax deduction is also different. Because of this, many hospitals ask that candidates receive a grant from their home country so that they can cover their expenses.

Finally, upon completing the academic program, the foreign resident does not take the final residency exam, as he or she will not receive the Israeli specialist license. This means that they're not allowed to work as a specialist within Israel. To receive that certification, they must return to their country of origin, revalidate the degree of specialist, and take the exams of the college of their respective specialty. If at the end of the specialty, the foreign resident decides they want to continue living in Israel, they must complete the process as a citizen.

Israeli citizens

This is where the formalities and bureaucracy begin. The first thing is to become a citizen. This is a separate process and, unfortunately, not available to everyone. Since the requirements are constantly changing and everything is carried out by Sojnut (Jewish Agency for Israel), I will not delve into the subject.

Once you receive the Israeli citizenship, following a process called Aliyah (/ a-li-ya /), you can apply for the National Medical Licensing Exam. This exam is the equivalent to the American USMLE, but with a completely different format. All procedures are carried out in conjunction with the Ministry of Health and the Israeli Medical Association. The exam is held twice a year and consists of two sections of 110 multiple-choice questions each. To pass, a minimum score of 65 is required.

Once the exam is approved, one must apply for the specific program of interest and be accepted. The length of residency varies between four to six years, depending on the specialty, but is not limited to that time. There's no annual hierarchy, but one must comply with a specific curriculum and two residency exams. The Shlav A (step A) is a multiple-choice exam that's taken once you've completed at least half of the residency. It's carried out at national level once a year and the minimum passing grade is, again, 65. The Shlav B (step B) is an oral exam with different synods that one must take at the end of the residency. You either pass or fail, and it's held nationally twice a year. Once both exams have been approved and all the residency requirements have been met, you receive the specialist certificate in Israel.

If a foreign resident wants to stay in Israel at the end of their residency, they must pass the National Medical Licensing Exam, the Shlav A, and the Shlav B so they can receive a specialist certificate in Israel.

Alberto Saltiel (Continues on page 133)

Luana Sandoval Castillo
(SPAIN, DENMARK)

I revalidated my degree as a surgeon in Spain[2], a fundamental requirement to take the MIR exam, which is like the ENARM and has on-site and distance courses[3].There are other prep courses, such as the CTO (http://www.grupocto.es), which are available in Madrid and Barcelona, among other cities; and also weekend programs, such as the one I took. Since I was part of the cardiology department of the Hospital del Mar, I was paid for on-call duty, and I could afford taking the course.

My recommendation is to be totally dedicated to preparing for the MIR, since you compete against Spanish nationals who have more

---

[2]   https://www.mecd.gob.es/serviciosalciudadanodecd/catalogo/educa- cion/gestion-titulos/estudios-universitarios/titulosextranjeros/homolo- gacion-educacion-superior.html

[3]   http://www.curso-mir.com/Informacion-para-edicosextranjeros/movimientos-migratorios.html

openings than us foreigners. You learn to turn answering an exam into an automatic skill. Once you pass, you choose a specialty based on your ranking of your exam and availability, so you must have clear priorities of specialty vs. place where you want to do your residency. These few years were very intense, with shifts where it was mandatory to be on call far from home, none of them similar to the ones I did during my internship.

During my first year of residency, the love of my life came knocking on the door of my house: my Dane moved with me to Barcelona. Some time later, Spain was facing an economic recession that forced people to take several jobs just to keep the standard of living, so the idea of migrating again started to become more and more tempting.

My first contact with Denmark was in 2013, when I was accepted for an external rotation, paid for by my residency in Barcelona. During my stay, I investigated the revalidation process for my specialist title and found out that everything works online. At the Ministry of Health (*Sundhedsstyrelsen*) (https://www.sst.dk/), they explained to me that, as a third country national (not a EU member), I needed a letter of good clinical practice issued by the College of Physicians of Barcelona (https://www.comb.cat/), and a certificate of compliance with Directive 2005/36/EC, with an explanatory point accrediting three years of professional practice in Spanish territory as provided for in Article 3.3 of the same directive and which is issued by the MECyD.[4]

In my case, this process lasted approximately eight months, and, by that time, I had already been granted Spanish citizenship, which meant that my case became that of a second country national, and my revalidation

---

[4]   https://sede.educacion.gob.es/catalogo-tramites/gestiontitulos/estudios-universitarios/titulos-obtenidos-en-espana/acreditacion-titulos-directivacomunitaria.html

was returned in full to the same level I had in Spain. Otherwise, I would have had to take a general medical exam, probably repeat the internship and service, called *KBU en Introstilling* in Denmark; repeat the specialty and accredit the mandatory Danish courses with a minimum of 7s and 10s, on a scale ranging from -3 to 12, which I finally did for my own benefit. Here's the direct link to the search for authorization as a physician trained outside the EU/EØS: https://stps.dk/da/autorisation/soeg-autorisation/laege/uddannet-uden-for-norden,-eu-og-eoes/#

It took me about a year to learn the language, so that I could communicate with patients/family *(lægmandsdansk),* colleagues *(læge dansk)*, and administrative staff, as when I arrived, they still used a dictation system. I had started to learn Danish back in Barcelona at the Intitut Nòrdic (https://institutnordic.com)where I lost my fear of the unknown. When I arrived in Copenhagen, I enrolled in the Kommune courses, which at the time were free for up to three years, but now each course costs almost 1400 kr for 8 weeks (https://www.kbh-sprogcenter.dk/da/). There's a basic orientation entity to turn to upon arrival in this country: International House (https://ihcph.kk.dk) welcomes you, lets you know what Denmark expects from you and lends a hand with logistics (identity number - CPR-, taxes, labor market, etc).

Luckily, my in-laws gave me a summer course to catch up on my Danish and later, when I was already in module 4, I switched to Hellerup Sprogcenter, where I did a specific course for doctors, *Lægedansk*, which in my case was from 8:00-14:00 from Monday to Friday at Gentofte Hospital. Here is the link to the course: https://speakspeak.dk/da/danskkurser/danskkurser-for-laeger/ and to information from Udlændinge og Integrationsministeriet (Ministry of Integration and Foreign Affairs) https://uim.dk/publikationer/laege-dansk .

After a year of unpaid work but speaking Danish daily, everything became easier. All my colleagues, patients and relatives were very kind and receptive and rarely stared back at me like saying "what do you mean?" After six months, I was offered an unclassified position where I could already be compensated as a specialist with on-call duty from 08:00 to 17:00. The rest would be home visits with extra payment per call made; in the case a ride to the hospital was needed, the payment was even higher, because it included transportation and aftercare at home. If I had a weekend shift, it also had its perks: the following week was free to compensate for the extra hours of work.

Ten months later, I was offered a permanent position as *afdelingslæge*[5], (junior attached physician) with working conditions from 8:00 to 15:00 without on-call and, if I worked overtime from 15:00 onwards, I'd be remunerated financially or with time off. My boss argued that my position should be section leader, and that I already had experience as a junior attached physician in Spain, so I could be promoted to *Overlæge* in 3 years instead of 5, have an administrative day and do 4–5 shifts per month with days off afterwards. Now, I have full flexibility to decide my schedule and a fantastic team. It has not been easy, but it has been worth every single minute I've invested.

I would absolutely recommend anyone to try and make a living in Denmark. Some companies that can help in the process are: https://medicarrera.com/; https://www.konzenta.dk/. Another option is to do a PhD or work with the industry as a medical advisor for companies such as Sanofi Denmark, Lundbeck or Novo Nordisk, among others.

Luana Sandoval Castillo (Continues on page 135)

---

[5]   https://www. laeger.dk/yngre-laeger-loen-tjek-din-loenseddel

Ilan Shapiro

(UNITED STATES)

Paperwork? I cannot fathom the number of trees that had to be cut in order to document the documentable. I have divided my experience with the procedures into two parts: first, the immigration part and then, the clinical tasks to revalidate six years of sweat and education. I knew very early on that I wanted to continue helping my countrymen in the United States. I saw that migrant communities were just as unprotected, but that the situation was aggravated by cultural and language differences.

I will leave the immigration part for the end but, before that, let me talk about the steps that, in my experience, should be followed when applying for a medical residency:

Revalidate your documents

a) All documents must be translated into English multiple times. In my case, ECFMG (the organization that validates documents for foreign doctors) contacted various Mexican institutions to make sure the translations were in order. However, this constant exchange of information usually took a lot of time.

b) Very important: Record the names of each of the agencies you send your documents to, the dates you delivered them, and the names of the people who received them. This documentation is often irreplaceable, and you cannot afford to lose it.

c) Find out if there's someone in your academic institution that can help you in this process. Constant communication with that person is key.

d) If you're a chart or diagram lover, I recommend the site: https://www.fsmb.org/siteassets/usmle-step3/pdfs/pathway-to-licensure.pdf. There, you will find all the information regarding the requirements for the Educational Commission for Foreign Medical Graduates' (ECFMG).

Take the exams

This was the most time-consuming part of the process, but it was also the least stressful one. I think the only difficult thing is to understand when and how to apply.

Find a residency and apply for a visa

Finding a medical residency and solving immigration red tape is an art in itself. For each country, this difficult process is different, but in the United States it's almost like getting a PhD. Laws change so often that when you enter, you must be familiar with them if you want to do a subspecialty. There's a great number of visas you can apply for, but the most important thing is where you are going to present yourself. Being accepted is something you have to anticipate in this process. It's also very important to know if your future plans involve a permanent residence in the United States. This is a very personal and delicate procedure, so I recommend talking to a lawyer to help you craft a strategy.

Go over your employment contract thoroughly

I wanted to make a brief review on a topic that will never be relevant in doing a residency or getting a degree: examining the employment contract. This document is extremely important, and you should read it carefully and ask someone who knows about the subject to read it as well. Your contract must include, in addition to your salary, all the benefits to which you are entitled.

Ilan Shapiro (Continues on page 137)

René Sotelo

(UNITED STATES)

Since the opportunity of coming to the United States came up, the first thing I thought of was how it'd affect us emotionally, but as time went by and the possibility took shape, putting the plan together became dealing with a series of formalities, paperwork and legal procedures. It was a matter of getting everything that a move implies under control: leaving the country, changing structure, home, environment, culture, manners, tastes, affections, landscapes, institutions, and legal systems. It meant considering how moving would affect each member of the family, the colossal dimensions of it, but all with common denominators: mixed feelings, great expectations and a lot of paperwork and documents to organize.

However, in the process of formalization and systematization, perhaps because it was a medical institution, the board took part in the process and made it much easier.

One thing led to another, and the journey's milestone was the recognition by the California Medical Board Division of Licensing of the extraordinary abilities that, as a foreign physician, had to be proven in order to grant the permit that would allow me to practice medicine, considering the possibility of performing surgeries without having presented or achieved the steps required by the State of California, as indicated in section 2,168 of its regulations.

While the University of Southern California had shown a tacit interest on hiring me as part of their staff, it was up to the state of California to determine if my credentials were valid. That was a bit inconvenient and, although my chances of success where really high —as I had been told by those who had shown interest in my work— it was still an unusually steep hill to climb, so the process had to, like everything else, start from the beginning.

Documentation, publications, papers, acknowledgments abroad, certifications of the times I had performed surgeries in other countries as a visiting professor, interviews that could prove my credentials before the Licensing Division of the Medical Board of California, all of it added to the formality of the consignment of the requested documents, and all of it meant a great effort of time, many sleepless hours, and a lot of order.

The submission and review of the documents, and the process as a whole, lasted about ten months, almost a year. That was the time it took for the committee to review the qualification of my credentials and grant me the special permit. Once those credentials were reviewed and the permit was granted, the University of Southern California proceeded to sponsor me to give me an O-1 visa and start the process of working in the United States.

At the same time, my family would be given the O-3 visa. In between, I had to make about three trips to conduct interviews with Keck Medicine's USC leadership. I had to put together an extensive presentation, which took months to prepare, to cast my vision for how I would approach the process from my position once I became part of #USC. In addition, along with my wife, we searched for what would be our new house, the children's school, and our new home.

René Sotelo (Continues on page 139)

Karla Uribe
(United States)

Migrating is easier said than done. It's not a simple process, there is always red tape, and it takes time and patience to complete. After doing some research and consulting with lawyers, my husband and I realized that it's easier to marry a foreigner in the United States than in Mexico. So, we decided that we would do the paperwork after I arrived, and I entered the U.S. on a tourist visa. A few days after our arrival, we got married. In such cases, you have ninety days to be in the country legally and ask for a change of immigration status. It's not all that complicated, it all boils down to filling out the forms and paying the fees and I was lucky enough to get my temporary residency in a few months. A year later, after proving to immigration that our marriage was bona fide, I was granted permanent residency and, after the time required by law, I became a citizen.

From the academic point of view, the path for me has been much more complex, especially because I got to the U.S. first and did the whole research later. Big mistake. If you, who are reading this, are considering changing your country of residence and practicing medicine, please inform yourself well before deciding.

Upon arrival, I was faced with a cumbersome and lengthy process. It was a slap in the face to realize that my specialty was practically not recognized at all; that I had to start over again, possibly with a different one. After a failed attempt, many days of frustration and always having my family's well-being as a priority, I decided not to follow the USMLE Steps, but to apply for a master's degree.

For any academic purpose, you need to revalidate your degree through a company endorsed by the educational institution where you plan to study. Most of the process is done from Mexico and takes quite a bit of time. You must remember to check the deadlines for your applications very carefully and take at least three months to prevent any unforeseen complications. Each university has different requirements, and, in my case, I had to take the TOEFL to accredit my English level, take basic science subjects at the university level and take a standardized test at the master's level, the GRE, Graduate Record Examination. The process is long, but the result is certainly worth it.

Karla Uribe (Continues on page 147)

Jeannette Uribe
(UNITED STATES)

The revalidation process in the field of medicine involves time, money, effort, dedication, persistence, and resilience. It's done through the ECFMG (Educational Commission for Foreign Medical Graduates). Once your degree is validated, you are authorized to take the exams and, thus, be able to apply for a medical residency. There were three exams: Step 1, Step 2 Clinical Knowledge (CK), and Step 2 Clinical Skills (CS).

It may sound simple but, back then, I had no clue where to start. I remember that, while I was studying, I would also check the ECFMG website hundreds of times. At first glance, it seems like an ocean of complex requirements. My pilgrimage through the whole process was because, at my university in Mexico, they had no idea what the Steps involved. In the beginning, I asked around. I went to the school administration, the rectory, external liaisons... Nobody knew what to tell me nor did they try to understand. A woman even told me that she would not sign anything because my degree was already issued and, if anyone had doubts about its authenticity, there was nothing she could do. No matter how much I urged her to, she would not sign it. I was frustrated and almost gave up. If I remember correctly, this was form 186, it was in English, and had to be signed by the authorities of the Faculty of Medicine. When I finally got the signatures, they rejected the form because the signatures did not match the ones they had on file (God knows what year they were from!). I was already living in the United States, and so my mom had to go to the university several times to get the correct signatures. The communication between the Faculty of Medicine and ECFMG had to be direct, meaning that my university had to be the one to send them the documents, not me as a student. Given their little availability, I would pay and do the shipping and put them as the sender. I even opened a FedEx account in the United States to be used by both parties. All documents had to be sent with their corresponding translation and certified by a sworn translator. I had to find the translators and pay them myself because my university didn't provide that service either.

To add insult to injury, my current last name in the United States did not match the one in Mexico. Although that's something very common in the USA, in Mexico it isn't at all. You live and die with the same last name. The whole mix-up wasn't even my husband's fault nor his intention, it was the mistake of the person who filled out my Green Card application. In the end, more paperwork, more explanations, more signatures until the ECFMG finally gave me the go-ahead to take my exams. I was finally ready to do what I love: studying.

Jeannette Uribe (Continues on page 149)

4

The essentials to adapt

Patricia Bautista Rivera
(United States)

How hard it is to arrive in a place where there are no familiar faces! Even more so if the customs are different from yours and, if the language is not the same. This was precisely the situation we found ourselves in when we first arrived in Kentucky (KY). Despite being a professional and a specialist, my command of English was minimal. I didn't get a chance to learn it growing up. During residency, I enrolled in a language course. Despite the efforts, financial investment, and persistence, learning a language as an adult is incredibly challenging. I knew that, in order to adapt more easily, I needed to be able to communicate with the people around me, so it was necessary for my integration that I not only learn but master the language. My husband, thank God, did speak English.

Mexican sayings and proverbs are based on popular wisdom and are a source of good advice. Although sometimes they may seem absurd or useless, in my case my mother's voice comes to my mind, who constantly repeats: *Al pueblo que fueres, haz lo que vieres* (when in Rome, do as the Romans do). And yes, without a doubt, to live in harmony with others, but above all with oneself, when one arrives in a new place, the best plan to follow is to accept that we are far from home and replicate the ways of behavior of the communities we arrive in.

When my husband and I arrived in KY, it was still winter. It was freezing and we were not prepared to face the cold. Preparation is also key for adaptation, and it includes acquiring the necessary clothing to make the transition easier. However, since our arrival in this city, we've been very fortunate, and we've met good people always willing to help us.

Upon our arrival, the coordinator of the bone marrow transplant program at the university hospital's cancer center was waiting for us at the airport and, from the moment we met, she became our guardian angel. She helped us look for an apartment, buy furniture, open a bank account, and get our bearings in the city. Although it's not easy to let down our guard and accept our vulnerability, adaptation is simpler when we trust local people who know how things work and accept help.

Since the first day we arrived, I was determined not to stay alone in the apartment so, together with my husband, I learned how to use the city bus system and would go downtown with him. His boss found a rotation for me on a pediatric service helping disadvantaged populations.

Since I was studying pediatric allergy in Mexico, my main interest was to get a rotation with allergists, which I, fortunately, did. At the beginning, I was only an observer, but as time went by, I was allowed to interview and examine patients and then present them to their treating physician to determine their treatment. The first consultation I did alone was with a patient who was an immigrant like me, who also had problems with English. It was a difficult interview, but one that I remember fondly; he was very cooperative, because he understood how hard it is to communicate in a language different from your own. Working this new routine, the months passed by.

Having the opportunity to interact with doctors on a regular basis allowed me to acquire more knowledge in medicine, especially about allergic conditions. Being constantly busy as an observer also helped me learn the language little by little, which was challenging but not overwhelming.

In my daily interactions, I would observe people, pay special attention to their facial expressions and, according to what I observed, I would answer "yes" or "no" to their questions or comments, most of the time without having the slightest idea what they meant. Once, my husband was there, and when he noticed, he intervened and said to me: "Are you sure? Because you were asked this." I don't know how many times I must have answered incorrectly without realizing it.

Another important aspect to consider when adapting is food. Although it's becoming easier in the U.S. to find the ingredients needed to prepare Mexican dishes, I encourage you to be receptive, adventurous, and explore the different types of food available in the place you find yourself in. Nowadays, among my favorite foods are dishes from India, Thailand, and Vietnam.

To close this chapter, I will mention something I believe to be essential in order to adapt. Look for like-minded people and create a circle of friends because, since you are far from your native country, they will gradually become part of your family. They will not only make us feel accompanied, but they will also be a source of affection and new experiences.

Patricia Bautista Rivera (Continues on page 151)

Edmundo Erazo

(THE NETHERLANDS)

Being an expatriate can be a very lonely experience, but it's relatively easy to get to where you feel comfortable with little. My advice to adapt is that you don't settle and explore all aspects of your new residence. Eventually, you'll meet people from your country of origin. In the stores where they sell Mexican products, you can bet you'll run into fellow compatriots. At work, it's also nice to interact with people who are empathetic to your circumstances or who are going through a similar situation.

Soon, you'll start to compare: "This was easier back home", "We're friendlier", and many other things that perhaps you'd never thought. Scientifically speaking, adaptation represents a period in which a trait, behaviour, or anatomical structure evolves. It seems that it also works that way when you're living in a country different from your own. At the beginning of the process, you'll want to seek comfort, touch base with what feels familiar, and establish a reference point to know where to go from there. Some achieve that last one, but not all.

During my experience abroad, I met all kinds of compatriots. Some constantly complained about everything: the weather, the way the locals eat, the customs, etc. They would always seek the company of like-minded people. I also came across those who shed their roots and adopted a different lifestyle. In conclusion, there are many ways to be an immigrant.

This also applies to the vast diversity of personalities and attitudes the locals have. You can have both wonderful and not so pleasant experiences. Some friendly people welcome you, and some don't care about your existence. Some have a preconceived idea of being Mexican or think we speak "Mexican" instead of Spanish. However, in general, I've always been treated with kindness and respect in the Netherlands.

Speaking of the Netherlands, adapting can be complex. My best advice: don't swim against the current. In Mexico City, I was used to driving everywhere and used the bike just for fun. In Rotterdam, it's the exact opposite. You bike everywhere and go out to have fun by car. Everything seemed perfect during the summer, but when the rainy season came, it changed abruptly: I was not too fond of the feeling of never being fully dry. You get ready, go to work, and halfway through, it starts pouring, and there's nothing you can do. You don't have time to leave your bike and hop on the bus or tram. Nonetheless, no matter what you do, you're sure you'll arrive at your destination with wet clothes. Eventually, you learn a few strategies to avoid the rain that make your life easier.

After a while, I changed my attitude when it came to rain. I understood it as something inevitable, and I looked for ways to avoid it. You can check the weather constantly or download an app that monitors the clouds. You can also buy raincoats, ponchos, or umbrellas. Well, scratch the umbrellas; in Rotterdam, the wind flips them over and breaks them.

In the end, you'll have to accept that, one day, you'll end up drenched. I decided that the main issue was an allegory of living in a foreign country: I knew it would be comfortable to meet people with whom I shared cultural, culinary or language traits but, eventually, I would end up "soaked" in the other culture; and accepting and enjoying that is amazing.

You can keep the good things, celebrate your national identity, and share it as well. The possibilities are limitless. Living in another country can be a great adventure that teaches you there are many different ways of doing things and that we all need help, companionship and friendship. You learn you can bike everywhere; no matter where you are, keeping an eye on the weather determines part of your day; that you have to visit four different stores to buy what in Mexico you could get in one; everything has been an excellent experience for me.

In my opinion, when you live in another place, you can decide to get to know the culture of that country, or you can commit and adapt so you can have the best experience possible and enrich your life.

Edmundo Erazo (Continues on page 153)

Sandra López-León

(ISRAEL, THE NETHERLANDS, SPAIN, UNITED STATES)

Adaptation happens little by little, but I think that if you learn the language and find something to study or work on, you adapt faster. It is also good to be part of a group or community and meet people you share interests with.

Before leaving your home country and arriving in the new one, it is well worth it to finish all the paperwork as quickly as possible, and get everything in order: house, job, car, school, etc. You basically have to close or sell everything from the country you are leaving, and open or buy it all again in the new one. There are lists online that seem endless once you see how many tasks need to be completed. Decisions that normally take years must be made within couple of weeks, like buying a house or choosing a school. It helps to know in advance exactly what you want. One of the best pieces of advice I've received is to take it all one day at a time.

The most frustrating part, however, is the bureaucracy. It exists in every country, but changes from place to place. One of the most practical

118

things I have learned is that if you hit a dead end with bureaucracy: "bureaucracy can only be beaten with bureaucracy". To understand this phrase, one has to understand what bureaucracy is: learning to play chess and being highly creative and flexible.

Once you get on the plane, you start flying and land on a great adventure. There is so much to discover: hundreds of new people, new stores, new restaurants, new traditions, new food, new beaches, museums, parks, tourist sites, festivals, rituals, historical places, and much more. Additionally, your day-to-day is also brand new: the house, the bed, the city, the car, the office, the history, the news, the government, the weather, the brands, the mealtimes, the bedtimes, the times the stores are open, the customs, the way people think, the way they drive, the way they communicate with each other, the rules, the holidays... Let's just say "everything". Everything is excitingly new, and you cannot assume anything at all.

The first year, all is very special. Each month brings something new, from seasonal fruits —in Mexico there are always fruits of all kinds, but this is not the case everywhere—to traditions, special dishes, parties, and activities. In each country these times of the year are unique. For example, December in Mexico, right before Christmas, reminds me of *Las Posadas*, but in the Netherlands, everyone focuses on *Sinterklaas*; in Catalonia there is *Caga tió* and, in the United States, there is *The Elf on the Shelf*. At this point, we have a very special mix of traditions and customs in my home, and we celebrate and eat everything. Speaking of food, December at home now means eating, among hundreds of other things, chocolate letters, *pepernoten*, *latkes*, *sufganiyot*, turron, candy canes, eggnog, ponche, tamales, *rompope* and *roscón*. The moment comes when one is no longer from here or there; one becomes a citizen of the world. The important thing is to take the best of each place and each person we meet inside of us.

After the first-year ends, a cycle closes, and everything starts repeating itself. That's when everything becomes familiar. The vacation year is over, and it's in the second year when you start missing what you've left behind. I remember bringing suitcases full of food, but little by little you learn to cook everything you like, find good restaurants with food from other countries, learn to substitute ingredients and find stores in the most remote places or online, where they sell everything you need and more. You also find different groups where you feel like you belong. It is not until the third year that you start to develop roots in your new country. At last, you find the best doctor, pediatrician, dentist, hairdresser in the world, and you no longer miss the ones you had before. I recommend that, if you don't like your doctor, look for another immediately, even if you must change ten times. Eventually, you will find what you are looking for. Around the fifth year, you start to consolidate real friendships and you feel you've finally adapted. By the time you turn around, you have been living in the new country for years, you speak the language, you have a job, a house of your own, a car with a driver's license (which is no small thing, since in some countries it is harder to study for a driver's license than for a final exam in anatomy).

One way or another, I can say that I adapted to every place I've lived in. I believe that, to be able to adapt to a new country, one must be flexible, tolerant, patient, and open to change. If you don't have these qualities, you'll eventually learn them, but probably the hard way. You must also learn to respect all kinds of customs, all possible ways of thinking and being. The golden rule is that we are the ones who must adapt; we cannot just sit around and wait for others to adapt to us.

Sandra López-León (Continues on page 154)

Rafael G. Magaña

(England, United States)

Moving to another country was something I'd planned since I started medical school. I wanted to live in New York, and I had in mind what I wanted to do. In the past, my family had migrated twice, and I knew this would be a big change.

When I got to New York, everything felt incredibly overwhelming. Huge, in all respects. I felt the weight of my decision and knew I'd have to study a lot, since the competition for places in the surgical residence was downright intimidating.

When I came to the United States to prepare for the USMLE exams and waited for the student visa, I had to find a place to live in New York. With persistence, luck, and thanks to the help of some friends who already lived there, I managed to find a small apartment for a good price.

For the first time since taking the course at Joe Blasco's Make Up School in Los Angeles, I found myself alone. I spoke daily with my family in Mexico, who had supported me greatly, but it was still a very stressful season: it wasn't just a change of country, but a culture shock that struck me from the very moment I landed at the airport.

The daily encounters with people from different cultures but, above all, the scams that you face on a daily basis (from renting an apartment, while on the subway or buying anything) turn this city into a real jungle.

My classmates' diversity was really interesting and, as time went on, I started making friends. I think the adaptation time for me was around six months. Having a group of friends was a huge support, since we were all in a similar situation, and we all helped each other study. Some colleagues came from Latin America; the rest from other parts of the world.

With a place to live, a routine, and a class schedule that filled my whole day, little by little I began to feel that the exams were less difficult, and I accepted the challenge with joy. I also met a very pretty girl who studied with me, and we started dating. That ultimately helped me feel less alone. From a difficult time, it turned into a memorable experience for which I now feel nostalgic.

I think that, when you are looking to migrate, it's very important to have a contact before getting there. In my case, that contact was Steven Cruz, the director of the program. He helped me out a lot and gave me valuable advice on how to carry out the procedures and solve everyday problems such as where to do the shopping, etc.

Rafael G. Magaña (Continues on page 155)

Nissin Nahmias
(UNITED STATES)

To adapt, something key, first of all, is to have a very positive attitude, and an adventurous spirit to start a new stage in life. I've always liked to travel and that helped me fit in.

You must also know the basics when it comes to organization and logistics, to plan your expenses and know the new place you're moving to. I got to know Philadelphia by walking the streets, and visiting every museum, building, and concert hall in the city.

During that time, I learned that I was very comfortable with myself, and that I didn't mind being alone. I was also fortunate that there was a Latino community in the hospital that was always coming up with new activities. In other words, it's good to be alone and it's better to be accompanied; it's nice to know yourself and others.

One must also accept that, no matter how organized you are, things are surely not going to go the way you planned. What's more, chances are that, most of the time, they'll turn out to be the exact opposite of what you had imagined. So, it's best not to take life so seriously; breathe and learn to develop a healthy sense of humor.

Finally, it's very important to understand that maintaining social relationships requires constant attention and care towards your family, girlfriend, and everyone who stayed back home. I recommend talking to them at least once a week; asking them what's going on in their lives and letting them know what's going on in yours.

Nissin Nahmias (Continues on page 157)

Susana Ramírez Romero
(SPAIN)

It's essential to be flexible, tolerant, persevering and always open to new possibilities; since arriving in a different country implies adapting to new customs and, in some cases, to a new language, or to new idioms, even when you speak the same language. In my case, I can say that the adaptation process was difficult at times. It entailed a period of questioning, relearning, and self-discovery.

Finding a babysitter and the ideal school was an arduous task and, at the same time, a bit unpredictable. We made choices and learned by trial and error. The first time we failed in the selection of the school, although the facilities were nice, the educational techniques were very obsolete, and the academic program was far from what was advertised. The main problem was that they didn't offer an integration program for foreign students. That took a great toll on my son, who started to suffer from nightmares every night, because he was not able to communicate properly in Catalan. The school never showed any empathy or interest to solve the situation. Even the school psychologist only said to let him cry it out in his room.

I questioned the educational system in both Spain and Mexico, and the way we exercise parenting in both countries, highlighting and applying the strengths of each culture.

On a professional level, I had to relearn how to ask for lab tests, write prescriptions, and ask for help. I discovered that being a foreigner is not necessarily synonymous with something positive, as in Mexico, where everyone's welcomed with open arms. I learned that, although history is Eurocentric, a European isn't superior to a Latino at all. In fact, growing up in a developing country forces you to be an artisan, creative and competitive. Here, people from my generation were used to having education and guaranteed work, until the crisis hit. Growing up with this ideology, compared to the Mexican ideology where "if you don't work, you don't eat", makes you have a different attitude towards life.

Having to leave everything behind taught me not to carry or accumulate material goods, only experiences. I stopped paying attention to the quality of the wood in my dining room and concentrated more on the conversations that originated during dinner. I own no famous paintings or expensive ornaments. There's no need for them because, little by little, the empty walls were filled with my children's drawings and creations.

I understood that it can be very enriching to live between two cultures, the more different the better, because you question a great deal more, and so you have more than one solution to any problem that may arise; in other words, you invent better recipes, since there are more ingredients at your disposal.

I jump for joy as if I were visited by royalty every time a friend or family member comes from Mexico, because I have grown to value immensely the closeness of the people I love. However, in both hemispheres we are now foreigners. Here, we are the Mexicans, and, in Mexico, we are the *gachupines* (Spaniards who live or settle in a Hispanic American country). As an adult, you can come to terms with the whole thing, but children have a tough time internalizing it.

What finally worked for us was to enroll our kids in an international school, where they interact with children of different nationalities who, like them, have left grandparents and cousins in another country and have had to make an effort to adapt culturally to new rhythms and culinarily to different flavors. I teach my children universal values such as love and respect; I have friends of all faiths, and I like my children to see that.

In this micro-environment, we're part of a multicultural group, where we all contribute and respect each other's way of viewing and living life. With the change of school and his integration to the new group, my son's nightmares magically disappeared.

Susana Ramírez Romero (Continues on page 158)

Luis Rodrigo Reynoso
(ETHIOPIA)

Once we arrived in Ethiopia, it was all "starting from scratch." It is easy to read. It was not the first time that I changed the country of residence, but on this trip the change was on another scale, almost like entering another dimension.

Anahí and I decided to come with blind faith: we did not investigate if the place where we would live had all the services, if there was enough food, we did not foresee everything that could happen. I think it was the best we could do. I sensed that this would be some sort of trip to the past, which would make me feel really alive.

In Addis Ababa, more than at any other time in our lives, we felt that we were building and transforming our present on a daily basis.

In Ethiopia, capitalism has not fully matured yet. There are shortcomings in all areas, in all imaginable sectors. Retail customer service is subpar, and there is little infrastructure in the cities. Only now, they begin to build buildings; they hire architects and engineers, but then they suddenly abandon the construction work;, they come and go. In general, there is a lot of cheap, unskilled labour that does not know what they are doing and does not commit.

And in the medical sector? There is work to spare! Specialists are scarce! Every day we operate only with local anaesthesia. For major surgeries there is only one anaesthetist nurse, one of a few in all of Ethiopia; so, we adapt the surgeries to her schedules. In Ethiopia, with its 109 million inhabitants, you can count anaesthesiologists with the fingers on one hand; medicines are very limited and there are no supplies; bureaucracy make it difficult to import them. A surgical mask is reused about 100 times; I was using cloth masks (which I had not done since the surgery workshop at the faculty).

I question, I investigate, I am very curious. They say that in the south of the country, on the border with Somalia, 500 children die of cholera every day; the disease is spreading rapidly, and the prognosis is that it will soon arrive in our city. For the staff of the orphanages and assistance centers that I visit, their eyes sparkle when they learn that I am a doctor, and that perhaps we can do something together: the children, residents, users of these centers have never been assessed by a doctor.

No matter where or whom you work for, the reality is that the health system in Ethiopia is almost nil, if not non-existent. Suddenly, an HIV detection booth or a health campaign financed by some foundation or international organization appears on the streets. But even those initiatives have issues: the vast majority of these are just looking for the spotlight. They ask for money, they appear on the news, they satisfy their ego, they fill their pockets. Then they help, but they help only for a couple of weeks to justify their existence with numbers, but they do not follow up with the patients, and therefore if they perform any surgery, they cannot verify that it has been successful.

–Numbers, they only need numbers...,

The population is heavily scarred, literally, and metaphorically speaking. Scarifications and tattoos that have been done in ancient tribal rites are the main reasons for the aesthetic and reconstructive consultation.

I am just beginning to understand some words, to repeat them, but I know that it will take me years to perfect my pronunciation, since there are sounds that I have never heard in any language. The only word that is identical in Spanish and Amharic is "tripa". I found out after trying them (here my "vegetarian self" has disappeared). From writing, am getting it ... I already know a couple of letters! They are a bitch! Sorry, complex!

"How radical can a change be? I remember that before leaving Mexico I thought: "We have it all! We do not need anything! It's time to change!"

And bam! Suddenly we were in this peculiar and enigmatic country. In Ethiopia, public services (drinking water, sewerage, public lighting) are practically non-existent. Here, we collect rainwater in large containers to anticipate shortages; blackouts are an everyday occurrence, and some can last up to two days. We must freeze cans with water as it is the only way to preserve food.

To dry our clothes, we must be careful and keep them away from the neighbors, since jeans can become a temptation and a cause of discord.

Burtukan - the lady who helps us clean the house - has had to retrieve our clothes from other people's hands. We only understand three words from Doña Naranja (yes, that is Burtukan's translation), but she gets very excited when she can watch a Turkish soap opera dubbed into Amharic on our television, and every day she carries bottles and bottles of tap water to her house.

- *How radical can a change be?*

To answer that question, we have had to ask that question ourselves not once, but several times, at each step we take, each moment we witness, and at each experience that we may never understand, but undoubtedly, all these together, will show us the way.

Here, I have to leave the phone by the window, waiting to get a signal and send a couple of messages. The internet service is deficient, plus, this country has numerous censorships walls and filters. Somehow the same thing happens in Mexico where we supposedly enjoy freedom of expression, until we realize that that is not really the case when some hidden truths come to light.

Here, a plate of strawberries and bananas with cream - all super fresh - make me the happiest man, and where the little moments are more meaningful than ever. Here is, where I have realized that a change can be as radical as you allow it to be! Thank you from the bottom of my heart!

– Get out of there… I recommend it!

I believe that the most essential quality to adaptation is to learn to let go, to unlearn; adapt to transform and thus situations will flow, and we can feel more comfortable with a new lifestyle.

Luis Rodrigo Reynoso (Continues on page 160)

Alejandra Rodríguez Romero
(UNITED STATES)

For me, adapting to this new country was not so difficult when compared to other people with whom I have exchanged similar experiences. That, at least, is how I see it. The reason for this is that most of my maternal family has resided in the United States for several decades. Almost every summer of our childhood, my sister and I would visit my family, and the customs of American culture no longer seemed so foreign to me. From the language point of view, adapting was also quite easy because, thanks to my parents, I was always in private schools that had a very good level of English. But even with these "advantages", emigrating presents a major challenge in all aspects of life. Things as common as having to put gas on your own, order food over the phone, or interact with people in everyday activities become a difficult task.

We arrive with so many plans and goals that are not always accomplished as we would like them to, so we must be flexible, persevere, and look for the positive in every situation. Another thing that's extremely important is to have a support network, preferably where we live, but family and friends, even from a distance, can also help us feel better. A few months later, when the excitement of "the new" fades away, is when we first feel the emotional impact of the decision to emigrate, and we'll need that help.

Facing the new culture with an open mind is key, as it will make situations we are not used to more bearable. This does not mean that we have to adopt ideas or behaviors that are not in accordance with our values and ideologies, but it's an excellent opportunity to become more tolerant. It's also important to take care of our physical and mental health because, at the beginning, we'll have to work really hard to achieve our goals and we won't get there if our health is mediocre. There are other relevant aspects such as obtaining a bank account to begin generating a credit history, and later be able to buy a car, apply for credit cards, take out loans, etc. Finally, the most important thing to adapt, in my opinion, is to be proud of who we are and where we come from; to always present ourselves with our heads held high and a friendly smile.

Alejandra Rodríguez Romero (Continues on page 163)

Jack Rubinstein
(UNITED STATES)

> "Reality is merely an illusion, albeit a very persistent one."
> -Albert Einstein

Theseus' paradox states, in one of its forms, that nobody steps in the same river twice since the person and the river are constantly in flux. Thousands of years later, Einstein changed the world, and also gave a relativistic twist to the concept, but the idea is the same. People —and the world— are constantly changing. I am frequently faced with two representations of this concept. On the one hand, I hear a voice saying, "this is the way I am"; on the other hand, I hear it contradict itself when it whispers, "but, I don't have a clue who I am or what I want to do". Both phrases are born from the same misconception that we are or should be a certain way.

Returning to Mexico is like stepping in a different river, but those I left behind often see only the person who left Mexico, not the one I've become. In Mexico, things evolve, but slowly. Outside of Mexico and, particularly within the medical environment, circumstances change rapidly and, in order to stay relevant, you must be prepared to reinvent yourself.

The first years I spent abroad marked me in a similar way to my first years of life. It felt like every day a pillar of my life fell, and a new (different and strange) one took its place. One of my first mornings post call I presented a patient we had admitted the night before to the team. As I presented the "A and P" (Analysis and Plan), the attached physician questioned a certain decision. In accordance with my training in Mexico, my answer was: "Because Dr. So-and-so gave that order." However, instead of receiving the approval of the attached physician and the group of fellows, I saw surprised and confused faces staring back at me. I don't remember the exact answer of the physician, but in summary he explained to me: "Things are not done here because a doctor *just says so*, they're done based on evidence. If you lack the evidence, they're not carried out." Those wise words were a great lesson and have generally served me well, both in my medical practice and in life. And I say generally, because many don't appreciate the search for evidence to treat patients, much less in everyday life. When I talk to Mexican colleagues, I realize that Mexico is also beginning to move from a medicine based on *eminence* to one based on *evidence*. The inertia of "this is how we do it" or "this is how my teacher/friend/parent used to do it" is hard to fight against in the medical environment, and even more so when the lack of evidence seems to hide behind political opinions or religious beliefs. However, slowly but surely, we all change.

Another pillar that quickly collapsed was my perspective on what a "good" doctor does. During my medical school training, I concentrated on memorizing as much information as possible and focusing my attention on the examination style of each doctor or teacher, but the teaching style of the American residency system made me rapidly change. Instead of memorizing seemingly immovable truths, I came across professors who taught me how to learn, how to analyze scientific articles, how and when to question information, and, most importantly, when to modify how I treated my patients. These changes in the professional field were so significant that they were not limited to my work, they spilled over into my personal life. Religious and political concepts that I defended tooth and nail for many years became difficult to justify. The first beliefs that crumbled were those underpinned by the a teacher's wisdom (also known as authority bias). These ideas were relatively easy to discredit. When someone gave me the answer: "Because so-and-so said it", my mind immediately knew that that statement should be questioned. Other concepts and ideas collapsed as my access to information increased and it became easier to confirm or refute ideas, proposals, and concepts. Sometimes all it required was a quick online search, others took books and months of study but, sooner or later, I ended up changing almost all the ideas with which I identified myself as a doctor and as a person.

In between all these transitions, I've had to deal with a fair amount of consternation from those around me. They accuse me, with ample foundation, of being a flip-flopper, of not having a value to live for, or of falling for the novelty of the moment. They are not wrong, I tell them. I've come to terms with the fact that, if someone changes their mind, others will see them differently. But today, as a doctor and as a scientist —and as a human, one might add—, there's no other choice. My children's lives will be substantially better than my parents' and will seem otherworldly to my grandparents. This is due to people who are willing to question the status quo, people who see reality as an illusion and their existence as the flow of a constantly changing river. In the medical and scientific environment, these are the people who change the world.

Jack Rubinstein (Continues on page 164)

Alberto Saltiel

(ISRAEL)

It's not easy to move to the other side of the world, to a country with another culture and a completely different language. It's of utmost importance to arrive with an open mind, willing to explore and learn. The first and completely essential (but not indispensable) thing is the language. Undoubtedly, a large part of the population speaks English, but not all of them do. Israel is a country full of immigrants from all over the world so, at any moment, you may run into someone who doesn't speak English. Ultimately, speaking the native language favors communication and understanding. Not being able to communicate creates confusion and stress. I remember that, when I arrived in Israel, I was not fluent in Hebrew and that made certain procedures difficult for me; even opening a bank account or getting a new phone number was quite a feat. Once the language is not a limitation, we can talk about what follows.

Israel is an extremely complex country when it comes to culture. There are multinational traditions that have accompanied all immigrants throughout the years and have become part of the national culture, but what identifies the Israeli culture is their peculiar way of living one day at a time. Let us remember that, since its creation, Israel's been a country deeply affected by terror and war. In a way, it means that its citizens have learned to value what they have now, because no one knows what tomorrow might bring. They live from day to day; they enjoy every moment. They go out, enjoy themselves, laugh, and fight for their dreams knowing that everything can disappear in the blink of an eye. This generates a certain level of stress that sometimes can translate into aggressiveness. The Israeli is passionate by nature. I don't mean a physical passion, but a mental and verbal one. They speak loudly, engage in conversations with strangers to give their opinion even if it's not asked, and yell. However, this passion is what also pushes the country to excel, to create, and to grow. And so, I learned that, in Israel, letting your voice be heard is synonymous with progress.

In order to adapt, friends are essential. When I arrived in Israel, I was alone. Fortunately, I had a group of friends that I had met on that kibbutz trip back in 2004, and they still lived here. They had moved to Israel from different parts of the world over the past ten years and now they had formed a very tight relationship. For me, arriving to that already established group was indispensable, and it allowed me to adapt slowly but surely. Obviously, this advantage is not always available, so one of the most important factors in adapting is socializing and looking for new friends.

Finally, not forgetting our roots plays an important role and opens many doors abroad. Yes, everyone wants to drink tequila with a Mexican. Growing up in Mexico, I never considered myself a tequila fan but, later on and especially since I've been here, I've learned to appreciate mezcal very much. Here in Israel, there's no event in which I am not offered tequila or, to which I don't bring it myself. Each time a Mexican comes to visit, I always have a bottle of tequila or two at my place so I can offer them a little sip of Mexico.

Adapting to any place is always a challenge with vicissitudes, regardless of the country. There will be days more difficult than others. You will create new stories, meet new people, and broaden your horizons. So, if you talk, share and drink, adapting won't be a problem.

Alberto Saltiel (Continues on page 166)

Luana Sandoval Castillo
(SPAIN, DENMARK)

No human is limited - Eliud Kipchoge

The main thing is wanting to do it. Even though I had already made a first one in Barcelona, to its Catalan, its people, its food, and its customs the second one was not a walk in the park. Every beginning is difficult.

Adapting to Denmark implied developing home-hunting abilities; sketching a map with the previously selected neighborhoods; calculating specific bike routes and spending many hours using Google Translate. That was the beginning of my adaptation process. Today, looking back on it, I'd have focused on being more patient and flexible; on enjoying those things that are different from our country and taking them just as they come. There are many little "routine changes", like how the weather redefines your new outfits. The Danes often say that there is no such thing as bad weather, just inadequate clothing. My theory is that it's a matter of time before you start loving or hating what initially surprised you. The mistake you have to avoid afterwards is turning it into monotony. Marvel at the snow, how little light there is, the different scents that fill the air depending on the seasons, and the unexpected new flavors. Make this experience your *hyggeligt* moment: a warm and cozy feeling, typical of the winter season.

My advice is: overcome the fear of going out in the street and face an unknown language, jump in with both feet and start with baby steps. You'll be surprised how easy everything gets after someone's first smile at you and, if not, it always helps to explain that you are not from there and if they do not understand you, you'll explain the situation some other way. Take advantage of every course (regardless of whether they're free or not), every possibility of language exchange, of socializing with locals; they don't bite, they're mortals just like you and me and, if you are lucky, they'll be as interested as you are in hearing stories from another world.

Travel, wander, get to know every inch of the country. That'll give you knowledge and will awaken the curiosity to know more about your new home, and it'll also give you an advantage in the new conversations you'll strike up with strangers. Make the most out of the few sunny days; do something new and get to know your new neighborhood. Hopefully, you'll find activities that involve your neighbors and will give you the opportunity to create a network of contacts. I recommend investing time in studying the language to have the necessary basics and update your CV to apply for jobs.

Set yourself a real and achievable goal in the time and place you're in. Set your sights on your next job and how you see yourself in a few years, apply without fear, the worst that can happen is that they turn you down and if you never try, you'll never know. Don't be afraid to start from the bottom or from a lower level than the one you had. A good friend of mine always says: someone who's a parakeet is green everywhere. Soon, they'll realize what you are worth and see you're an asset to their team.

Put your resourcefulness to the test. I think that's something that characterizes Mexicans wherever they go: we can achieve great accomplishments with scarce resources, so we already have a chance to win if something gets stuck while our papers are being approved. You will see that after a while of tightening your belt, you'll be able to feast, but always save for a rainy day.

Eventually, you'll feel nostalgic and suddenly you will find yourself listening to mariachis and *banda* music but try to see the positive side of the dark days. When it comes to social benefits, this new country will offer you better possibilities for parenthood, health, education and even the freedom from unending on-call shifts that our country still lacks.

This chapter starts with a quote by a Kenyan marathon runner who broke his own record by running a marathon in less than 2 hours. No human is limited; practice, excel, surround yourself with admirable people and enjoy every step taken.

Luana Sandoval Castillo (Continues on page 167)

Ilan Shapiro
(UNITED STATES)

Let's get one thing straight: we cannot ever have absolute control over anything! The most important thing changes have taught me (Mexico -> Miami -> Mexico -> Chicago -> Florida -> Los Angeles) is that, in order to adapt, we must be flexible. At first, the mind seeks stability, and desperately tries to find familiar shapes, colors, and flavors. And so, we levitate toward that corner of normality, which I call "local anesthesia." However, I don't recommend staying there. We must move forward and start a new adventure. You can start from scratch if want to: no regrets, just opportunities.

Among the changes experienced when migrating, I've seen the following stages:

The honeymoon

You struggled to get to that place or maybe you just landed there. Once you're settled, everyday life takes gives you basic tasks where you develop daily routine. You're excited for what's to come and, to be honest, it's all very subjective. You're living the dream right now, and that's when you must take all the knowledge in.

Sincerity

After the honeymoon period (which can last from weeks to months), life begins to emerge objectively. As much as we long for the familiar comfort of what we're used to, reality kicks in. You begin to see cracks in the dream, a couple of fears and worries begin to bother you, and you begin to question what you're doing there. Nostalgia becomes a constant companion. Without realizing it, you are approaching the next stage (my favorite one).

Being present

There comes a moment when fears, passions, energy, and dreams come together. And you realize that the most important thing is not what was or what will be: the most important thing is to be present! Everything changes so fast: energy, life, time... We end up damaging our mental health obsessing over roads that are never going to be traveled. Here are a couple of tips to understand this:

1.Everything is new.

2. Taking care of yourself is imperative.

Cut down: I call it Dr. Shapiro's special diet, which consists of limiting everything that gives us extra calories (and, as a Mexican, for me this means chips, candy, and tequila).

Develop a routine: Exercise, sleep, and having a good relationship with your family are a must.

Move: It's very important. As a doctor, sometimes it was contradictory for me to prescribe one thing and do the opposite.

3. Stress management: We're all stressed from time to time. In fact, a little stress is good; it makes us more agile, and it's helped us survive for thousands of years. We ran faster when there was a lion chasing us. However, we must not let that stress become toxic. That can lead to depression, anxiety, and fear, and it can consume us. Making meditation and religious activities an important part of my routine helped me live in the present. Our best assets are our body, mind, and soul. If we align them, we'll be more efficient and happier. The best advice I can give is this: never forget that the only constant in life is change.

Ilan Shapiro (Continues on page 168)

René Sotelo

(UNITED STATES)

Adaptation is a difficult process. It's challenging. It means turning your life upside down. This is true from the day-to-day changes of the landscapes and surroundings, all the way to a harsher reality: realizing you know nobody at all.

This process is, without a doubt, a painful one. One that forces you to face this whole new reality you now live in but, as is the case with all challenging events, also pushes you forward in the pursuit of progress. Moving implies adapting to all kinds of new things, like the new city's air quality, what you see, what you eat, a new language that constantly reminds you that you're away from home and, of course, a brand new working environment that immediately makes you get your feet back on the ground, and reminds you time and again that your life has changed.

Professionally, it's incredibly difficult to admit that your go-to working teams are no longer there. That, in the midst of the unending medical labor of this new routine, newfound teams will come together and develop, and that's exactly where the adaptation process starts.

You start to miss the former members of your team, the facilities you worked in. Maybe they were not perfect, but you knew them like the back of your hand. You were in your comfort zone. Emotionally, what hits you the hardest is being a complete stranger in a gigantic and unfamiliar hospital. And then, another uncomfortable reality: the US-medical system is not really prepared for newcomers that have not been trained in the country, since those cases are rare.

You argue with anesthesiologists, colleagues, and team members in each case you work on. Going through that first phase is tough, because it constantly reminds you that you don't really belong there, you're the new guy, and there's an extra mile you have to walk. There is no other way but to adapt and make yourself known. What used to come natural no longer applies, because no one knows you, and you must fight to be visible.

The second step is facing the fact that you work in a hospital of top academic level, where there are highly trained and prestigious doctors. Even though a wide variety of patients resort to the hospital, many of them come for a regular appointment with their lifelong physicians, who are local specialists. That's when reality pulls you back to Earth and reminds you the marketing strategies that must be part of your day-to-day life: using self-promotion tools so people know what you do and what makes you stand out is not only necessary for early survival, it's essential. That's what allows you to go from "Doctor Who?" —the subtle nickname I had been given to remind me that my last name was unknown, as was my reputation— to Dr. Sotelo.

Every day of every minute, this new reality kept highlighting the need to build a network of social contacts that would support me on the path of making a name for myself, of providing my face, my name, my work, and my identity with meaning. That was essential so I could adapt and continue to move forward.

In addition to this, there was also an issue of ego. Oh, powerful feeling, how you make the mighty fall! Especially when you are used to the acknowledgment and appreciation from your homeland.

Then, all the sudden, you end up in a place where nobody knows you, where making a simple phone call to give medical instructions is an action questioned by everybody. That is a red light that seems to yell "these people do not know you. You have not been around enough to make them know who you are or feel reassured by you". It's logical: you still have not earned the necessary trust amongst the group so they can welcome you in properly. In that moment, you realize that your name, at least during that first phase, is none other than Doctor Who. That's when your lack of identity and the feeling of not belonging anywhere really hit you, especially when you reach a certain age and realize, with disappointment, you must start all over again. Then you play the scenario in your head again and again: you make a call, *"Hello, good morning. This is Doctor Sotelo speaking. Could you please...",* only to be interrupted, on a loop, by a ruthless, call center-like question: *"Doctor who?"*

As a result, your survival instinct, and the desire to stop feeling invisible kick in, and the marketing tools to shout out who you are —specially through visually appealing channels— become decisive. Two elements have been a part of my professional arsenal ever since: the first one, clearly, was my white medical coat with my name sewn to the chest, glimmering like a neon light. The second one I turned into a kind of promotional merchandise of my identity: a backpack I had specially made with my name on it as well. Two simple shields that protected me from anonymity and kindly but firmly shook hands with those who approached me. Little by little, I became a sort of "walking billboard", but the results paid off. Everyone was starting to notice me, and they gradually learned to call me by my name. Dr. Sotelo was beginning to replace Doctor Who, and I appreciated it. It made me smile. It made me feel like I was part of the job and the routine.

Undoubtedly, one of the greatest difficulties for me was adapting to the new style of medical practice. I had come to the United States to observe, to improve surgical techniques, to acquire skills and new ways of performing robotic surgery, but I was unfamiliar with the administrative issues necessary to create electronic medical records, the informed consent forms...

Medical records must be documented and all the legal issues that surround them must be considered. It takes time to learn and get to that point where you feel at ease because you're certain you documented what was necessary. When you're new to this, you pay very close attention to what you write down or not; you're particularly aware of taking notes of the results that, although negative, are relevant to leave record of the patient's examination. There's a feeling of anxiety that accompanies you for some time, but it's precisely after you've done it time and time again that you're thankful for the structure. It's only with time that serenity, in this particular case, is regained and becomes permanent. Time, that silent but implacable and helpful companion is, in the end, the best lever to achieve change.

It wasn't just about learning how the hospital and the procedures associated with medical records at Keck. It was also a way to get acquainted with the United States healthcare system. You need to puzzle out how insurance companies work to understand exactly where the patients who belong to certain networks are, and what benefits they have. It's necessary to identify those benefits in order to make them tangible for the patient and achieve —from a doctor's perspective— that everything comes together properly. This process is complex, and it must be learned and mastered to ensure that everything fits and works.

Something that also plays to your advantage is that, even if the new system is unknown and the markets are different, if you have a track record, you recognize the similarity between prescriptions, and then you can apply that strategy to move forward along the way with what you have learned and add it to what you bring, what you are. The Latino and Caribbean factor also began to be a differentiating and linking asset, as well as convenient in connection and networking. These particularities, although different from ours in the American culture, were also well received. It contributed to the adaptation process, as it also helped me join the Latino doctors who are part of Keck Medicine at USC, eight in total, out of a staff of one thousand physicians. Spanish as a means of communication also played a huge role, since fifty percent of the Los Angeles' population speaks it. This, undoubtedly, comforts you, even though for me the English language was another battle to conquer, since I had to go beyond the technical medical jargon to communicate with patients and with the other fifty percent of the people in Los Angeles.

Patients are used to a different kind of medical relationship. Our warm Latin style is well received, but it's very important to know that, because of their culture, they react differently and expect information in another way than we tend to give it. These patients generally possess a much higher level of medical culture, more accustomed to seeking concrete information and, therefore, they expect to receive more specific details.

The process of adjustment also involves discipline and extra effort in the face of the academic pressure of generating publications of every procedure that is performed. Although I frequently used to do this in Venezuela, I did it for pleasure, because I wanted to, and I decided the pace along the way and, although I still do enjoy it, the tension increases when it's a duty. It becomes part of your responsibilities, because everything must be accounted for so that, at the end of the year, an academic productivity evaluation can be conducted and, thus, set contract renewals or any increase in benefits. In Latin America, you generally start working in a center and you will probably work there for life. Here, you are reviewed for how productive you've been, how much you have contributed to the academy and, based on that, you are encouraged and acknowledged. This is, without a doubt, a structural element in every physician's career that leads to levels of excellence I'm pleased to have achieved and for which I am profoundly grateful.

Something that definitely helped me to get used to Los Angeles and Keck Medicine, and that's directly linked to the benefits of teamwork, is the sectorization, the specialization. In Venezuela, I handled all topics related to urology, but here in #USC, I've dedicated myself exclusively to robotic surgery. I refer the rest of the pathologies to my colleagues, who have developed greater expertise in other areas. This is an excellence-oriented strategy that drives you to focus and enjoy those areas in which you have developed more skills. That allows me to sit back and exclusively enjoy what I do. In my case, my relationship with the robot enables me to enter that state where everything flows, and I lose track of time. My commitment, once in front of it, comes alive through the action of operating, of having a positive impact on each of my patients. This loss of the sense of time, once I start operating, I've learned to appreciate as a great ally for my particular adaptation process. In the United States, that uniqueness of orienting specialization in such a sophisticated way has given me a sense of progress as a professional, of refinement and at the same time of rest, which I deeply treasure.

Overall, I can say that the sense of belonging was gradual: it took me about two or three years. Adaptation takes place as you get to know people, when they start to remember and recognize you through the results of your surgeries. You discover and connect with locals, establishing bonds and putting together a new family. When you move, you don't know anyone. When we enrolled our children in school and were asked who to call if something happened, we wrote down the phone number of a secretary at work, because we had no family to refer them to. You grasp just how lonely you are, you realize the ties and support networks you've abandoned, the close family you left behind.

Getting involved as director of Keck's international department forced me to contact and get to know specialists in other areas; starting a postgraduate degree in management also led me to relate and interact with new and more people. Getting to know them, developing that interpersonal network that you can count on at any given moment, is what really gives you a sense of belonging that helps you move forward.

Missing the flavors, the food, and the day-to-day kindness. That was another important element: having left the comfort of your routine. Having left behind the rehabilitation wing of the medical institute, the one that I had developed and from which I directed a great part of my operations in Venezuela. I'd think about the reliability and peacefulness it represented in many ways: the tasty soup, hot and on time; that dish you craved, so affectionately prepared; the arrangement of the furniture according to your taste and specifications; the gallery of bromeliads that brightened up your rest time and that had been arranged so they'd please the eye... Memories that are always in the back of your mind and force you to look for temporary and similar substitutes in your current home.

The new environment that imposes itself on the familiar city that you're leaving is also a bit shocking and takes some getting used to. And suddenly, you realize that you're in a continuous struggle to identify elements in the city that share similarities with what's been your home. I saw in some mountains the resemblance with the Ávila. I was looking for it all around me. That glorious and monumental shape that decorates Caracas and says good morning in such a beautiful way to all those who wake up there.

I would go to the beach and try to find the sunsets that reminded me of my home in Margarita. Discovering Amara Café was like finding a corner of Caracas in Los Angeles. Eating arepas, listening to the Venezuelan accent coming from the tables next to you. You realize you've become a citizen of both cities, and that, at times, your memories fly to where you will always belong, without stopping to consider the anguish that comes with thinking about your loved ones, the business you still have in your country and the socio-political and economic struggles it's going through.

One element that certainly helped me in the adaptation and that was particularly interesting was realizing the importance of the Venezuelan Armenian community in the area. I know many Venezuelan Armenians. Finding a teacher responsible for reviewing the adaptation process was exciting and very helpful. When the community found out that we were Venezuelan, it supported us on how to navigate and learn about the education system in Los Angeles. That's how we were able to choose the right school for the children. It was also key to have another teacher. She introduced me to the dean, originally from Holland, but who had lived many years in Maracaibo –the oil city par excellence in Venezuela–, and it was also she who introduced me to Amara Café, that gastronomic space that has become my home and the refuge I turn to when I want to take a breather and feel the "Venezuelanness" that stems from the tables around me, that pours from the flavors that are tasted in the food, that lives in the particularly melodic Spanish spoken in Caracas, in what's seen and felt. We have made this place so much our own, that there's even an arepa called "Dr. Sotelo." Once again, our particular ways and the time spent together become anchors that reinforce the process of achieving a sense of belonging and identity.

René Sotelo (Continues on page 170)

Karla Uribe
(UNITED STATES)

If I had known how difficult it would be to adapt to my new life, perhaps I would not have moved at all. The language and cultural issues have not been as much of a problem for me because, since we live on the southern border of the United States, I'm surrounded by Mexicans. There are always tacos, tamales, *fiestas*, and we all speak Spanish.

The hard part was adapting to the stay-at-home mom life. Putting my professional life on hold to take care of my daughter was a well thought-out decision that I don't regret, but it wasn't easy to overcome the frustration generated by my professional void.

The first few days were great: a little vacation, a wonderful break! I hadn't stopped studying since kindergarten, so I enjoyed it at first, but after three days, the confinement exasperated me. I had no one to talk to and nowhere to go while my husband was at work. It drove me crazy to feel like an outsider to absolutely everything.

The key to my survival and adaptation was my daughter's early stimulation classes, which began a year after I arrived. There, I met what is now my "McAllen family": a group of first-time moms, Mexican, and newcomers to the city just like me. What started as setting up a playdate became a support network that changed my life forever and made me feel part of the world again.

Adapting to the American medical system has been a challenge as well. Everything is different here. You don't just step into the doctor's office merrily waving hello. You have to spend a long time waiting, and then go through three little rooms, three interrogations. In each one you spell out the name of the medication you take, they want to take blood and urine each and every time because it's "protocol", and, in the end, you talk to the doctor for three minutes and, due to the rush, you forget what you wanted to ask in the first place. Not to mention that you pay a fortune. It has been hard for me to learn on the fly to say "no" without fear and to not allow them to follow their protocol when it comes to my children without first having them examined by the doctor. It's also very important to make sure that any procedures they perform are covered by the insurance and, above all, to trust what I learned in school. Making my medical opinion heard. It took me ten years, but I managed to find doctors I can trust and with whom I have been able to establish a doctor-patient relationship that gives me peace of mind. It's so hard to be on the other side of the desk!

Living in a different country, managing to adapt, finding balance and inner peace... All of it has been one of the most complicated processes I've ever faced. I think that, over time, I have managed to see this country with different eyes and today I feel at home, grateful, and at peace with the nation where I decided to raise a family and where my children were born and are growing up.

Karla Uribe (Continues on page 172)

Jeannette Uribe
(UNITED STATES)

"It's never too late to learn a new language." Just as it's never too late to move to a new city or country. It's difficult and challenging, of course, the road is full of ups and downs but, at the end of the day, they are adventures and experiences that make you grow as a person in a myriad of aspects.

My first and biggest obstacle was the language. Before moving, I thought I knew enough to be able to communicate but, when I arrived, I realized that I didn't know the basics that well. It was frustrating at first; my ear was not trained at all.

For a year, I took English classes for adults. The program was called ESL (English as a Second Language). It was free, and luckily for me, they also had childcare, so I had no excuse. I attended morning and afternoon classes, sometimes in the company of my baby, and I tried to make his nap match the class schedule. I followed my teachers' advice: even though I had no close friends whose native language was English, I tried to strike up a conversation with anyone I met. I listened to music and watched television in English with English subtitles and tried to read non-medical books, even if I only understood half of the story. At the same time, I was studying to take my revalidation exams.

On weekends, I volunteered in the ER of the local hospital, nothing medical related but it was an opportunity for me to talk to the people of the community whose native language was mostly English. It wasn't easy for me to be in a hospital without being able to practice medicine, especially on Friday nights or Sunday mornings, because that was when my husband was home and could take care of our baby.

Part of the requirements to apply for the residency was to obtain letters of recommendation from American doctors. I knocked on many doors; several of them never opened. We even had to move from Michigan to Florida to complete my rotations (which came with the challenge of learning to drive in a city like Orlando). A few months later, we returned to Michigan, where I did more volunteering and studied for the two exams I had left. This time around, I did it alone, without my husband and son, but the sacrifice was worth it: my grades went up.

Once I finished taking all the exams, I applied for the medical residency but was unsuccessful. Then, I started my first formal job in the United States, in the same hospital where I volunteered, as a phlebotomist. My command of the language was improving little by little, and now I had a salary which, although it wasn't much, helped us financially because now there were four of us. This last baby brought us nothing but joy and hope. Before his second birthday, we were already planning another move, this time to New York as an OB/GYN resident... Finally!

Jeannette Uribe (Continues on page 173)

5

What I left behind in my country

Patricia Bautista Rivera
(UNITED STATES)

It's been many years since I moved to the United States for the first time, and I can say that the hardest part of migrating has been being away from my family.

In Mexico, I left most of my family: mom, siblings, cousins, aunts, and uncles. At the beginning of our life on this side of the border, it was hard to cope with that. Knowing they were so far away made me feel empty. Even though I was by my husband's side, I always felt my family's absence. We were alone, my husband had me, and I had him. When my daughter was born, no member of our family was present, and that was really painful.

Being away not only in times of celebration, but also in times of difficulty, illness, pain, and death, bore heavily on my heart. Facing the illness and deterioration of the people you love from a distance causes great sorrow.

Although it does not happen to all those who migrate, it's frequent that those who accompany their spouse or partner for love, as my friends would say, leave their professional life in Mexico. I left, due to a combination of circumstances, the opportunity and privilege to practice medicine, at least to do it the way I planned, and to earn a living from my work. That hurt for a long time. It's one of the negative impacts that our migration has had on me personally. However, although I have not been able to earn money practicing medicine, I feel very fortunate to have had the good fortune to meet the group of allergists who allowed me to work under their supervision for a long time. In the beginning, I attended the different offices 5 days a week. After the birth of my children, it changed to one morning a week for several years.

Over time and with the development of the Internet and social networks, the ability to keep in touch not only with family but also with friends, whom I had also left back home, improved a great deal. I feel that I've been able to renew or even initiate new relationships of friendship and affection with former classmates from medical school or even high school. I can be there for them in moments of joy and also in moments of sadness, no matter the distance.

If someone were to ask what I miss the most about Mexico, I'd answer, without a shadow of a doubt: my mom. Fortunately, talking on the phone is cheaper now. We can talk frequently for hours and, sometimes, we can even see each other through phones or computer screens.

Patricia Bautista Rivera (Continues on page 175)

Edmundo Erazo

(THE NETHERLANDS)

Leaving Mexico was complex. In my case, it meant leaving the hospital where I felt at home both professionally and personally and where I had good friends and colleagues. I believe that, at some point, all doctors feel connected to where they were trained, as interns, residents, or subspecialists.

After graduation, you start to wonder where you'd like to work. Professionally, I stopped working with my internal medicine teacher. For me, he's a mentor rather than a teacher, and he later became my friend, but we all seek to dedicate ourselves to what interests us the most, and I always wanted to do research, so I looked for a way to do it in Europe. However, whenever we choose, we're giving something up simultaneously, not only professionally but in all aspects of life.

I left my family in Mexico, and, sometimes, years went by until I was able to visit them. The COVID-19 pandemic also made it extremely difficult to meet again. You renounce being present in the life of those you grew up with (friends, colleagues, etc.). People go on with their lives if you're not constantly there, and time doesn't stand still just because you're gone. That's something we have to come to terms with: sometimes, you feel like time has stopped in Mexico and that at some point, when you return, everything will be just as you left it.

Despite that, just as I left people and experiences in Mexico, I gained new ones when I arrived in the Netherlands. By venturing into the unknown, I gained friends, faced challenges, and most of all, I was able to achieve my personal goals. You take risks in life and decide what is and isn't essential for you. I knew that I could live somewhere other than Mexico and away from my family. Still, the idea of never having tried to pursue my passion for doing clinical research in another country was unbearable.

Edmundo Erazo (Continues on page 178)

Sandra López-León
(ISRAEL, THE NETHERLANDS, SPAIN, UNITED STATES)

When my grandfather arrived in Mexico from Spain, he never saw most of his family again. Decades passed before he was able to see his parents and the only news he received were letters that took a month to arrive. At that time, when you left your country, you disappeared almost as if you had died.

Now it's a whole other story: we can communicate faster with people on the other side of the world than with the people sitting next to us. We can talk and see them daily on our phone and we can visit them several times a year. That keeps us close to the ones we love.

When I left Mexico to go to the Netherlands, I had no prior expectations. I was simply ready for the next adventure. I never asked myself when I was going to come back, when I was going to see my family again, or if I was leaving for good. At first, I didn't even miss anyone. I began to miss my family and friends in important situations and on important dates: celebrations, birthdays, graduations, weddings, baptisms, illnesses, and funerals.

It wasn't until my first child was born, three years later, that it dawned on me that my children were not going to have grandparents or aunts and uncles around in their lives. From that point on, all my savings went into trips to Mexico so I could spend New Year's Eve and summer near my family. We'd spend a week together and say goodbye as if it were the last time we'd ever see each other again.

I often talked to my parents, and we were closer emotionally and intellectually than ever before, but I missed them, and they missed us as well. Life is so short and the time we spend with people goes by so fast that it is illogical to live so far away from them. My parents are only children and my siblings lived in the United States, so there came a moment when they realized they didn't want to grow old away from their family and that it made no sense for them to be alone. My father is Spanish and had his medicine and psychiatry degrees revalidated there, so we made the decision, all of us, to move to Spain. We were the ones to arrive first, and my parents followed shortly after.

A few years later we had the opportunity to go live near my two brothers in the United States. It was very nice that, for the first time, my children had aunts, uncles, and cousins nearby. The more time goes by, the more I value my family. They give us the strength that supports us, they are there to celebrate as well as to embrace. For me, it doesn't matter which country I live in, what matters is being close to the people I love.

Sandra López-León (Continues on page 179)

Rafael G. Magaña
(ENGLAND, UNITED STATES)

Moving to another country was something I'd planned since I started medical school. I wanted to live in New York, and I had in mind what I wanted to do. In the past, my family had migrated twice, and I knew this would be a big change.

When I got to New York, everything felt incredibly overwhelming. Huge, in all respects. I felt the weight of my decision and knew I'd have to study a lot, since the competition for places in the surgical residence was downright intimidating.

When I came to the United States to prepare for the USMLE exams and waited for the student visa, I had to find a place to live in New York. With persistence, luck, and thanks to the help of some friends who already lived there, I managed to find a small apartment for a good price.

For the first time since taking the course at Joe Blasco's Make Up School in Los Angeles, I found myself alone. I spoke daily with my family in Mexico, who had supported me greatly, but it was still a very stressful season: it wasn't just a change of country, but a culture shock that struck me from the very moment I landed at the airport.

The daily encounters with people from different cultures but, above all, the scams that you face on a daily basis (from renting an apartment, while on the subway or buying anything) turn this city into a real jungle.

My classmates' diversity was really interesting and, as time went on, I started making friends. I think the adaptation time for me was around six months. Having a group of friends was a huge support, since we were all in a similar situation, and we all helped each other study. Some colleagues came from Latin America; the rest from other parts of the world.

With a place to live, a routine, and a class schedule that filled my whole day, little by little I began to feel that the exams were less difficult, and I accepted the challenge with joy. I also met a very pretty girl who studied with me, and we started dating. That ultimately helped me feel less alone. From a difficult time, it turned into a memorable experience for which I now feel nostalgic.

I think that, when you are looking to migrate, it's very important to have a contact before getting there. In my case, that contact was Steven Cruz, the director of the program. He helped me out a lot and gave me valuable advice on how to carry out the procedures and solve everyday problems such as where to do the shopping, etc.

Rafael G. Magaña (Continues on page 182)

Nissin Nahmias
(UNITED STATES)

For me, this chapter is especially emotional. Everything I've ever known, everything familiar and who I was until then, I left in Mexico. I left the places I loved during my childhood and teenage years, I left many friends and beautiful times spent together that are now gone forever.

I left the daily routine of living with my parents, and the city where I grew up. Mexico is dynamic, ever-changing; but the Mexico that lives in my memories is static. Whenever you move someplace else, you keep an idea of what your home represented and the people you left behind. When you return, you realize that everything has changed, that places evolve and people too, friends grow, have new families, move away... That's why, every time I return to Mexico City, I encounter a brand-new place. There's something familiar about it, and, in it, there's a big part of me. Nonetheless, each time I go there, it's always a different city.

Nissin Nahmias (Continues on page 183)

Susana Ramírez Romero
(SPAIN)

We left everything in Mexico: family, friends, colleagues, professors and even the prestige gained during the years of hard work and study. In our case, migrating meant starting from scratch. We had no academic or family ties in Spain.

The first Christmas was austere and difficult. With so many expenses generated by the move, So the only decoration we had was a nativity scene of cardboard figures made by me and illuminated by my eldest son.

Here in Catalonia, they don't celebrate Christmas Eve, only Christmas Day. I missed celebrating on the 24th with the *punch*, the music, the piñatas; and then reheating everything on the 25th with the whole Mexican family, which includes uncles, cousins, nephews, nieces, grandparents, and party-crashers.

For this reason, two years after we moved, I decided to go to Mexico every December, which meant tightening our belt financially and making arrangements when it came to school and work.

Going to Mexico is a celebration framed by sparks of joy. We relish every part of the trip: packing the suitcases, buying presents to let the family know that, despite the distance, a day hasn't gone by that we haven't thought about them. The process of boarding a plane with children is quite an adventure. We've traveled with stopovers in Frankfurt, Paris, Amsterdam, Madrid, and London and there's always another Mexican mom on the flight whom I quickly identify by her accent and because she has the same sparkle in her eyes as I do; the same enthusiasm that spreads to the kids each time we visit our beautiful, noisy, and colorful Mexico. Upon arrival at the Mexico City airport, there are always smiling siblings and aunts, grandparents with balloons waiting for the grandkids they only see a few times a year. I'm a romantic; I celebrate not only my own arrival, but also the coming together of hundreds of Mexicans who, for various reasons, live abroad. We are a loving and enthusiastic people whose concept of family has no limits or borders.

I cherish that my children feel the shelter of their grandparents, the complicity with their cousins, the optimism of Mexicans; that they taste chili and learn to eat tacos with their hands, that they are invited to *Las Posadas* (a traditional nightly celebration in the days leading up to Christmas Eve), that they make new friends, that they know how to break a piñata, that they feel loved in the most authentic way.

Today, social networks, cell phones and Wi-Fi have become invaluable tools, especially for those of us who live far from our family, as they allow us to shorten distances. An aunt who lived in England in the 1980s told me: "In my day, when I wanted to communicate with my sisters, I had to spend a lot of money on a phone call or send a letter that took several months to arrive, so that by the time the letter arrived announcing the pregnancy, the baby had already been born."

However, with all the technological advances, remoteness weighs heavily, especially when it comes to health-related issues. Since I moved to Spain, three family members —my mother, my aunt, and my nephew— have been diagnosed with cancer: another difficult stage in our lives. In these circumstances, I wish I lived near them, I wish I could be there, so I could hug, accompany, and guide them, but it's not always possible. But fortunately, thanks to the fact that we live in the digital era, we can share the blood test results, CT scans, and medical reports and send instant messages to my family or even to medical colleagues involved in the diagnosis and treatment.

Once again, I'm grateful I studied medicine because, even at a distance, I've been able to intervene in some way in my family's recovery. I never imagined that I would cross the corridors of INCAN (National Cancer Institute) again, where I did my social service in research, only now as a patient's family member. I was lucky to have met the pathologists of that hospital years before, because now, they would again lend a helping hand, no longer reviewing slides for my project, but corroborating my mother's diagnosis.

I will be infinitely grateful to my friends, especially my physician friends, who were close to my family, showing their professionalism, their love and their wonderful vocation to medicine. To all of them, a thank you that goes beyond what my mouth can utter, and my heart can hold. And, of course, to all that rollicking and united family that has always been there, that has always stood by our side and made us whole.

Susana Ramírez Romero (Continues on page 184)

Luis Rodrigo Reynoso
(ETHIOPIA)

From the very moment in which the opportunity to emigrate to Ethiopia presented itself, I was exhilarated. Just thinking about facing something unknown brought me satisfaction. But knowing that I would be surrounded by tribes was also a great motivation to me. Either way, I did have much time to think about everything that I was leaving behind.

Although I must admit that, from, my long history as a nomad has taught me to detach myself. Although I can pack my whole life in a 23-kilogram suitcase, there are countless people you miss, but it is impossible to bring along with you: family and friends. And you always have the hope that when you return nothing will have changed.

A shared trait among Mexicans who emigrate is food nostalgia. When I travel, I carry mole paste, tortillas, jalapeños, chili powder, sauces, traditional tamarind, and chili candy with me in all their presentations. And this trip was no exception. I do it for myself and now for my wife (who is living outside of Guadalajara for the first time ever); but also, because I like to show off a sample of our gastronomy to our hosts. In addition to the food, this time I packed some of my favorite clothes, the most comfortable and practical, four surgical scrubs and as many sutures as possible, medication, pencils and cautery patches, and whatever material could be used. A suitcase of over 23 kilograms was filled by materials and surgical supplies donated in solidarity by colleagues from the health area who supported us in this great decision.

My wife and I sold one of our cars and we left the other one on consignment in the hope that its sale would allow us to have some savings, in case of an emergency. We vacated the "madhouse," our love nest, which made us realize how unconsciously we had filled ourselves with belongings and memories.

But leaving family and friends is the most painful thing. Without a doubt, when you emigrate, you always have the desire to see them again, to hug them, and to be able to share with them all your anecdotes. It can be said, however, that the family situation for my wife and me was ideal: with our parents alive and well, and with the certainty that our siblings would be in close proximity to them, we were able to make the trip with some peace of mind.

So, without thinking twice, we organized a very unusual asks for a hand in marriage, we introduced both families, we shared our intentions to marry under a Mayan ritual - against my fervent Catholic mother's wishes and in spite her tears, -, and we also notified them that after getting married, we would move to Ethiopia. The reaction of both parents translated by their facial expressions is one of those things in life that are priceless, my in-laws mainly, as my parents could say that they were already used to it . But no, my mother still cries before each one of my trips, takes out her holy water and begins to repeat aloud: «In the name of the father, the son and the holy spirit, Sacred Heart of the good path, bring them safe and sound to their destination". She rigorously does this at least twice, and she could continue giving you blessings until the drops drip down your forehead, because they are never enough. I once accumulated up to eight blessings right before a trip.

We also leave Mustafa, our cat. We had made all the arrangements to take him with us, we had even paid his travel fee. However, the lack of food and cat litter, the non-existent veterinary attention (we had been informed that if we needed a veterinarian for our cat, we had to travel to Kenya), as well as the little respect that the country has towards pets made us desist.

We decided that it was best for us to explore the place before deciding whether Mustafa could travel later. A couple of friends promised to take him if possible, and in the meantime, he stayed at home with Nananina, my mother-in-law, who to this day resents me, as she had just upholstered her furniture.

Thus, with four suitcases – but without packing the molcajete mainly because we could not - and many mixed feelings, we left our native Mexico. When uncertainty invaded my mind, I remembered the song by Facundo Cabral and reaffirmed that it was time to go: «I'm not from here / I'm not from there. / I have no age / or future / and being happy / is my identity color ».

When fear oppressed my heart, I listened to Abraham's command: Leave your native land and your father's house and go to the country that I will indicate to you, I will make of you a great nation, I will bless you and for you, all peoples on earth will be blessed as well».

—Thank you Mexico!

Luis Rodrigo Reynoso (Continues on page 186)

Alejandra Rodríguez Romero
(UNITED STATES)

My parents, my sister Regina and I have always been very close. My first separation from them was when I left to study medicine in Guadalajara when I was 18 years old. Three years later, my sister decided to go study the last year of high school in Houston, Texas, where my maternal family lives, and finally decided to move there. For that reason, only my parents, a little of my paternal family, and childhood friends are currently still in Mexico. Fortunately, I currently live in Tucson, Arizona, only 4 hours away from my hometown of Hermosillo. However, I miss my parents' home, its smell, and cozy atmosphere. I miss my friends and their families. I miss the delicious food, the warmth of the people, the *fiestas* so full of life and color, the folklore, the customs, the music and even the Oxxos (grocery stores). Something I admire and miss about Mexicans are our family and moral values, much firmer and deeply rooted than those of other cultures I have lived with, where everything is disposable. This doesn't only mean interpersonal relationships, but also to jobs, studies, and many other things.

I try to go to Hermosillo at least two to three times a year, enough to soak in the love of my family and friends and eat all the cravings I accumulate over the months. Unfortunately and inevitably, these visits remind me every time that Mexico is no longer like I remember it, and I would be lying to say that I'm not glad to have left behind things like the insecurity, the fear of walking in the park or to the corner store. The fear of being kidnapped or raped and, even more frustrating, having to stand impunity and corruption in the face of these acts. To be honest, I'm always a bit worried about my relatives and friends who live there.

I left many beautiful things in Mexico. My country is the source of the unique customs and roots that shaped me into the person I am today. For this very reason, I feel responsible for making sure my children spend enough time there so they can know my origins and so I can give them a bicultural and diaphanous perspective of life. To date, my daughter Zoe has spent several weeks on vacation with my parents over the course of her 5 years of life, where she has begun to learn and experience part of Mexican history and traditions, and soon it will be my son Jeffrey's turn. It's been 11 years since my arrival in the United States and I still miss my *México lindo y querido* very much, but it comforts me to know that, by sharing my customs with my children and integrating them into my family, I will be passing them on to the next generation.

Alejandra Rodríguez Romero (Continues on page 190)

Jack Rubinstein
(UNITED STATES)

> "Poor Mexico, so far from God and so close to the United States."
> –Attributed to Porfirio Díaz, but probably written by Nemesio García Naranjo

For me, returning to Mexico means regression and, at the same time, an opportunity to reevaluate the choices I've made throughout my life. The personal and social repercussions of living abroad are clear and sometimes painful. Leaving my family behind meant not being present at key moments of their lives, including the deaths of my grandfather, father, and father-in-law. These losses undoubtedly came with opportunities for personal growth but, taking stock, I'm still not sure I made the right decision regarding my personal life. In contrast, the professional repercussions have been enormously positive. My visits to Mexico —the last one after my father died— make it clear to me that, from the point of view of medical and scientific training, the United States and Mexico are two completely different worlds.

This chapter is guided by the question "What did I leave behind in my country?" and, frankly, I left a punitive training system for medical residents. An archaic, hierarchical, and aggressive method, focused on trying to break the young doctor through excessive work, punishing shifts, and schedules that, under other circumstances, would be considered war crimes. This system remains inflexible and is based on a principle that (only) veterans defend ("If I survived it, they can, too"), painfully ignoring the inherent survival bias and with little sympathy for the doctors in training.

What did I leave in Mexico? I left a public healthcare system where residents and employees work for a precarious salary, one of the lowest in the world. A salary that forces all doctors to prioritize private practice and insured patients in order to survive financially. What did I leave in Mexico? A private healthcare system where older doctors control the entry and exit of younger ones. These "eminences", abusing their position of power, compete with other doctors and don't allow them to move up the ladder so they won't lose their jobs. This struggle to keep patients and to refer them only to their allies or buddies results in a bubble of safety for the doctor, but a careless handling of the patient. What did I leave in Mexico? An arthritic scientific and medical research system, which deteriorates, not because it lacks intellectual capacity or scientific imagination, but rather because it falls short of political vision and economic sustenance. Cutting-edge research requires that science be stimulated and supported in all sectors, from elementary school to laboratories in national institutes, and that's impossible when the scholarship for the highest-level researcher within the National System of Researchers corresponds to the weekly salary of a technician in the United States. What did I leave in Mexico? My hopes that the Mexican healthcare system can one day move forward.

Jack Rubinstein (Continues on page 192)

Alberto Saltiel
(ISRAEL)

Mexico is, and always will be, my home. I was born and raised in a beautiful country; a place I love and miss every single day. When I emigrated, I left an incredible culture full of warmth and tradition. I left my home, the comfort of my routine, and everything that I enjoyed there. I left the *tacos al pastor*, the *carnitas*, the *micheladas*, the *cochinita pibil*, the *chiles en nogada*, the Day of the Dead altars and the men we called *viene-viene*, who mastered the art of parking a car. I left the tamales and the *atole*. I left the Mexican people, who help their fellow man without second thoughts. I left the Mexican who smiles in the face of adversity and finds creative solutions to the problems life throws their way.

I left the security and peace of mind of everything I know. The easy way of living my day-to-day in autopilot. The possibility of going to the corner store to buy that little part I need to fix something at home. I left the feeling of freedom. Yes, of course, Israel is a free country, and I am a free man, but since I left Mexico until I fully adapted to Israel, I gave up the freedom to move without limitations. In Mexico, I did not feel restricted by language, culture, or lack of national knowledge. I was used to moving freely back home, in the cities and even across the country, but, when I got here, everything was different.

I've always been a very sociable person and one of the biggest difficulties of migrating is leaving the people you've grown up with behind. Leaving all the conversations, including the ones we'd have with our eyes and surrounded by an air of complicity, was undoubtedly one of the most difficult things for me. They're the people I grew up with, my people, who stood by me through failures and achievements, laughter, tears, and arguments. They're the ones who accompanied me in the process of becoming who I am today and, whenever I must leave them behind, it weighs heavy on my heart. However, they're never forgotten, and only distance separates us.

The most difficult part of migrating and the most valuable thing that I left in Mexico is, without a doubt, my dear family. I grew up in a very close family circle, in the company of uncles, cousins and grandparents. I left behind family meals, festivities, and Shabbat dinners. I gave up the chance to watch my nephews grow up and enjoy spending time with them. It's tough to live new experiences, achievements, challenges, and failures without being able to share them in person with your family.

Fortunately, today's technology helps us shorten tremendous distances. Today, we can enjoy our families, be part of the festivities and share new virtual experiences and, although it's not the same, we're there somehow and feel closer to each other. What we leave behind when we migrate is of great value and importance, but what we acquire makes the sacrifice worthwhile.

Alberto Saltiel (Continues on page 194)

Luana Sandoval Castillo

(SPAIN, DENMARK)

In Mexico, I left colors, aromas, spices, an ancestral culture, home remedies, music, sunshine, a warm sea, mariachis, unparalleled customer service, dear friends and my beloved family. I left the long after-dinner conversations that filled me with satisfaction and warmed my heart. I left the talks in the dark with my sister, who's my partner in life. Even though it's been more than 15 years since I left home, I still miss the Mexican wit as much as the day I went away. Mexicans seek to treat you as best as they can. My countrymen work with honor, they know what they're doing and do it with gratitude. We are noble people.

On the other hand, I also left insecurity, corruption and cheating, inequality, the advantageous levers, the stress generated by constant traffic, earthquakes, and sexism. At least I thought I did. I left an overwhelmingly hierarchical healthcare system, where respect was earned through experience and punishing on-call shifts. I left how normalized it was for my colleagues to be humiliated or abused. I left a country where Mexico's worst enemy is the attitude of conformism and waiting for someone else to provide an answer for your problems.

After so many years, I no longer know where my home is. I am from here and I am from there, a combination of experiences and feelings that make me who I am and I'm immensely proud of that.

Luana Sandoval Castillo (Continues on page 196)

Ilan Shapiro
(United States)

I begin writing this chapter with tears in my eyes. I don't know if it's due to how complicated it is to reflect on one's life or to the pain that contemplating the past involves. For me, Mexico means refuge, growth, and experimentation. The foundation of what I am was formed in Mexico City, in a country in the making, with many contrasts and inequalities.

For more than 25 years, I made memories and experienced adventures in Mexico. I will start by telling you about my family and friends, and then I'll talk about other things close to my heart that I had to leave when I ventured out into the world.

Family

Family is one of the things I miss the most. I come from a family with many connections and stories and alongside which I grew up. I miss the weekend discussions to decide which relatives we'd visit, or more importantly, who we would spend Friday dinners with. I miss my immediate family, uncles, and friends, the dinners full of passion and food. Although I feel that, on the one hand, I am distancing my children from their roots, on the other I'm absolutely certain they're Mexican. For me it was really important to spend time with my family at births, graduations, birthdays, and holidays; but also, to stand by them in difficult moments, or when someone died. All this was part of a cycle of laughter and crying that, unfortunately (or thank God, who knows), my children will experience differently.

Friends

How I miss the activities that started at nine or ten at night! And to think that, nowadays, dinner at half past six seems late. I left many friends on the way, for some the gasoline just ran out, others left us too soon. At first, the only requirement to belong to a group of friends is to be present. Today, there are no requirements. A friendship just is.

The incredible thing is that, whenever we call each other or meet up, it's as if not a day has passed. It feels like I still live around the corner, and only went out for some snacks. This same cycle made making friends easier in Chicago, Florida and finally in Los Angeles; places where I've benefited from the quality rather than the quantity of new friends.

Memories

I left my beloved Scouts. For at least fifteen years of my life, I was part of an organization that filled me with an immense amount of knowledge. I was part of a family that taught me leadership skills and group management, planning and execution skills, and the need to work for the common good. I hope that the camping trips, the endless hikes and, above all, the wonderful memories, never fade away. On the other hand, my relationship with different schools in gatherings, dances and festivals was key to developing friendships that will last forever.

Ilan Shapiro (Continues on page 197)

René Sotelo

(UNITED STATES)

It's difficult to know what you leave behind when you emigrate, because the truth is that you take with you your background, experiences, memories, the essence of the country that makes up who you are and left its mark in you. Along with you, you carry in your suitcase the places, the smells, the flavors... What encompasses your identity. But it's exactly that, those feelings of rootedness, what remains in hundreds of longings and thousands of stories, anchored in the path that was forged and in the footprint that was left. You leave a life behind but still carry it with you, to start again, to contribute, to move forward.

I left my home in Venezuela, that space where I built my life alongside my family. I left years of having practiced medicine with my colleagues, catching up with the man in the parking lot every morning, the coffee served by the same smile for years, and the good morning welcomes of familiar faces. I left behind a gallery of bromeliads among which I would walk if I wanted to take a break during the day, and the orange, yellow, purple, and fuchsia colors of the hibiscus, those flowers so characteristic of the mansions of La Floresta, an area of Caracas that, for years, was also my home.

I left behind the peace of mind of knowing that you have the affection of family, friends, neighbors, and co-workers; that network of people that is woven over many years and that provides you with security in times of adversity, because you know that you can count on them whenever you need them. Without knowing it, that'll be perhaps what you miss the most, and exactly what you'll strive to build again wherever you are.

I left behind the Venezuelan way of communicating, its sense of humor and friendship, the quickness to crack up a conversation with a stranger and that pleasant feeling you get —after fifteen minutes— when you receive a card together with the greatest honesty and the phrase: "Call me, or get in touch to have a coffee soon, because it was a real pleasure meeting you."

I left behind a legacy of work, a group called UNIC (Unit of Robotic Surgery and Minimal Invasion) that I had put together, and that continues to provide medical services and research to bring academic value from the experiences of patients I managed to accumulate in decades of study and medical work. It functions as an extension of who I am, and it's still part of the history of those who, for so many years, have placed their trust in me as their physician and health consultant.

I also left behind the wonderful rehabilitation wing of the medical institute, a recovery center for patients undergoing postoperative processes, made for those you want to pamper in a special way, and for the ones who want to take a break before starting over again.

I left my haven, Piedras Blancas, anchored in the town of La Guardia, that magical place that always accompanies me in my memories and awaits my return: my home right in front of the Caribbean Sea. Piedras Blancas is, perhaps, one of the things that I had the hardest time letting go of and that, at the same time, is the best reason to rejoice when I come back.

It all stayed the same, everything is in its place, and welcomes me every time I return to Venezuela. Four times a year I rescue what I left behind, and my heart smiles when I find it once again.

René Sotelo **(Continues on page 200)**

Karla Uribe
(UNITED STATES)

Now that I'm away, my heart constantly misses Mexico, its traditions, its gastronomy, its beaches, and the warmth of its people. Mexico is, undoubtedly, one of a kind.

Blood beckons and it's hard to attend family events through social networks or screens. It's difficult to understand that, after you went away, life did not remain as you left it. With time, although it never stops being difficult, the heart hurts a little less. You may even learn how to live with the longing but, in the end, no matter how much time passes, goodbyes are always painful.

I dare say that the hardest part for me about moving, with the implication of not having a medical license in this country and dedicating myself to being a wife and a mom, was the disapproval of my parents. Recriminations hurt. "This is not the life I prepared you for", "What? You don't have money?" or "You're not a doctor anymore", were some of the phrases I had to hear. Now that I am a mom, I understand that it's inevitable that parents have certain expectations when it comes to their children, and it must be difficult to accept when the mental scheme you have of them collapses. However, words carry a big weight, they are not easily forgotten, and, without a doubt, they hinder the adaptation process. Time is the best medicine; through it we have tried to respect and value each other as independent families, but also as a single, united one.

I also left my friends back in Mexico, the ones with whom I grew up and who became family. Although technology enables contact and closeness despite the distance, it cannot replace the warmth of a hug, something so simple, yet sometimes so necessary.

I have thought about what our life would be like if we decided to return to Mexico. I think that, at this moment, it would be as hard for me as it was when I arrived in the United States, because nature took its course, and our life is here now. Home is built with the love and dreams of those who share it. Although a piece of my heart is always there, I take my home with me wherever I go.

Karla Uribe (Continues on page 202)

Jeannette Uribe
(UNITED STATES)

I didn't leave my country behind. I can't. I don't want to. Mexico will always be my country, and its people, my people. There I have my house, the house of my dreams, that I built alongside my husband. Every year, we try to make renovations and improvements, so the place is not abandoned, even though we only visit one or two weeks a year.

The U.S. is different. There's, for example, the peace of mind that comes from knowing that, if life rewards you with financial stability, you won't have to hide under a rock or conceal your assets for fear of being a victim of crime. In the States, you know that the police are there to help you, not to extort money. In almost every job, your effort, besides being paid, is rewarded and acknowledged. You don't feel repressed by your supervisors but, rather, celebrated. If you wish to continue your education, most companies support you and even pay for your postgraduate studies. The big difference in salaries is relative: you earn a lot more but spend a lot more. Taxes, basic services, daycare, food, medical services, education... absolutely everything is more expensive when compared to Mexico.

Leaving the country with that feeling of separation but, at the same time, with plans and many dreams to fulfill, leaving behind your history, your roots, friends, family, parents, and siblings, is a decision to be applauded regardless of the circumstances. A change of this magnitude will transform you and, if it doesn't work out, no harm done: at least you tried.

Even today, I still miss my beloved Mexico, the eternal afternoons at the ranch, where listening to the birds at dawn and watching the most beautiful sunsets and a sky full of stars wasn't a privilege or something unusual but, simply, your day-to-day life.

Jeannette Uribe (Continues on page 203)

6

My new life and my family

Patricia Bautista Rivera
(UNITED STATES)

A few months after we arrived in Kentucky, we found out we were pregnant. It was a surprise... a shock, to be honest! It's so ironic that a couple of doctors would be caught off guard by pregnancy, but that's what happened. I had an uneventful pregnancy, although it should be noted that the discomforts associated with pregnancy can make married life complicated. I must admit that my husband worked overtime on his patience and goodwill towards me.

The birth of our daughter was one of the most challenging moments of our lives — not only were we alone, but we also faced complications. My baby and I were hospitalized for several days and, when I left the hospital, she had to stay a while longer. Luckily, that bumpy arrival had no negative consequences.

Once she was born, I became a full-time mom, but it wasn't easy; I felt terribly lonely. The pediatrician came to the rescue and connected us with a Spanish lady who also had a baby, and soon were surrounded by the most wonderful company. So, little by little, we found friends, people with whom we learned different things: the importance of playgroups, gardening, walks in the countryside, etc. When it was time to choose my daughter's godfather, I asked the allergist who had accepted me in the rotation with his medical group, with whom we had developed a friendship, and who also visited us in the hospital. He gladly accepted. Little did he (and we) know that, eventually, he and his family would become our family in Kentucky, and we would be his new-found Mexican relatives.

As for the language, at home we decided to keep Spanish as the first language, because it's easier for the children to learn English from their schoolmates and friends. My daughter attended a preschool program twice a week and gradually learned English. By the age of 3, she could switch from one language to the other depending on the situation.

When she was 4 years old, we became pregnant again, but this time, due to the threat of premature labor, I had to stay on bed rest for 12 weeks. Thank God for my kid's loving godmother and my dear neighbors, a Swedish family with a little girl my daughter's age, because they helped us a lot. They alternated taking my daughter to and from school and accompanied us as much as they could.

Within 6 months of our son's birth, my husband finished his training and we returned to Mexico. Two of us had arrived in the States with only a few suitcases, and now a family of four was returning to Mexico with everything they needed to build a home. We were very happy to be back. However, two and a half years later, we returned to Kentucky.

Over the years, in addition to being a full-time mom, I've been involved as a volunteer at my children's schools, with parent organizations, after school activities, and also at our church. Volunteering offers the opportunity to interact and learn the customs of the new society we're now part of. In my weekly rotation in the office, I learned to see not only pediatric allergy patients with allergies, but also, adults. Unfortunately, due to the fact that the practice was sold, my increasing busyness, and the arrival of the pandemic, I stopped going to the office.

Speaking of extracurricular activities, my family joined the hustle and bustle and continuous busyness that characterizes Americans and my children have participated in ballet, a percussion group, soccer with the school teams, cello, field hockey, track, marching band and more. So, I had to find the time to drive my children from here to there and to support them in whatever they needed.

Now that they're adults and independent, I've been slowly taking time for myself. I do yoga regularly, walk my dog, earned a master's degree, and started working. I've also participated in book clubs and continue to be a catechist at my church.

One of the activities I enjoy the most is running with my children and my husband. I don't run at the same speed, of course, but it gives me immense pleasure to follow them and feel the challenge of finishing the routes we plan. I also really enjoy cooking with them, all three of them, because each one has their own style and preference and I love nothing more than being their assistant.

When I mentioned gardening, I didn't mention that I love growing and taking care of my plants. I grow organic vegetables: tomatoes, chilies, peppers, cucumbers, etc. I also have blackberry and raspberry plants, and planters only with decorative plants and flowers that I also love greatly.

Patricia Bautista Rivera (Continues on page 207)

Edmundo Erazo

(THE NETHERLANDS)

My new family is diverse; I have friends from Mexico and many other countries. Getting used to a new life takes time and patience. At first, the culture seemed interesting to me, and everything was new, which motivated me to get more involved with the Dutch and adopt their customs. It was essential to realize that not all of us new to a country adapt at the same pace; you must enjoy the process and take your time. That's how I met my best friends, by taking it easy and genuinely enjoying my new life.

Luck also plays a role. I met my two best friends while chatting with another friend in a park. Suddenly, we realized that we all spoke Spanish and were from Mexico. My advice is not to think of adaptation as a one-way process or feel like meeting new people is a chore or obligation. Just enjoy the journey.

I learned quickly that you should not hold onto a preconceived idea of what your life "should" be. You must be open to the possibility of change and take risks to get the best experience, not only professionally but personally. When leaving Mexico, the first place you go may not be where you'll end up.

My new life is different in many ways from the one I led in Mexico. Still, there are things that I enjoy and value: for example, not having to spend up to two hours stuck in the traffic of Mexico City and having the possibility of achieving a balance between work and my personal life.

Edmundo Erazo (Continues on page 210)

Sandra López-León

(ISRAEL, THE NETHERLANDS, SPAIN, UNITED STATES)

In every country I've lived, it sometimes seems as if I've led a different life. I went to Jerusalem when I was twenty-three and lived there for a year. The first few months, I lived in the dormitories of the Hebrew University and attended an ulpan to learn the culture and the language. I was surrounded by people from all over the world ranging in age from eighteen to twenty-five. It was non-stop partying and traveling. On weekends we went on organized tours to different parts of Israel and stayed in various kibbutzim. The second leg of the trip, however, was my medical internship at Hadassah Hospital, where I spent most of my time. I had to rotate in the gynecology, surgical, internal medicine, and emergency guard throughout the year. I ate lunch and dinner in the cafeteria, studied in the library, and the other interns and residents became my friends. My days were spent checking on patients and attending surgeries.

I came to live in the Netherlands a year later. I had just gotten married and was fresh out of medical school. I knew that, to adapt, I had to learn the language, so for the first ten months, I went to a university to learn Dutch. Our daily routine looked a little bit like this: my husband went to work, I studied Dutch about eight hours a day and often I'd walk around the city and discover every corner of it. I had two favorite places: the central library in The Hague and the Scheveningen beach. I was used to going to the beach once a year; now, I could go every day. I loved walking with my husband along the seashore, watching the sunset and eating *haring* and *paling* (herring and eel). Not even a year later, I had already passed the Nt2 (the Dutch as a second language exam) and was a doing a Masters of Science at the Erasmus University in Rotterdam. My new colleagues were physicians my age, with interests common to mine, and they came from all over the world. I was very happy to have found the place where I belonged.

The next five years I basically went to the university from 08:00 to 17:00, took classes, studied, did research, and ate with my friends. Then I would go pick up my husband from work, we'd cook, have dinner, and go to sleep. Saturday was the day we had to go shopping because all the stores were closed on Sunday, so together we'd get the groceries for the week. On the street where we lived there was a cheese shop, a flower shop, a bakery, a fish shop, and a snack bar where we bought fried food and croquettes. It was incredible that, in less than four hours, we could visit France, Belgium and Germany.

We moved to Barcelona in 2007. My oldest son was four years old, and my middle son was about to be born. My parents had just moved there, and we lived right across the street from the American School my children would later attend. We lived in the buildings of La Mallola: a residential estate of very nice houses and buildings, full of gardens and parks. Below my house there was a supermarket, a bakery, a fish market, a bar, my dentist, and the hairdresser. We lived in an area famous for its foreign community in Barcelona (Esplugues de Llobregat). Many celebrities also lived near La Mallola; once, in the bar below my house, we saw opera singer José Carreras and the Barça player, Piqué.

My day consisted of my husband walking my children to school and me going to work, where I did research for a pharmaceutical company. Its cafeteria, like everywhere else in the country, had healthy and delicious food. I loved that every Thursday they had paella or *fideuáà* on the daily menu. I would leave at 16:00 and go to school to pick up my children. Every afternoon we would go to the park in front of the school and spend about an hour there. While the children were playing, I'd catch up with my friends. Most of them I'd met at the kids' school, because they also were families that had emigrated, and it was with them that we felt most comfortable.

Every Friday we would go to the bar all afternoon. The kids would play soccer and run around, and we moms would sit at the bar eating *tapas* —serrano ham, Manchego cheese, and *tortilla de patatas*— while drinking wine or beer. If I wanted to see friends, I'd go to the bar downstairs; if I wanted to eat well, there were plenty of restaurants near my house; if I wanted culture, there was Barcelona and, if I wanted to travel, I could go anywhere in Europe at affordable prices and within a couple of hours.

Now we've reached my current life in the United States. We live in a neighborhood full of children, with a swimming pool, a park, and sports fields. The housing costs are three times less than in Europe. In the U.S., children usually go to school where they live, so we first chose the school where we wanted our children to go to and then the house. We are also surrounded by nature; plants, flowers, forests, and lakes abound in the area. There's also the most diverse fauna: bears, deer, rabbits, squirrels, birds, and turtles. You can go fishing right next to my house. There are also many farms where we buy fruit, vegetables, milk, eggs, and cheese. We live in the countryside, but if we want to go to the city, within an hour we can get to Philadelphia or New York City.

My job is forty minutes away from my house, but if I want to, I can work from home. I love going to work because that's where I have the most friends. I like to go to lunch with them and chat. Besides, it's an incredible place, very nice and modern. It's in a small town with many coffee shops, stores, gyms, pharmacies, and recreational areas. I enjoy everything immensely because I know that nothing is forever, and no one knows what the future holds.

Sandra López-León (Continues on page 210)

Rafael G. Magaña

(England, United States)

Filled with uncertainty but excited to improve myself, I began my residency in general surgery. I wasn't really starting from scratch; I had already done a year at the 20 de Noviembre Hospital in Mexico City.

As time goes by, a residency becomes not only a way of training and improving, but also a kind of home where the family is made up of residents, students, teachers, etc. I spent six years of general surgery residency in New York, and, during that time, I made many friends I still hang out with, both inside and outside the hospital.

When it comes to my relationships, those years were more or less stable. As time passed, and with the difficulties of obtaining a place in the specialty I wanted, I had to do several specialties, so I became a nomad: every year, I switched residencies while I trained to become a better physician. This reminded me a lot of my childhood and teenage years. In each of these changes, I experienced new things, met new places and people, had new girlfriends, succeeded, and failed.

After finishing general surgery in New Rochelle, I went to New York to do two years of reconstructive burn surgery. From there, I moved to Salt Lake City to do a year of craniofacial surgery, and, after that, I decided to return to the East Coast to do a one-year specialty in breast reconstruction. From there, I moved to Augusta, Georgia, to complete two years of plastic surgery.

Every time I returned to New York in between specialties, I visited my friends, who were always there for me, my "regular" friends.

Along the way, I forged a lot of friendships and made sense of many things. The time I spent in Salt Lake City was one of the hardest. On the one hand, the director of the program could've perfectly played a dictator in any film production; but, at the same time, the people I met there were the kindest I had ever met. That contrast was a bitter-sweet circumstance amidst a tremendous academic experience.

I currently live in Greenwich, Connecticut, where I've lived for the last five years. I think this is the closest thing I've had to a home in the last 20 years. I'm also fortunate that my brother and his family now live in Greenwich as well. Furthermore, after my mother died five years ago, my father also moved here. We are all together again, and I think I've finally found a place where I'd like to stay forever.

Rafael G. Magaña (Continues on page 212)

Nissin Nahmias
(United States)

I've lived in the United States since 2002, in Florida, Pennsylvania, Virginia, Connecticut, and New York. When I finished my specialty in Virginia, I moved to Connecticut, got married, worked for several years in private practice and later in a hospital.

I had three wonderful children: Albert, Stella, and Jacob. Their laughter is the soundtrack of my life.

Unfortunately, after countless attempts to keep my family together, things took a different turn and I got divorced seven years later. That was probably one of the hardest moments of my life, because of how far away from my family and friends I was, but more because of the uncertainty the whole situation entailed. One wonders if the divorce will affect the children, if they'll be fine, whether they'll resent your absence of be angry at you; in short, in a divorce, you question a lot. I think the most important thing is to let your children know that you love them more than life itself, and that you'll always be there for them.

My dear children suffered no sequels in this regard, but what they did develop was a very curious mind and an excellent sense of humor, in addition to learning how to take great care of our dogs.

After my divorce, I met Hanna, my current girlfriend, and her three children. Every weekend, we have a "full house" between the two of us. Now, loneliness is a thing of the past and I even feel weird whenever the house is still or silent.

Nissin Nahmias (Continues on page 214)

Susana Ramírez Romero
(SPAIN)

We've been living in Spain for ten years now and our routine consists of getting up at 08:00, as classes start at 09:30am. The system promotes that the school is close to home, which is appreciated, as it's more fun and environmentally friendlier. Classes end at 17:00, which, in winter, leaves little sun to enjoy the afternoon and we end up at home doing homework or reading.

In my opinion, education in Catalonia leaves much to be desired in any type of school, whether private, subsidized, or public. Therefore, it's common for parents to load their children with extracurricular activities, trying to make up for the gaps left by school, so it's normal for some children to get home at seven in the evening. Personally, I have managed to adjust my work schedule to take advantage of the two hours they have at noon so we can eat together, talk for a while, and practice music. That way, in the afternoon, in addition to doing homework, they have time to play, be bored, create, and rest. I believe kids have the right to a childhood without stress and pressure.

After taking them to school, I go to work by metro, which usually runs well and punctually. However, driving in Barcelona is quite easy. Of course, you have to pass the tedious driving test.

At work, I get to choose my schedules, but not my fees. In Spain, private medicine practically does not exist. Everything is taken over by the insurance companies, who are the ones who set the rates. The doctor's work in general is not well remunerated. Despite budget cuts, we usually work with more supplies than those currently used in a public hospital in Mexico, and the salary is slightly higher.

As in any European city, it's common to live in apartments, and one of the things that caught my attention was the neighborhood coexistence law, which stipulates that you must not make noise after 22:00, among other things. I learned about this law due to a very famous case of a lady who sued her neighbor for playing the piano and blamed the pianist for causing her anxiety disorders This lawsuit seemed absurd to me because, when I was a child, my neighbors constantly played the piano. It was a bit annoying at first, but as they got better, we enjoyed it when they practiced. I also remember that another neighbor across the street would play domino on Thursday nights and had music on until late. I just got used to the fact that, on Thursdays, I'd go to sleep with music playing in the background. I never imagined that people could be so intolerant as to sue the neighbor for being loud.

At first, I lived in fear of my children making noise. Having to shut them up for laughing out loud, screaming with excitement, or even not allowing them to cry at ease if they were sad or angry, that made me feel inhumane, so we moved to a house with no downstairs neighbors.

However, all this is something to take into account if you decide to emigrate to a European country. Spaces and houses are almost always small.

Now that we have friends, as good Mexicans, we organize parties a couple of times a year, even though they end early.

It's worth mentioning that the lawsuit against the pianist did not prosper and the artist did not have to pay the enormous amount requested, thanks to the fact that someone at court was sensible.

This is my life abroad, missing all the beautiful treasures we have in Mexico and, on the other hand, enjoying the security of being able to walk alone at any time; the tranquility of wearing shorts without fear of being raped; the certainty that no one will kidnap my children or that the police will really do everything to find them; the simple peace of mind of crossing the street knowing that the driver will stop and not run me over. These little details are what keep me here.

Susana Ramírez Romero (Continues on page 217)

Luis Rodrigo Reynoso
(Ethiopia)

Every day I ask myself: What is this place? Which place are we standing at? Every day I feel that we adapt more, but the more we delve into the culture and history of Ethiopia, the more it surprises us and the less we understand what is happening around us.

Ethiopia lived in total secrecy with respect to the West, until the Italians arrived at the end of the 19th century. They invaded the country in 1936, using mustard gas and the most powerful weapons of the time.

Thus, they annihilated more than 250,000 Ethiopians and occupied the country for approximately five years. The resistance, supported by the British government, achieved the country's independence in 1941.

Until 130 years ago, in Addis Ababa – the capital of the country – there were only straw huts and the first imported eucalyptus trees from Australia were planted.

Just 40 years ago, there was a bloody war against fascism that put an end to the Solomonic dynasty that ruled the country. Known as the Red Terror campaign, this repression claimed the lives of 500,000 martyrs, who were tortured with hot oil, hung alive with their hands and feet tied. Today the Memorial Museum of the Martyrs of the Red Terror exhibits the horrors of that war with a goal that has been inscribed in the memorial: "Never again."

Touring the streets of Addis Ababa today is a surreal spectacle: on the streets you can see hundreds of Soviet cars adorned with flowers, transporting Orthodox, Muslim, or Christian wedding couples. The brides wear veils or crowns, and the grooms garrison caps, both wear clothes with exquisite embroidery. When there is a wedding, the bride and groom and their entire entourage gather in the only wooded park in the city.; There they drink beer, play drums, and sing ancient songs. They clap and make tribal sounds that one can only possibly hear on National Geographic.

Being on the street is overwhelming: barefoot children and young people, covered up in dust, with visible malnutrition. Some are friendly, others harass you like birds of prey, they try to get closer, sell you candy, and suddenly they grab you by the arm: "Money, money," "I'm hungry, give me a *birr* (local currency)." Others greet you: «Hello, Hello, my friend», they approach with the intention of selling you a magazine, and suddenly you already have their hands rummaging in your pockets, looking for a coin. They had already warned us of these situations, but it is different to live through them.

The city grows and grows, disproportionately compared to the quality of life. The shortcomings are visible, but suddenly, two steps away you are inside a capitalist oasis; you breathe deeply, you analyse your surroundings, you meditate... We are living in Ethiopia! If they had told me, I would not believe it!

My wife tells me that I am crazy, I tell her that she is crazier, for coming with me on this adventure. And suddenly, the unimaginable: Ethiopian Luis was born. I leave the house each day calmly, having had fresh and delicious mangoes and bananas for breakfast, ultra-organic strawberries, and the best coffee, the most aromatic I have ever tasted.

Now dress how I want. One day is a guayabera with linen pants; another day I opt for something more indigenous. I've even gone to work in my baggy, colorrful Thai pants. Patients do not care how I dress: they would never rule out a surgeon for his appearance or for not having his office in the best neighborhood of the city, let alone which car I drive.

Why? First of all because they don't have prejudice. Second, because there are very few doctors in the country. In a country of 109 million inhabitants and only six plastic surgeons.

I had been told that there would be a lot of work here, that the operating rooms were crowded, that there was a waiting list of approximately ten months. I was able to confirm all these!

In the three days I devoted to consultation, I got to see about 45 patients, and I do between six and eight surgeries a day for the remaining three days of the week; that is without counting the cosmetic procedures that we are recently introducing to people.

I have come to Ethiopia to learn, to unlearn what I have learned. Although on the outside it seems that we are different from Ethiopians, in reality we are the same. Underneath their chocolatey skins there are the same musculoskeletal structures, their blood is the same and it has the same smell, but for some reason everything seems fascinating to me now.

–We stay here!

Their canons of beauty are as diverse as the tribes that make up this nation. Even now, many of the villagers have scarifications and tattoos on their faces, neck, and thorax. Most had them done during childhood, and they are part of their ethnic identities. But now they want to eliminate them through plastic surgery: not only because to have a job it is necessary not to have them, but also because they remind them of unimaginable times of genocide.

But I do just do plastic surgery. Here I have had to perform varicose vein resections, to create of arteriovenous fistulas, to place catheters, to filter the blood in cases of non-functional kidneys. They say that I will also have to do hernia surgeries, and that the work will increase once a new surgical center is completed.

I still remember when I was just beginning the specialty in general surgery and laparoscopy. There was always a teacher or a colleague who questioned me for not going straight to plastic surgery: «Well, you are going to end up operating boobies and buttocks». Thanks to my training in general surgery, I can do almost any operation. It is not because I feel like God, nor because I believe that I can monopolize the entire market. There is simply a lack of trained personnel to operate.

"That's how different my life is today."

Luis Rodrigo Reynoso (Continues on page 218)

Alejandra Rodríguez Romero
(United States)

Before coming to this country, my biggest goal and dream was to practice my profession as I had envisioned it since I was a child and as I had seen my parents do it. After 4 years of dedicating myself almost entirely to enter the medical residency in this country and still not having achieved it, I decided to take a break from all activities focused on that and, although it's still a goal I want to achieve, my priorities have changed. There's a quote from an unknown author that I read somewhere on the Internet some years ago that has come to revolutionize my thoughts and shake who I thought I was, my essence. The phrase goes something like "the world needs less professionals and better human beings". Having been able to experience this society for several years and seeing the world and its current situation, it is clear to me that the concept of this phrase is part of the change society is in dire need of. Convinced that what will give me the greatest satisfaction in the future is not to have been a great doctor, but to have been a great human being, everything I have or haven't done since then has followed this conviction.

In July 2013, I got my first job in the United States in a pharmacogenetic company. The job lasted a scant 6 months, which were very productive and in a very pleasant work environment. Subsequently, I joined the American Red Cross to work for the biomedical department for 2 years. I was able to realize that, although I was not yet practicing my profession, I was very satisfied with my life. This realization allowed me to focus even more on my happiness and to feel very grateful for all the experiences I had, which left me with a great number of lessons and sincere and true friendships. Further complementing my existence and rekindling a part of my life that had been absent for a while, in June 2014 I met my now husband, Jeff, and we began our journey together.

With great joy and excitement, in March 2016 I became a mother to a beautiful baby girl, Zoe Isabella, and, in September 2018, Jeffrey Jr. came to complete the family. Becoming a mother came to place those aforementioned ideals more firmly in my mind and heart.

Currently and by choice, I find myself totally dedicated to my family. This makes me very happy and gives me peace of mind, because my main priority is to be present for my children in their first years of life, which are the most important in the formation of their values and the foundations that will remain with them for the rest of their lives. The situations and circumstances that have presented themselves to me up to this point have been somewhat unfavorable for my professional life. However, this is not a cause for any regret or disappointment; on the contrary, I consider my situation ideal, as I find myself living in a society and time where I witness the need for a closer relationship between parents and children.

The chapters of my life have been written in a unique and perfect way up to this point, and I am confident that that will continue to be so. My professional life is on pause, but not forgotten. Knowing that in this country professional opportunities are available regardless of age comforts me and opens the door to a possible future goal. I've found a myriad of positive qualities in this country that is home to so many wonderful cultures and people. Being able to go out to the park or for a walk without fear of violence, and the academic and professional opportunities are priceless treasures. However, the best thing about coming here has been finding who I truly am and where my happiness lies. To this day, 11 years after I started this adventure of emigrating, I am still not professionally where I would like to be, but personally I am fulfilled and, when the time is right, I know that I will give all my effort to achieve my goals.

Alejandra Rodríguez Romero (Continues on page 221)

Jack Rubinstein

(UNITED STATES)

> "Love one another, but make not a bond of love:
> Let it rather be a moving sea between the shores of your souls".
> -Khalil Gibran

My dog doesn't really pay much attention to me. Sometimes he curls up next to me at night and often lies at my feet but, unless I offer him some food, the chances of him following my orders are slim. Sometimes, I bump into my neighbors and their perfectly trained dogs that catch balls thrown at them with their snouts while my dog trips over his own leash. When I see him —his huge eyes, genetically engineered to produce a loving reaction in me— I can't help but think about my children, and how little I can influence their actions.

My children clearly have greater decision-making powers than my dog but, compared to the level of authority that past generations had over their children —particularly within a relatively enclosed community—, mine are on the brink of rebellion. The same goes for my wife: while we raise our family, we rarely ask each other's permission, we go about informing each other and comparing calendars so we don't trip over our leashes of life. Could it be that my family is nothing more than a product of modern reality? Or could it be that, through the years, our decisions slowly shaped the current result? To answer these questions, my scientific mind requires a control group to compare. This technique is the foundation of modern medical science. To assess whether a medication works, at least two groups are established: one is given the medicine and, the other, a placebo. The classic example in cardiology is the study called CAST (Cardiac Arrhythmia Suppression Trial). The study was based on the clinical observation of people who had suffered a heart attack, and those with the highest number of arrhythmias (erratic heartbeats) were more likely to die. Therefore, a study was conducted with the drugs that best suppress these arrhythmias to assess which was better, but the crucial thing about it was that a placebo group was even included in the first place (that is, a group that took sugar pills instead of the drug).

I read studies like this almost every day to try to better understand how to handle my patients. In the same way, I think it would be easier if I could contextualize my family in comparison to others, just as I compare my dog to a dozen similar dogs in my neighborhood. Clearly, if other dogs are well behaved and do tricks while mine can hardly find his food bowl in the mornings, the problem is his lack of training, not his nature. But what can I compare my family to? There are not many Jewish Mexicans in the world, much less in Ohio (although there are a few). There are also not many families with parents with university degrees who have emigrated from Mexico to this specific part of the United States (although there are also a few). Therefore, I have no choice but to try to assess my family decisions through other variables. So, once again, we return to the question that arises in any clinical study: what are the important variables? In general, the variables must be constantly and consistently quantifiable, and they must also be stable over time. The CAST study did exactly that: assess the usefulness of different medicines in reducing arrhythmias. To evaluate life, many use earnings, wealth, or assets as criteria; others focus on how attractive their partner is, or on the grades and achievements of their children. But this strikes me as similar to judging my dog by the number of tricks he does, or his ability to respond with a bark when a stranger approaches him. Is it quantifiable? Certainly. Is it easy to measure? Undoubtedly. Is it stable over time? Yes, but for some reason none of these variables seem relevant to me.

Going back to CAST, and the hundreds of clinical studies that flood modern medical journals comparing a drug against a placebo, researchers often measure surrogate variables (say arrhythmias, which decreased with all the drugs compared in CAST) and rarely measure important variables (such as death, which surprisingly *increased* with all the drugs in CAST compared to placebo). This sounds like an odd scientific case, but it's very common to find that the intervention improves the surrogate variable but worsens the important variable.

I think about this while I read lying in bed, and my dog or one of my children curls up next to me. Will one of them be able to catch a ball in the air? Do they have any special abilities? Will they make more money than their peers? Probably not, but these are surrogate variables. Useful, but not important. To feel them comfortable by my side, confident that no matter what they accomplish, do, or don't achieve, they will always have me by their side to curl up next to, that's the most important unquantifiable variable.

Jack Rubinstein (Continues on page 223)

Alberto Saltiel
(Israel)

It's hard to refer to this as my "new life". For me, it's simply a new chapter, because life is made up of different stages and, thanks to that, we create our path and become who we are. I can certainly say that this chapter of my life has been extremely fruitful.

I came to Israel in 2013 and I integrated fairly easily. I had the advantage of having friends who lived here, who welcomed me warmly and included me in their lives. With this group of friends, we started new traditions and had numerous adventures. We formed a road cycling team, we participated in different events, we supported many causes with altruistic rides, and, in fact, we founded a new "family", since each of us had migrated to this country without their own. Over time, each of us found our own way and formed our own families.

At this stage in my life, I no longer suffer the wear and tear of spending hours in traffic while moving from one place to another. Now, I'm lucky to be able to get to the hospital by bike, calmed and unhurried, or to walk home while enjoying being outdoors. At this stage of my life, I worry much less about insecurity or pollution. I enjoy time outside the house, in open spaces.

I've met many people from various places with traditions and customs different from mine, and I've learned a great deal from them. Now, much of my own traditions and customs have been positively influenced by these people. I strengthened my Latino pride; I fell in love with the Spanish language, and now I get excited whenever I hear it on the streets.

During this chapter of my life, I also met my incredible partner, and, with her, I formed a beautiful family. We have two wonderful children, a boy and a girl, who fill the house with laughter, joy, and invaluable lessons, and who motivate me to grow and be better every day. Being in a country far from home and starting a new family is an enormous challenge, since we lack the possibility of our families being there to support us, but this, in turn, strengthens us as a couple and as a family, and unites us even more.

I would love to be able to share more about this chapter of my life, but it's still being written.

Alberto Saltiel (Continues on page 225)

Luana Sandoval Castillo

(SPAIN, DENMARK)

I went through a period of uncertainty because the revalidations were taking forever to be ready. My nationality was still pending, my Spanish maternity leave was coming to an end and I was already a mother to a four-month-old baby girl. In Danish institutions, they do not accept children under six months old, so since we had made the decision to leave Spain I started working for free wherever they accepted the papers I already had. I would go to the hospital for a few hours while my husband took care of the baby.

My best friend was the breast pump that accompanied me at feeding time. After a few months, my papers were in order, but my Danish was still pathetic. My mentor and friend managed to convince the department head to open a specific position for me, where I would work only on Mondays from 08:00 to 15:00. It's worth mentioning that, with just that one day of work, I earned almost the same as in one of the hospitals in Barcelona for five shifts per month. However, to make ends meet, I had to travel to Barcelona on occasions to do holiday shifts, still breastfeeding my baby girl, while I continued to improve my Danish and my husband was looking for a better job.

Today, I thank each of the people who were fundamental pieces of my growth and who contributed to my constant professional development. To PP, the person who gave me a chance to work an on-call shift, because thanks to that I was able to make a name for myself in the Spanish work system; to BD, the one who recommended me in *lægedansk* a highly recommendable course with endearing professor IMH. To all those admirable mentors, LM and SVM, who could see in me the potential that I had not even discovered, who opened the doors of their homes and their hearts and filled me with knowledge. To SF, who took me by the hand on the road to learning; to MW and EP who did not let me escape; to my dear Mexican/Peruvian and Danish family and, of course, to my life partner and exceptional team, who also experienced my constant frustrations and joys. Thank you for dancing with me and not letting go.

Thanks to all of them and many more, today I am responsible for the peri-operative optimization unit for hip fracture patients. We have undertaken some Mexican colleague rotations and joint publications. I'm part of an incredible team and I have caught myself smiling in the corridors at work.

We have been able to plan long parental leaves, so we can travel back to my homeland and the girls can get a taste of what it's like to be Mexican. They have perfected their Spanish, had the opportunity to enter the educational system and have been pampered by their grandparents. This second season was a little different, as we went a year after the pandemic started and experienced restrictions and closed schools. However, we were able to live in Acapulco for a whole month and enjoy the process of my sister's wedding, from the dress fitting to the bachelorette party. It's been 15 days since we returned from that trip to a sunny summer-like Denmark, with street-music and people enjoying the sunsets at 22:30. The recommendation to wear masks has been withdrawn and you can enjoy the strangers' smiles again.

Luana Sandoval Castillo (Continues on page 227)

Ilan Shapiro
(UNITED STATES)

Three regions, one goal: to thrive. Our family has practically never lived in Mexico. With two suitcases and millions of experiences, my wife set out on a new adventure just twelve hours after our wedding. In that moment, more than fear, we felt that we were ready to conquer the world. We felt the excitement that came with beginning to live a dream we've been wanting to reach for so long. From then on, every lesson, tear, sweat, and smile depended entirely on us.

We are proud to say we've built our family on our terms and in our image. At first, we arrived in Chicago, a completely different city where I understood that snow completely differed from the flavors and colors I had associated it with in my head. I understood what it means to work entire days without seeing the sun and, above all, I learned how to transmit love and honesty to my partner. When your bubble bursts and your expectations are shattered, you begin to depend on your partner. I had my wife, who was my best friend, confidant, lover, and the voice of my conscience. We realized that, though some friendships might be temporary, many times they last forever. Chicago taught us to appreciate the weather, and the turning of the seasons. It was our first adventure. I'll never forget my fellow residents, the sleepless nights, and the delicious sandwiches that my beloved prepared at 5:30 in the morning to give me strength for my next shift. I learned what it's like being in love with a demanding but yet incredibly rewarding profession.

At that time, I approached the Hispanic community —in area where I worked, most people were Mexican— and I was able to observe that regardless of the side of the border we were in, old patterns had a tendency to repeat themselves.

During our first winter in Chicago, Nikki came to our lives. I'd always had big dogs (around 100 pounds or so), but now, size aside, we were looking for a hairy friend that would accompany us through the endless winters and infinite summer afternoons. Nikki arrived from Los Angeles (ironic because, years later, she would return there). She was a mighty 10-pound, lion-resembling Pomeranian who became part of our pack and adventures.

After I finished my residency there were invitations, promises and tears, but the constant need to broaden my horizons and to be part of this new bicultural world fascinated me. So, we looked for a place where we could settle down and have enough stability to increase our family, and not necessarily with more Nikkis.

I ended up applying for a job in Fort Myers, Florida, a place I'd never heard of. This job marked the real beginning of our growth and happiness in a warmer place (my wife would later point out that humidity had made her life impossible for five years). Fort Myers was a very interesting place surrounded by swamps. There, among lizards, spiders (did you know brown, black widows existed?) and snakes, our family built its nest.

Around that period, we dealt with the first deaths in the family. We feel the helplessness of not being present. Opening so many books without being able to close the chapter hurt me greatly. Being on a new adventure brings responsibility and challenges and this one in particular was one of the hardest I've faced.

In the blink of an eye, our family went from having three to five members. Time flew by and the children grew up. Now we had a family and we had to see to their well-being and development. We also wanted to keep our promise to continue working for the benefit of our community, so we ended up in the most unexpected of cities. A place in constant motion and filled with stars and icons. A city that, in some way, resembled Mexico City, with a hint of Miami and the beaches of Acapulco: Los Angeles.

We have relatives in California, and we were able to choose a school in line with our values and cultural background. I thank God every day for the gift of being present with my family, of making them part of my crazy ideas, of witnessing their triumphs. I'm not done learning and, although it's been a bumpy ride, the scars it's left us are medals that symbolize the unity and growth of our family.

Ilan Shapiro (Continues on page 228)

René Sotelo
(United States)

My new life focuses mainly on a new style of work, to which I am totally adapted, and that I enjoy enormously. It's associated with colleagues and faces that are no longer foreign but familiar, spaces and shapes that are now part of everyday life, tastes and smells that make you happy and that are now part of you.

It's already been five years since I left Venezuela and, in that time, we've collected stories and accomplishments that we celebrate individually and as a family: My oldest daughter, Andrea, already graduated from the University of Southern California with a degree in Neuroscience. My daughter Daniela finished high school in Los Angeles and is in the middle of her degree, also at USC. My youngest son, René André, is still in high school, but each of my children already has a sense of belonging, friends, community, and a future that, each day, they make a bit more their own. Seeing them progress steadily from each of the decisions they make not only fills me with pride, but also reinforces my conviction that they're in the best place they can be now. This is a great encouragement as a father and as a professional. Alongside them is my wife, Patricia, who unites us all and who is now also a student.

We've already been granted the Green Card and a visa that would also allow my wife to work if she wanted to. In the beginning, we were only allowed one income associated with the O-1 visa, which was the one I had.

Realizing that you've legally reached the status of having the Green Card is the best proof that time has gone by, and you're in a new country permanently. You realize there's a new reality and a new life, and the role of someone who emigrated is now in the past, because the present claims your presence in body and soul and that's where you want to live.

Los Angeles has also been very kind and generous to delight us with its architecture, the gala of its shows, its culture, and its climate. It has proven to be, in every sense of the word, a city right out of a movie. The opportunities it has given us as a family have been extraordinary and, in short, each one of us has strived to surpass our limits and become better, and although we will always carry our "Venezuelanness" in each of our hearts and every fiber of our being, I can say for certain that we can learn to craft our souls not only out of what we are, but out of what we can be, no matter where we find ourselves. Being Venezuelan becomes a two-way asset: you contribute because of what you bring and add value to what you'll bring back.

In this new life, that network of friends, those special people who become your family by choice, play a relevant role. They turn into support, calm, and joy. You can certainly rely on them to lend you a hand if necessary. Gone are the days when the emergency phone number for René André, my youngest son, was the secretary's.

Gone are the days when, like a kind of nomadic placard, the ID card and my backpack with "Dr. Sotelo" written on them were the preamble to avoid the off-key tune of "Doctor Who?"

The days come together in ways and forms you get used to and evolving is a challenge that's assumed with the confidence and conviction that you'll succeed in a home that you've already made your own.

René Sotelo (Continues on page 230)

Karla Uribe
(United States)

It's been more than ten years since I left Mexico, full of uncertainty, but also full of hopes and expectations; with many plans and with the conviction of practicing medicine in a country that was not my own. I knew very little about the process to follow to obtain a medical license in the United States, but I knew I was headed for the right path.

However, it was not long before I realized that I was in a different stage of my life; that I was now not only a doctor, but also a mom. At that moment, my notion of my place and my mission in life changed forever.

My greatest commitment was now to that little person who was completely dependent on me. My heart and my mind would not allow me to leave her in anyone else's hands. My idea of being a mother was not only to have a daughter, but to take care of her. So, my dream, my life project, changed from being Dr. Karla Uribe, to building a family. That's what I had become: the mom, the wife.

I am deeply grateful to my life partner for accompanying me every step of the way in the process of identifying with my new self, of finding myself again. The transition from the adrenaline of the operating room to lullabies, cartoons, and bedtime stories was difficult. Changing the sleepless nights to fevers or new teeth instead of emergencies and postoperative patients. It was surprising to realize that the most tiring thing I had ever done in my life was not the internship or the first year of residency, but this new adventure where a mom's work never ends; where money is not for trips or new clothes, but for bows, dresses and little pink shoes, where when you grab a cup of coffee with your friends you don't talk about last duty's patient, but about your children's triumphs or breakthroughs. It took me ten years of inner struggle to find my comfort zone and feel at peace with my new role as a mom.

When my youngest son started school, a group of women came into my life that changed it, the *Doctoras con Alas*. Belonging to this group has made me feel there are other women in the same position I can relate to, and it has reminded me that life is a constant challenge. It gave me the encouragement I needed to get out of my comfort zone and resume the search for my professional development. Thanks to this group, I found my first job in the United States as a medical scribe. And although being a working mom has been more tiring than just being a mom, I feel happy and accomplished. It feels good to return to work, dust off my mind, and proudly realize that, what you learn well, you don't forget.

Today I am convinced that the transition from doctor to mother has been my greatest challenge, the hardest thing in my life. However, I can say that I feel very satisfied with the decisions I have made.

Karla Uribe (Continues on page 232)

Jeannette Uribe
(United States)

I currently live in New York City, and I'm in my third year of residency in OB/GYN. I'm extremely happy because, ever since I can remember, this has been my dream. Doing a residency is no joke. It not only consumes your time, but also your energy. One thing is getting it over with in your 20s and a whole different one is doing it in your 30s and with children. I am, nonetheless, enjoying it a lot. It's my passion. To get to this point, I've had to overcome many obstacles, big and small.

I have two beautiful boys: an eight-year-old and a four-year-old. They were both born here, in the United States and, even though they might be physically similar, they have very different personalities and, thank God, they're both healthy. It wasn't that way at first. My little warrior was born at thirty-four weeks and, due to his prematurity, he had to remain in the ICU for ten days. It was depressing to go home after my delivery without our son. Thank God, there were no complications and now he's as strong as an ox. My oldest boy is noble and loves to be cuddled by his mommy.

At home, we mostly speak Spanish. The children learned English in daycare and pre-kindergarten. We try to keep Spanish present at home because it's important for them to communicate well with their grandparents, to have at least two native languages and, if we don't push them a bit to at least try, their Spanish will fade away, because it's easier for them to speak the language they use all day at school.

We're very fortunate to be in NY; the city is amazingly diverse, and the children benefit from it: they grow up with the mentality that it's normal to see different skin colors, languages, and customs. It's interesting how they notice that other people who speak Spanish don't speak "the Mexican kind", and they've learned there are many ways to be a Spanish-speaking country. They're enrolled in a bilingual program where they're taught to read and write in Spanish, and they love it. The schools are safe, the food is not very healthy but, for them, it's absolutely delicious.

We also try to keep them active; since moving to NYC, due to traffic and rather tight schedule, they only practice swimming and mixed martial arts and have a gym bar at home where little Mr. Muscles practices his tricks.

It's not easy to decide the best path for our children but, as parents, we have a plan, which is to educate them in our faith. We want to instill our values in them, transmit our Mexican customs and traditions, make them participate in them and, most importantly, give them the necessary tools so that, when the time comes, they'll know how to make their own choices.

Jeannette Uribe (Continues on page 234)

7

My failures and achievements

Patricia Bautista Rivera

(UNITED STATES)

After the birth of my daughter, I was no longer able to work at the doctor's office. We were in the middle of winter and going outside was difficult due to the intense cold and weather. Even when we had the car, going out meant dressing in several layers of clothing to go to the mall. We had no family. All our new friends were working.

When my husband would come home from work, he'd find a wife who'd confront him and ask him if he had enjoyed his day seeing patients. I wished I could do what he did! For a long time, I was upset and unhappy, because my dream of being able to practice medicine seemed to slip away from me more and more each day. It was many years before I could appreciate and value the privilege and importance of staying home to care for my children without worry; and to accept, however painful, not being able to work as a physician in this country.

However, always eager to interact with patients, I returned to the office. I had the opportunity for many years to practice medicine under supervision, my knowledge of allergy grew, and my ability to speak and understand English also improved. Although I did not earn any money, the peace of mind that came from seeing patients, and the knowledge and experience gained were priceless.

I took and passed the USLME exams and obtained the ECFMG certificate that recognizes me as an MD in the U.S., which gives me great satisfaction.

After being on bed rest for 12 weeks, my second child was born. Soon after, my husband finished his training and we returned to Mexico City. Then, we moved to the States again. The validity of my exams was coming to an end. Unfortunately, I could not go back and retrain because I had two little kids to take care of, so my certifications expired. It was very painful.

I dedicated myself to being a full-time mom, doing my best to guide and educate my children in the best way possible, as well as accompanying my husband on the path we decided to follow in this country.

Once my son reached high school, I was faced with the reality that he would soon be going to college. For a long time, I had considered taking the exams again, however, as the years went by, the possibility of being able to obtain a residency placement was more and more unlikely, so, as a temporary solution, I decided to go back to school. I enrolled in a master's in public health with a specialization in health promotion at my local university. When I arrived at the student services office of the medical school in Mexico, I was shocked to discovered that my academic record was in the dead file! Nevertheless, things worked out, even though I had to learn biostatistics again, now through sophisticated electronic programs (and suffered a little, like any good student). I graduated and had the happiness of having my mother and sister overflowing with joy and pride present at the graduation ceremony, accompanied by my husband and children.

After graduation, I worked as a project advisor on the evaluation team of a research project on the influence of mindfulness on children's behavior that the University of Virginia was conducting in my city. Due to the pandemic, the project was put on hold, though the preliminary results are promising.

Around the same time, the executive director of a non-profit organization, La Casita Center (LCC), serving the socially disadvantaged Latino migrant community in my city, invited me to participate as their summer camp's academic advisor. After the camp, she offered me a job as a community liaison and, step by step, we began taking advantage of my medical and public health knowledge. We have organized talks on healthy eating, hygiene measures, vaccination campaigns for the migrant population —updating vaccination records—, talks for pregnant women, etc. Since the pandemic, LCC has developed cooperative partnerships with the city's health department and other community organizations. We have conducted campaigns to promote preventive measures through videos and radio programs, promotion of diagnostic tests, and vaccination. LCC nominated me as a spokesperson and representative of the Latino community to promote vaccination against COVID-19. I received the first dose of the COVID-19 vaccine as one of four representatives from the international community in the state. We were vaccinated in front of the press, in a ceremony in which the keynote speakers were the governor of Kentucky and the mayor of the city. The event celebrated the state's diversity and promoted vaccination. I was also selected by the governor's office to participate in the statewide immunization promotion campaign.

Patricia Bautista Rivera (Continues on page 239)

Edmundo Erazo

(the Netherlands)

Most of us are used to listing and going through our accomplishments. We remember the path we had to travel and the challenges we faced and overcame. However, it's not common for people to keep track of their failures. I once read Dr Adam Cifu, an internist at the University of Chicago. He said that, on his desk, he has a resume of his failures, like the scientific articles that never got published or the medical schools that never accepted him.

Defining what's a failure or an achievement can be very subjective. Some think that failing to enter the desired medical residence or obtain the job they applied for are failures. Among the successes on my list are receiving professional, personal, and social experience in Europe. One of my failures was turning down a job opportunity, which led me to reflect on what I wanted to do. I learned from both experiences, and the important thing is always to move forward.

I don't think sharing a list of each of my failures and achievements would do any good. It's irrelevant. I think it's more helpful to say that it doesn't matter what others define as such, especially in an environment as competitive professionally and personally as medicine. The important thing is for each of us to express our purpose in life.

Edmundo Erazo (Continues on page 242)

Sandra López-León

(Israel, the Netherlands, Spain, United States)

Every single one of our achievements has a failure behind it. The stronger the failure has been, and the harder it has been to reach the achievement, the more we value it. Just as there is no light without darkness; there is no success without setbacks. The point is not to dwell on failure, but to learn from it, to learn from our mistakes, to build, to improve ourselves, and to grow. Maybe in the moment we feel that the failure is too big to recover from, but once we have turned it into success, it no longer exists.

In retrospect there is nothing I regret or that I would've done differently. But I can say that whenever I have fallen, I have always gotten up: I have always moved on, and I always try to learn from my mistakes. Let me tell you a failure-achievement that reflects very much my way of facing challenges and defeats.

When I came to live in New York, I got the idea of running the New York Marathon. You could say it was a crazy idea because I had never run before and was almost sedentary. But I like new experiences and challenges, and this one seemed difficult and different from the ones I'd faced before. A few months after I started running, I did the New York half marathon. I was obviously not prepared. To finish I had to take ibuprofen and walk (more like crawl) the last few miles. The first half of the marathon I enjoyed intensely; the end, I hated. After I was done, I had to stay in bed for a week. I hurt my IT band and got plantar fasciitis. I'm sure many people would have given up and said running wasn't for them. I didn't agree. I realized this challenge was tailor-made for me.

There were 30 weeks left until the marathon. The first thing I did was read 20 books on how to run properly, starting with *Running a Marathon for Dummies*. I went to rehabilitation to fix the muscles I had injured, and I got an expert strength training coach. I also got a dietician who guided me on what to eat before, during and after training and running. With 16 weeks to go, I started the New York Road Runners training. The plan told me exactly how many miles to run daily and which days to rest. I continued with my weight training and started doing yoga on rest days. I did everything to the letter, and it worked for me. Most of all, I learned to love and enjoy running.

Marathon day finally arrived, and I was completely prepared, recovered, and excited. I enjoyed every minute of it, and, most of all, I enjoyed crossing the finish line. Now I can say that it takes a bit of a masochism and a lot of discipline to be able to run marathons.

That was 5 years ago. To this day, I love running. I like to run 5 kilometers a day first thing in the morning, as it is my way of clearing my mind and getting my thoughts and plans for the day in order.

Sandra López-León (Continues on page 245)

Rafael G. Magaña
(ENGLAND, UNITED STATES)

My graduation from general surgery residency was one of the happiest moments of my life. My whole family came to New York, including my grandmother, Nayma Habib, who had always inspired me and whom I loved deeply.

I savored that event as a personal rather than professional triumph, since the director of the program who gave me the diploma was the same one who previously assured me that I would never be a surgeon in the United States. In the end, he gave me a chance, which was all I needed, and things worked out well. My residency graduation was the last time my entire family was together.

While applying for plastic surgery training, I did two years of reconstructive burn surgery, but did not get interviews for plastic surgery. That was very demoralizing, and I perceived it as a professional and personal failure. I even thought my personality was to blame for it.

During medical training, it's difficult to separate your personal from your professional life. Therefore, there's a blurry line that doesn't allow you to see clearly where your failures and successes belong.

I think my biggest flaw is summed up in these words: "a decade behind." There are various reasons why I feel that way: many of the things I worked so hard for would've been more effective if I had focused more. Hating paperwork and red tape cost me a decade. I think I could've done more to speed up my academic process, like writing more articles and worrying about having a more robust résumé. Had I not hated writing so much, I would've progressed faster.

I made several wrong decisions. For example, having done a specialty in reconstructive burn surgery for two years, instead of one. If the following year I'd done a specialty in hand surgery, that probably would've made me a more apt candidate to compete against others for plastic surgery positions.

These decisions cost me time, because I knew what was sought academically in plastic surgery programs, and some key elements were publishing, participating more in academic events, and impressing the right people at the right time so they could advocate for me.

It was largely a lack of personal maturity and vision. However, good things also came out of being "a decade behind," such as gaining surgical and clinical experience as a resident and fellow, without the responsibility of being an attached physician.

I was more inspired during the plastic surgery residency and began to write and publish chapters and articles on topics that I was passionate about, but I was already late. So, not anticipating these things cost me time and academic achievement.

At the time, that's how I interpreted why my life unfolded the way it did. However, now I see that situation differently, because as an attached physician I do things that perhaps under other circumstances I wouldn't be doing.

Now I'm single, without obligations outside the hospital, and that's made me mature professionally. I have fewer obligations and more time to do the things I like. Now, my philosophical, academic, and artistic reflections have grown. At this point in my life, I think what I'm doing has a bigger impact than what I did as a young man, when I didn't know what to study or what to focus on.

I think the questions I currently ask myself are more valuable thanks to my experience, so that "decade behind" has become a "decade earned."

Rafael G. Magaña (Continues on page 248)

Nissin Nahmias
(United States)

I've learned way more from my failures than from my achievements. I've always been highly self-critical, perhaps due to insecurity or because of a constant need to improve myself. Let me start with my failures.

During my residency, I learned to care for my patients in many ways: I'd visit them, check on their lab results, refer them to other physicians, and correct abnormalities. I remember an episode as if it were yesterday: night had fallen, and I still had a long to-do list. I came to the floor of a patient whose tracheostomy tube had to be exchanged for one of a smaller size. I had all the necessary equipment and proceeded to change the tube when, suddenly, the patient's oxygen saturation began to drop. I had never faced a similar situation before and started to get really nervous. I increased the oxygen and called the emergency team, but they were in the trauma center, and were taking a long time to arrive. Oxygenation continued to drop, and the patient was unconscious and on the verge of respiratory arrest.

The patient stopped breathing and, at that precise moment, the anesthesia team appeared and intubated him. I put a central IV line in his right jugular vein, and we transferred him to intensive care in critical condition. The patient improved, but we realized that the central venous catheter was in the carotid artery and not in the jugular vein, so we had to consult an interventional radiologist to remove the catheter and place the central line in the right place.

The first time I put a gastrostomy tube, I was a third-year resident. I had performed an operation on a patient who suffered brain trauma after a road accident. He'd been stabilized and was receiving nutrition through a nasogastric tube. At the time, there two residents, me, and an intern. I made the incision, found the stomach easily, and put the tube in the right place. After that, we sutured it, so everything would stay in place. Once we checked all was in order, we closed the abdomen and the patient returned to the ICU. The next day, however, we noticed that the nasogastric tube wouldn't come out, which meant that it had been sutured together with the gastrostomy tube. We then had to call the gastroenterology team to release the tube so we could remove it.

Fortunately, my successes outnumber my failures, especially when taking into account the thousands of patients I've satisfactorily operated with great success during twelve years.

During a move, my friend Pedro cut his hand with a glass from a table that had been broken. Being a urological surgery resident, that accident was devastating for him. He looked at his right hand and it was bleeding a lot, so I applied first aid and rushed him to the hospital. I remember not moving from his side and urging the medical staff to do something, until he was taken to the operating room for a plastic surgeon to operate on him. Fortunately, thanks to the promptness with which he received help, everything turned out just fine.

During the residency, there were two events that shaped me: the first was during a night shift. It was about four in the morning when we were called to the trauma center. A 17-year-old boy had been stabbed in the chest and his life was hanging by a thread. I opened his thorax and found the wound at the tip of the left ventricle; his heart was still beating. I initially controlled the bleeding with my finger and a surgical stapler. That gave him enough time to be taken to the operating room where his left ventricle was repaired.

The second event happened on the very last shift of my very last year of residency, with a patient scheduled to receive radiation therapy for a large neck tumor. The patient went into respiratory arrest, and I immediately called a team and performed an emergency tracheostomy directly in his hospital bed, thus saving his life.

Also, through weight management surgery, I've been part of the transformative miracle in my patient's lives countless times. Through their gratitude and affection, my life has improved tremendously.

Today, I am a happy and professionally accomplished man. I direct a program of bariatric and minimally invasive surgery in New York, I'm coordinator of the surgery rotation for students of two medical schools, and I've been invited as an expert guest speaker to numerous conferences of the different surgical societies in Mexico, England, Austria, Israel, and the United States.

Nissin Nahmias (Continues on page 251)

Susana Ramírez Romero
(SPAIN)

Academically, physicians submit to an unimaginable series of exams, many of which open or close fundamental doors for our professional growth. The first time I failed an important exam for which I had studied a lot, I felt like a failure and was shocked because I considered myself an outstanding student. In fact, my grades were what allowed me to maintain a 90% scholarship throughout college.

At that time, I was a big fan of Michael Jordan and two of his quotes helped me overcome these tough times:

"I've missed more than 9000 shots in my career. I've lost almost 300 games. 26 times, I've been trusted to take the game winning shot and missed."

"I've failed over and over and over again in my life. And that is why I succeed."

Since then, I've had to deal with different blows on a professional and personal level. I've learned that, after failing, what's important is getting back up, although it's also the most challenging thing to do. It's hard picking up your dignity from the ground, dusting it off and moving on, sometimes in a different direction.

To fail means being unable to produce the desired or intended result. So, there are only two options left: either to stand up again and face the challenge or to accept that perhaps not getting the expected

217

result leads us to explore new paths, sometimes with very pleasing outcomes.

That's possibly my greatest achievement: learning to be resilient and showing my children by example how to adapt as well. Teaching them that failure hurts, but it can also empower us and lead to reflection.

I've also learned to celebrate my victories because, sometimes triumphs, if shown in excess, were regarded as an act of vanity. But it's been proven that neurons are more receptive to learning after a success and that, the more triumphs we accumulate, the greater our motivation and energy to keep moving forward.

Susana Ramírez Romero (Continues on page 253)

Luis Rodrigo Reynoso
(Ethiopia)

In Ethiopia, my life is surreal! There are things that I cannot even explain myself. Sometimes I question my physical and mental state. Everything that my wife and I experience is exceptional; it elevates our senses, makes us feel more alive than ever, and reminds us how lucky we are. We continue to learn every day in constant exhilaration.

Between the undergrowth that still invades the streets I have seen radiant colours bloom; I stop to observe the perfection and beauty. Friends holding hands, totally intertwined, regardless of gender and without prejudice. Someone else comes singing and dancing and makes my day with his enviable curly hair.

I take care of my hands from the attacks of the stray dogs, which unlike the ones I knew these do not let their skeleton show even a little bit, when you question their source of food, they show up parading around, showing off freshly abandoned carcasses between their powerful jaws that in most cases, exceed their own size and weight; they, rummage around beyond belief, and rest alongside their prey. And I am still here, trying to understand my mission. There has not been a single day that I did learn something.

I keep trying to understand my mission here. There is not a single day that doesn't teach me something, a promise, an answer, a photograph. I like to fantasize in a big way, to let my imagination flow and suddenly find myself in majestic settings, and then start infinite dialogues with myself.

Today I believe that I have primarily come to break chains, to light candles, to turn off sensors, to correct attitudes, to modify patterns, to trust my intuition, to recognize my strengths, to take advantage of my abilities and to collaborate. Here I have come to distance myself from parasites, pests, and inhuman people.

This trip, for me, has represented one of the most authentic spiritual retreats I have ever experienced.

Suddenly in ecstasy and in less than a second, they could take you to the extreme ... but there, right there, we ask one of my favourite questions: "What do I have to learn from this?"

And so, the days go by, between consultations and surgeries. Generally, I like to know a little more about my patients, to know a little more about their history. But language can be a barrier. Sometimes even the translator cannot understand my patients. No matter how many signs and gestures you make, it is impossible to communicate.

Thirty-five years passed for her and I to meet. The stigma from her cleft lip had almost extinguished the light in her eyes, but still she was anxiously waiting for me to be her surgeon. And so, I found her on the surgical table. I tried to get her to speak to me, but neither my English nor my poor Amharic manage to get a single word out of her.

After the procedure was over, I was happy. I showed her the result. She remained motionless, almost catatonic, expressionless… I gave her the last instructions and she left.

We had a post-surgical review meeting. She remained distant and warned me that she would not return, she had to return to her region. She left without saying thank you or goodbye, and that made my head spin: Did I do something wrong? What did I miss?

Out of nowhere, 22 days later she came back: "I have an itch." I explained that this was part of the healing process and that she should use a moisturizing oil (I miss medical samples, they are needed here!). She was nodding along and suddenly she said to me in a soft voice: "Konyo …"

I immediately understood that word, which means beauty, beautiful, pretty, well… Come on, I need you to smile. She pretended not to understand my request, I asked for a translation: "Smile, I need to see that the muscles we rebuilt are working." She made all kinds of attempts to understand but could not. I started to laugh at her gestures, and then it happened, spontaneously she laughed at me.

That smile has remained as one of the greatest lessons in life. Blessed itch. Konyo. I hope the strength and power of healing go with you. She represents for me one of my greatest personal and professional achievements.

And that is how I gleefully experience these kinds of surgical events. I must also admit that another of the adventures lies in the conditions in which we live. Here, public services (drinking water, sewerage, public lighting) are practically non-existent, each step reminds us of where we come from, where we are, and it is captivating to imagine where are we going?

At this time in Ethiopia, I have seen my wife cry with helplessness when she turns on the water tap and mud falls on her head, after getting lost for three hours in the city. I have heard her scream in terror while some children tried to rob her. But we have also died of laughter when we saw Mrs. Burtukan (who helps us clean the house), chase after a neighbour who tried to steal my jeans that were drying in the open air. Emotions are many, and everything we are learning is clear to us.

Luis Rodrigo Reynoso (Continues on page 255)

Alejandra Rodríguez Romero
(UNITED STATES)

Despite already considering this country my home, there have been two very difficult stages that have made me question whether the decision to emigrate was the right one. The first one was when I realized that no matter how much effort, time, and money I put into continuing my professional life, my goals were farther and farther away from becoming a reality. After two years of intense study and certification with ECFMG, I started doing hospital rotations. These were necessary to obtain practical experience and letters of recommendation in the United States. This part constituted the biggest effort of all, paying large amounts of money and having to travel to different cities, leaving me with mixed feelings. On the one hand, I was happy to be able to integrate into the American medical system, but at the same time I felt nostalgic for having to leave my home and husband for months at a time. Having all these requirements in place, I applied to the medical residency system. This process, besides being very stressful, is extremely expensive. In two years, I received a total of 7 interviews, a very unfavorable number for a foreign physician. I went through this application process for two years without being selected by any hospital. Despite receiving a lot of support and encouragement from family and colleagues, my hopes were almost nil. This stage, which lasted approximately 4 years, left me disappointed and with a deteriorated marriage due to the time dedicated to my professional life. This led to the second difficult stage, my divorce, which presented a great challenge because, coming from a functional, Catholic, and Mexican family, getting divorced is something almost unthinkable and very criticized. However, because there were already irreparable differences and Chris' family values differed a great deal from mine, that was the only possible outcome.

After overcoming these hard times, I decided to take a break from medicine and focus on finding my happiness and enjoying life intensely. These experiences made me develop a different mindset and learn priceless things. Among others, I learned that life is too short not to do or be what makes you smile. I learned that true friendships last forever and are essential to get through rough patches. I learned that I can make myself happy on my own and understanding all of that is a tremendous accomplishment.

Another of my greatest achievements has been being able to be my son Jeffrey's advocate in his battle against cancer. In May 2018, being Jeffrey 8 months old and after surgery and many radiological studies, he was diagnosed with stage 3 alveolar rhabdomyosarcoma. My world fell apart when I heard the words "your son has cancer", especially knowing how aggressive that particular cancer was. At that point, I said I would only allow myself a few days to grieve because, after that, my mission would be to read and soak up medical articles, ask for opinions from my dear co-authors and doctor friends, who always supported me, whether it was from a genetic, pediatric, oncological, or simply empathic point of view. I have kept myself updated on therapies and studies, suggesting on several occasions to his treating physicians alternatives to lessen adverse effects, or genetic studies to make his treatment more personalized and maximize his chance of remission.

During all the time that I hadn't practiced medicine, I always wondered the reason why I studied it in the first place and if someday I could actually put it to use. Now, in these years of continually visiting the hospital and seeing him in remission, I am convinced that the most important reason was to help my son; everything else is a bonus. I could not describe how different it would've been to navigate this diagnosis if I hadn't had the medical knowledge and help of so many doctors willing to lend a hand. We still have a long way to go, and I will be sure to always look out for the health of my little big warrior. And, of course, another great achievement and one of the most current ones, is to have participated in the book *Doctoras con Alas* (and now in its English translation) alongside excellent physicians and people. I know that this movement has contributed and will continue to help many doctors or professionals in the process of emigrating, and that's something that fills me with satisfaction and brings a smile to my face.

Alejandra Rodríguez Romero (Continues on page 257)

Jack Rubinstein
(UNITED STATES)

"Good judgment comes from experience; experience comes from bad judgment."
-Robert Byrne

There's no way around it. We can only develop good judgment through bad judgment. That time I shouldn't have had that last shot of tequila: bad judgment. When raising your voice to a nurse: bad judgment. When I didn't pay attention to the patient's name before entering the room: bad judgment. Most of us try to avoid moments of bad judgment and especially their repercussions but, is this the best way to live? Mistakes, bad judgments, and failures in life can either make us wiser or haunt us for the rest of our lives. The difference between getting ahead and staying behind is not in the mistakes made, but in what one decides to do with them. It sounds trite but, if we analyze the process of an error, we can see important differences between the "traditional" and the "modern" way of dealing with mistakes. Both forms are exemplified by the concept of "M and M", or morbidity and mortality conferences. These conferences began in Boston in the beginning of the 20th century, where surgeons would meet and review cases in which a physician had made a mistake. The purpose was to learn from that mistake so that others wouldn't repeat it. These conferences were often exalted and were (and in some places still are) used to settle scores or damage a physician's reputation but, as society advanced, so did the conferences. Today, most specialties have some type of morbidity and mortality conference; and each of them is governed by the stereotypical temperament associated with the specialty (those of pediatricians are cordial; those of cardiologists, irritating; those of psychiatrists, sarcastic). However, many conferences have stopped focusing on the mistake of the physician to reveal the faults of the system.

It doesn't seem like a big deal. What does it matter if the system worked or didn't work when the doctor was the one who punctured the coronary artery? That's a valid question, but one can also analyze the role of the system that put the surgeon on call two nights in a row, or the technician who gave the wrong catheter, or the resident who did not maintain adequate control of the incision site, and so dozens of other variables.

These conferences are like a societal microcosm where the focus has changed: rather than blaming the physician for his or her actions, we now evaluate a process in which we are all partly responsible and where we can all grow and learn from our mistakes. This open, non-punitive and inclusive culture has also influenced daily activities in the hospital. What was previously hidden or discussed behind closed doors with managers, today is openly communicated within the specialty and, sometimes, if it's of general interest, even shared via email with the entire institution (without naming those involved). Personally, this way of facing mistakes and overcoming them allows me to be a better doctor and teacher. Almost daily, when I see hospitalized patients accompanied by a team of residents and students, I highlight a mistake I made regarding the patients we're treating. In this way, I can correct my mistakes and, at the same time, make that error a learning experience for others. Can I be sure that they will learn anything? Maybe some of them will but, ultimately, by remembering them, I am sure that at least I will not be the one to repeat them.

Jack Rubinstein (Continues on page 260)

Alberto Saltiel

(Israel)

Someone who's succeeded once, has a thousand failures behind them. We always celebrate the triumphs, sometimes even brag about them but, in reality, it's the failures that shape us as human beings, which teach us and push us to keep going forward and try again. Therefore, you should be as proud of your failures as you are of your achievements, and we should celebrate them both equally.

My first achievement begins with having fulfilled a lifelong dream and graduating from medical school. Of course, along the way, this path was accompanied by multiple failures, but they were small and not worth mentioning. However, all those failures helped me get to where

225

I am now. They taught me to study more, to be more persistent, and, therefore, to prioritize.

One of my biggest failures this far was failing to pass the Medical Licensing Exam in Israel the first time. In retrospective, it's not a huge failure, but it delayed my training. At that time, it was a hard blow but, thanks to the support of my loved ones, I was able to come to terms with it and move forward. In the end, the great achievement was, of course, to have obtained the medical license in Israel and to have been admitted to a very demanding and coveted residency in the best national program.

Throughout my career, during the specialty, in surgeries and with patients, there have also been failures. Some of these were minor, but others had serious repercussions. One of my great teachers always said, "Behind a great surgeon, there's a cemetery full of patients." It's our job to learn from each of our failures so as not to repeat them, and to avoid them in order to help the next patient even more.

Another of my accomplishments has been to have been appointed as chief resident for vascular surgery, a demanding position that carries a lot of responsibility. At the same time, during this period I learned a lot about the specialty, my colleagues, and myself. All that fills me with pride and satisfaction.

It's also important to be successful in your personal life. Among these achievements, I cannot fail to mention that I formed a beautiful family, and I enjoy their company. They're the ones that give me strength to keep moving forward, who push me every day and from whom I learn the most. What's essential is that, regardless of what life throws my way, we'll always celebrate each failure and success together.

Alberto Saltiel (Continues on page 262)

Luana Sandoval Castillo

(SPAIN, DENMARK)

I've decided not to keep track of my failures, although I have surely been through enough to learn how to overcome them. However, the most important thing for me has been to try again, to turn them into achievements. I'm proud to speak Catalan and Danish. I don't consider myself fluent at all, but I get by and make myself understood. Best of all, I can be myself.

If you had asked me 10 years ago if I could imagine being where I am today, I would have raised my eyebrows and looked at you in disbelief. Today I can say that every stage was necessary and has taught me that destiny is not a goal to reach, but every step taken and the best thing we can do is enjoy it. I have managed to balance my personal and professional life and enjoy both, but it has required endless changes and adjustments and, of course, a great team: my family and friends, both here and on the other side of the world.

For me, the most important thing is to never stop setting goals for myself. I enjoy cycling to work, making the most of my time and getting a little exercise. I have managed to run a half marathon and now I am preparing for a full one and a triathlon. I have also managed to get rid of the pain in my fingertips when I play the guitar: what matters is perseverance. I managed to write a book and now we are working on its translation to reach more people and pave the road for them, so they'll have it easier than we did.

Luana Sandoval Castillo (Continues on page 265)

Ilan Shapiro

(United States)

My, this is a tough one. There have been so many achievements and failures in my life these last few years that I couldn't possibly name them all.

Failures

Master of Public Health: Learning about projects, management and how to be a leader, put me at a crossroads: everyone around me had many academic degrees and titles. Because I worked for the public, private and federal sectors, I felt the need to increase my education. Among the options I had, I thought that a master's degree in public health would give my career an interesting boost.

After applying, I started my master's at John Hopkins. After a couple of months, I realized that the skills I lacked in order to help more people were not medical, but rather financial and numerical. My training had given me the ability to save lives, but not to balance financial statements that are key to high-level conversations in creating projects and strategies. That's where I am these days: about to finish my master's degree in public health.

Negotiation and finances: As doctors, we're taught how to perform surgeries, apply vaccines, prescribe treatments and, above all, how to communicate with our patients. But they never explain to us that, sooner or later, we'll need something called money to help other people. Treating someone in critical condition, operating, or simply calculating the dose needed to save a life is something innate to me. However, I've always felt that my profession is a privilege that allows me to help, which is why it costs me a lot to negotiate both for the salary I receive and for the support I request for social programs.

Today, I recognize my value and know what I'm worth. I'm no longer afraid to raise my voice and be clear in my expectations regarding finances, but this journey left me with a couple of scars.

Achievements

Media: I'm fascinated by media. Helping in a massive way with key messages is essential within public health programs, and I strive to reach that goal. As a doctor, in an office, I can see a limited number of patients a day, but by using mass and social media, I've been able to reach out to millions of people these last few years with the sole objective of improving their lives and those of their families.

Aid: I humbly say that I have had the opportunity to help society. I've put in sweat, tears, and time. On both sides of the border, I've come across different groups of binational physicians that can care for and, most importantly, understand the challenges immigrants face in terms of health and well-being.

Binational projects: One of my great achievements has been building bridges and connecting people. You must put weight on the bridge to test its resistance and prepare in case it starts to bend. At some point, we all need help. Coming from a family that migrated, I understand the importance of creating collaborative networks. One of the projects I worked on was helping patients who were on the waiting list for a kidney donor. At that time (and these prices are just examples) dialysis cost around 70 per year, while a transplant from a related, living donor —performed at a center of excellence— cost 150, plus 10 more a year for medications. Taking all this into account, it's clear that a kidney transplant from a related living donor is the most convenient option. The project sought to create community funds so that relatives residing in Mexico of patients waiting for a kidney could travel to the United

States to make the donation. Unfortunately, due external problems, the project did not take off. However, this effort led to the creation of two associations that fight for our patients' rights.

Family: I can't thank this phenomenal achievement enough. My wife. Without her I would not be the person that I am today, both physically and emotionally. More importantly, she's the source of the energy that characterizes me.

In addition, she has created a safe space in the house so that I can continue putting my crazy ideas in motion. I love coming home to enjoy the fruits of my hard work and to share the experiences of the day with my family.

Ilan Shapiro (Continues on page 273)

René Sotelo
(United States)

Talking about failures is hard because I really feel I haven't had any. And it's not about arrogance or pretentiousness, it's more like focusing on being grateful for what I have achieved, on celebrating every step taken, the big and the small, because I've earned a living in an honest way. I've relentlessly worked for it and continue to do so every day.

I like to focus on the work. I always tell my fellows: "Make the most of your time." When they assist me in a surgery and I see they're not writing anything down, I ask them: "Are you taking notes of what you are observing and learning? Ask questions, focus on every single trick, every single detail involved in a surgery". My desire to share knowledge, and support them, vanishes when I see them distracted, talking about other subjects in the operating room, stealing time and concentration from the rest of the staff, when they should be aware that this is a room where the only thing they should be focused on is the patient. At that moment, their job should be to take advantage of every second they're given, to learn through observation. That's my way of telling them they should be on their toes every nanosecond and gain knowledge from it.

I use time to the fullest, I squeeze it until it runs out. You won't see me chatting in a coffee shop, passing the time without making the most of it. Being aware that time goes hand in hand with work allows me to value things even more. To be honest, I never imagined that I would get to where I currently am, and the truth is I feel there's still a long way to go.

Looking ahead, imagining all the things left to do, the sheer adventure it represents, the people on the road waiting to be discovered, not only encourages me, but enables me to move forward. And I think that's the point: preparing to win in the face of adversity. Whenever I go through a rough time, I remember approaching my mother and getting the same answer time and again: "Well, go on, go ahead, keep at it." From her I learned that that's the only direction: forward. Perhaps that reflects that, along the way, we'll find more strength and possibilities of learning, not failures, but new lessons that will empower us and make us even better people.

I think success lies in working for your dreams, in looking at the road ahead and envisioning what you want to achieve, imagining it and moving towards that goal. I firmly believe success is a journey, not a destination, and that's why working tirelessly, every second, every minute, is of vital importance. Enjoy and be conscious of every step taken, so when you look back you can identify the lessons learned and collect the smiles of every moment along the way, because sometimes life's roads are not paved, there are not always highways. Sometimes you need to slow down, and other times you can speed up and resume the intensity of your journey at a faster pace.

In this adventure called life, my main concern is being absent someday and, at that thought, I need to be certain that my family has the tools to keep moving forward. I strive to teach my children the value of things, to appreciate their friends for who they are, for their affection, and not their belongings. They have enjoyed many pleasures early on in their lives, they've visited many countries thanks to my work, grown up surrounded by opportunities, and met famous personalities. Besides a father, I've always wanted to be an example for them when it came to work ethic. I've wanted them to view effort as a value, so they work for what they want with dedication, giving it their all. They've had —and currently possess— all the necessary tools for success and must capitalize on them. In life, it will be up to them to decide which of these instruments they can rely on to move onward in the best way, but always committed, always eager. In this journey, without the shadow of a doubt, moving forward accompanied by friends, is definitely the best way to go.

René Sotelo (Continues on page 277)

Karla Uribe
(UNITED STATES)

The first twenty years of my life, I had a life and a professional career that went according to plan. I entered medical school on the first try, and, most importantly, I graduated without any setbacks. I took the specialty exam and was also accepted right off the bat. Four years later, I obtained my certification from the Mexican Board of Otolaryngology and Head and Neck Surgery and, by then, I ran a successful private practice that allowed me to be financially independent.

It was when I knew that my daughter was coming into the world that I lost the script I had for my life. At that moment, I had to make decisions that, like everything else, have wonderful aspects, but are not without downsides. I chose to start a family and be a full-time mom. I consider myself brave for having decided to leave what I had worked so hard to achieve, to bet on love and start again from scratch. The problem was that my parents did not agree with my decision, and they constantly reminded me of it. Not living up to their expectations made me feel for a long time that I had failed. Now, ten years more mature, I understand that I decided to engage in a cycle of complaining about the things I could be doing but wasn't, because, from their perspective, I am wasting my talent, and my socioeconomic level, according to them, is below me.

Now I have two children. They are the greatest gift life has given me. It's a true privilege to be their mother and they are my way of contributing to the world. One day, when my daughter had a fever, she told me: "Mommy, when I see how you take care of us when we get sick. I would like to be a doctor too, so I can take care of my children like that". Moments like this make me think that I am doing things right. I also have a strong marriage and a family built on solid ground. That, so far, is the happiest of my achievements.

I haven't yet reintegrated into my professional life as I would like to. Among the things I have considered, I decided to apply for a program to become a PA (physician assistant), which I thought was the best option for me to be able to practice my specialty at least partially. To meet the eligibility requirements, I went back to school to take basic science courses that were not required for my university education in Mexico. I took classes in algebra, statistics, chemistry, and much more. So, I had the experience of being the older lady in class among twenty-year-olds and witnessed how things have changed between generations. My classmates no longer took notes in a notebook, they just took pictures of the teacher's slides and had to wait for me, the older lady, to finish writing. I still wonder if that really helps them process the information properly. At that stage, I got a taste of what it's like to work, study, have children, and be married. It was very tiring. I learned to take it one day at a time, to make every minute worthwhile. With that philosophy, I got a 4.0 GPA and got into the Honor Society. I always knew that the PA program was very competitive, and I thought that my background and grades were enough to get me accepted. But that was not the case, and it really hurt my pride a lot when I read the email that said more or less: "Thank you for applying. We don't mean to imply you're not good, but our program is in high demand right now". Oh, well. No matter. It's back to trying again.

My most recent academic achievement was completing a tinnitus retraining therapy course with the Jastreboff Foundation. Thanks to the new technological tools we have adopted since the pandemic, I had the opportunity to take the course via Zoom and with the kids at home. I am preparing to offer it remotely in the near future as I continue to look for options and opportunities.

Karla Uribe (Continues on page 278)

Jeannette Uribe
(United States)

One day in high school, first thing in the morning during math class, the classroom was filled by a very strong smell of skunk. The teacher took all the students out, and called us back in one by one, until she discovered the stinky culprit. After identifying the person, she took the student to another classroom to see if other children could also notice it, and, well, after being singled out, I was sent home. At that time, we didn't have cellphones, nor did we have a phone at home. Since there was no way to get a hold of my parents, I had to return in a cab. My mom was outraged, and she almost went back to the school to complain to the teacher for exposing me in such an insensitive manner. Well, not almost. She did go; you know what moms are like. What had happened was that, in order to go to school, I had to walk down a poorly lit street, and I probably stepped in skunk urine by accident. I got rid of the smelly shoes and thought I'd be known as "the skunk girl" forever. In the end, that wasn't the case. Actually, I think I was remembered as one of the smartest girls in the class (or so I think).

I tried to play soccer. I kind of sucked at it but I really liked it. I could never get my dad to say, "Great game!", but at least we shared the passion for soccer as a family. As a team we almost never won, but I made a lot of friends that I would never have met otherwise.

I also tried basketball, but I was almost always benched, and one day, a ball hit me right in the face. My god, I thought I knew what pain felt like. I was wrong. However, every cloud has a silver lining: that's how I met the love of my life, my now husband.

In medical school, the senior students organized fundraising events for graduation. I lived right next to the school and usually I spent my time in the library studying. One day, when I was heading out, I saw that there was an arm-wrestling match going on, and my eyes sparkled. I signed up in the women's category. My mom had taught me some tricks and my dad had made sure I had good biceps by putting me to work in the cornfield. And that's how I easily won some tickets to a nightclub that I later sold.

My life has been filled by insignificant failures that have paved the way to enormous achievements. When I was young, I remember thinking "Why me? Why can't I be faster? Why am I not taller? Why did my dad put me to work in the fields? Why didn't they give me more money? I got my answers when I had to leave home to study medicine when I was 16 years old, and had to cook my own food, wash my white uniforms by hand, clean the house, sleep on a cot, and appreciate every single peso I was given.

And so, I managed to graduate from medical school as the second best score of my class and with honors. I passed my residency exam in Mexico on the first try and, at 26, I finished my specialty in Obstetrics and Gynecology, also with honors, and made great friendships along the way: nurses, teachers, and my dear fellow residents.

I had grown used to giving my best and seeing results. Then, I came to the United States and oh, surprise, the real failures were yet to come.

My dream was to practice gynecology but, in order to do so, I had to repeat my residency. Repeating it was not the problem, the tough part was getting in. Besides the language and the tedious paperwork, the biggest challenge was how incredibly difficult the exams were. Being able to focus on studying while experiencing a cultural shock, living in someone else's house, becoming a first-time mom, giving up a life where I was already someone and starting from scratch seemed like an impossible task. I never lost hope, but there were many moments when I wanted to give up my dream and go back to Mexico. My poor husband bore witness to the frustration I felt.

However, I kept moving forward, passed all my exams on the first try, and looked for rotations. Some of them were free, others cost money and involved moving to other cities. Fulfilling the basic requirements took me two years, which wasn't too bad. Now, I was ready to apply for residency, a process that takes place only once a year on specific dates. I applied to many hospitals and spent more money. Normally, the invitations for interviews arrive by email, so I would anxiously stare at my computer screen. When I got the first email, it said something along the lines of "Thank you for applying, but we cannot offer you an interview." I felt that nothing I had done had been worth it, but there was still time and there were still 99 hospitals that hadn't replied yet. I received many emails exactly like the first one. Finally, I had an interview, which involved a trip, spending more money and, in the end, I didn't match.

I was already working at the hospital as a phlebotomist when I applied for the second time. More money, one single interview and nothing, I didn't match either. That same year, my second baby was born premature. We went through difficult times. We moved into our own house after living with my brother and his wife, who had helped us through the past difficult years. We worked overtime as much as possible, we were now a family of four, and we still had to save money for my residency and for the last exam (in a series of four) which also costs a fair amount of money. Taking this test was risky because, if I didn't pass, I wouldn't apply again. One agonizing month later, I received my result: I had passed with a decent grade. I was excited; there was still hope.

When I applied for the third time, I was interviewed twice. One of them was in New York, and I traveled on October 31st because my interview was on the Day of the Dead. On the flight, the two seats next to me were free, which I interpreted as a lucky sign. I was interviewed by Dr. Riess, Dr. Mishra, and the director, Dr. Mikhail. When I returned home, I told my parents, my brother, my sister-in-law, my husband, my children, and my nephews about the whole experience. Everyone had a hunch that this interview was going to work out. They were right. On January 8th, I received a call from Dr. Mikhail to be part of the resident program.

I thought this would be my greatest accomplishment. Now, I realize that my greatest accomplishment has been by my side all along: my parents, my siblings, my in-laws, my friends, my two beautiful children and a husband who has always supported my decisions and taken care of our family.

Jeannette Uribe (Continues on page 280)

8

Life during the pandemic

Patricia Bautista Rivera

(UNITED STATES)

When the first images of the health crisis in Wuhan appeared on TV, followed by the announcement of the border closure and the large number of people trying to leave the area, I can only say I felt alarmed and worried.

At the beginning of February my family and I traveled to Mexico City to celebrate my mom's 80th birthday. We enjoyed her party very much, and she was thrilled to have her children and grandchildren all together in the same place. Two weeks later, I traveled to Los Angeles to meet a fabulous group of women, co-authors, at the presentation of the book *Doctoras con alas*. I had the most wonderful trip.

Given that La Casita Center (LCC) was visited daily by dozens of people seeking help, guidance, or accompaniment, it seemed urgent to me to implement preventive measures. In late February, we started to promote hand washing through videos on Facebook. Two weeks later, we promoted the avoidance of kissing and hugging when greeting, a custom deeply rooted in our culture. Days later, we started using hand sanitizer when entering the facilities.

When the lock-down was declared, my job became virtual. Gradually, like the rest of the world, we learned to hold videoconference meetings, and to use the telephone and computers as our main work tools. We reaffirmed the importance of sharing truthful and accessible information to the community through videos on LCC's Facebook page.

Meanwhile, at home, considering the unprecedented events the world was facing, I began to prepare myself by stocking up on food: beans, rice, cans of tuna, and pasta. The stress caused by the pandemic triggered hoarding behaviors, so I did my best to buy only what was necessary, but it was easy to succumb to the generalized hysteria.

My husband continued to see patients, both in consultation and in the hospital. I urged him to wear a mask, and he agreed hesitantly, since most of the doctors and nurses at his hospital did not wear them. On March 21st, *The New Yorker* published an article describing how doctors in Hong Kong and Singapore prevented infection through the correct use of masks, hand washing, and social distancing. We shared the article with friends and colleagues, and began promoting these measures, which later coincided with those adopted by the CDC (Center for Disease Control and Prevention). My husband occasionally entered the COVID-19 unit and thankfully did not get infected.

My daughter was in graduate school in our city, and working at the same time, so she was at home when the lock-down began. My son, on the other hand, was attending college in Boston, and needed to get home. My husband flew to Boston and rented a car to bring him back.

The college, which had previously announced that it would remain operational, closed the next day, leaving many students stranded.

My son and daughter continued their education online, while my husband left every day for work. The first time I went out to buy groceries, I had an accelerated heart rate and felt extremely anxious. For a long time, I was the only one going grocery shopping. When I got home, my children would help disinfect each of the things I had brought. We used disinfectant wipes and washed fruits, vegetables, and anything else we could rub soap on.

On the other hand, our family in Mexico had us extremely worried. The grandparents refused to stay at home, my mom complained and said she felt imprisoned in her own house. She gradually came to terms with the situation and, by the second wave in the winter, she then understood the importance of staying at home.

The concern for our community was growing, many of the jobs considered essential or front-line jobs are performed by Latinos/as, who had to continue working, because many of them depended on their jobs to survive. So, at LCC, we began to plan the best ways to promote preventive measures.

At LCC, we hand out food to families in need and, once the center closed, we relied on volunteers to distribute it to their homes. More and more people were out of work and in need of help. In my city, where there are a large number of restaurants, a well-known chef, Edward Lee, organized a whole movement to provide food and assistance to restaurant and hotel workers.

Because the number of sick people in our community was increasing, we organized virtual forums for Latino restaurant and store owners, in which we clarified doubts and promoted preventive measures. We also held information sessions with church leaders and pastors who offer services in Spanish.

Weeks later, LCC began working with my city's health department. Contact tracers refer Spanish-speaking patients who test positive for COVID-19 to LCC. My job is to call them and follow up on their health status, share prevention measures, and guide them on what to do (symptom surveillance, etc.) while sick. Affected families are sent food, sanitary products, and sometimes medicines to treat pain or fever. Even now, I still record informative videos about the virus and other health topics for LCC's Facebook page to educate the community. LCC has conducted campaigns to promote the importance of PCR testing when the disease is suspected. The communities have been provided with tests and, in coordination with the health department, also with flu and COVID-19 vaccines.

The pandemic has allowed my family to spend more time together and to face this difficult situation side by side. We've learned a lot in terms of communication and virtual interaction.

Patricia Bautista Rivera (Continues on page 283)

Edmundo Erazo

(THE NETHERLANDS)

The times we're currently living in are strange because of the pandemic. During this crisis, being a doctor and outside of Mexico is hard to describe.

My most significant concern are my family, friends, and colleagues. My first instinct, realizing the magnitude of the situation, was to return to

Mexico to help and be around in case of a family emergency. It's been hard for me to accept that there's a big possibility that one of my relatives or friends will get seriously sick while I'm away. Each day there's more and more uncertainty, and worst-case scenarios are constantly popping up in our minds. The distance means that I wouldn't be able to get to my country fast and, therefore, I'd lose valuable time not accompanying the ones I love.

Along with my partner and family, I decided not to return at that exact moment but to keep in permanent touch. I was still worried that I was not helping enough. I was not practising clinical medicine at that time, so I enlisted as a reserve in the Netherlands. The first days of confinement were simple. I kept a routine of exercising at home in the mornings, working in the afternoons, and calling my friends and family in the evenings. As time passed, I felt the need to help my country, so I collaborated with some colleagues to publish an article about COVID-19 in Mexico. I also went to work in a company in Mexico City to offer free online consultations as a strategy to avoid saturating the national emergency services. After five weeks at home, during which I went out only when I had to, I noticed that it was difficult to keep my sanity without pillars such as human contact, reflection, and the balance between recreation and constant work.

Sadly, the illness disrupted the lives of my loved ones. My best friend and brother by choice, Abner, lost a very close relative. We're like family, so I immediately wanted to return to Mexico. However, I had to see reason because, even if I'd been there, it would not have been possible to attend the funeral, and I would've had to remain in quarantine. I felt sad and anxious, and then doubts haunted me: Had I made the right decision leaving Mexico?

I took refuge in music, one of my great passions, and while listening to "Iron Sky" by Paolo Nutini ["To those who can hear me / I say, do not despair"], I was thinking about the answer to my question. I finally realized that it depended on the moment and the situation.

When you start the adventure of living in another country, you don't know what the result will be, and only time allows you to see everything in retrospect. So, I decided to take control of my emotions and thoughts. I accepted that "what if" isn't real, and I tried to be positive and face whatever came my way the best I could. However, I'm confident that the moment I decided to leave my country, I made the right choice because it has allowed me to learn and grow immensely. I cannot judge that decision based on current reality. I must go back to the moment I decided to leave.

It was in November 2016 when I applied for a scholarship abroad. The following month, even though I was in Mexico, they assaulted me a couple of kilometres from my house, and for me, that was the breaking point when I decided to go live in another country. So, I got my strength back and decided that it was best to find new paths. All of this helped me feel better about my decision to live in the Netherlands and focus on helping Mexico to the best of my abilities.

Living outside my homeland during the pandemic also allowed me to put into perspective other aspects such as how difficult it is to adapt and understand the changes beyond our control, no matter where we are. I've learned different lessons: how overwhelming the infodemic can be, the importance of how a message is conveyed, how the fear of the unknown does not respect borders, how being aware and seeking the common good is reflected in the individual interest, how listening to the Mexican National Anthem while away from home will always provoke feelings that words cannot express. I also understood that no matter which country a Mexican lives in or what they do for a living, they will always be willing to help.

Edmundo Erazo (Continues on page 285)

Sandra López-León

(ISRAEL, THE NETHERLANDS, SPAIN, UNITED STATES)

I was one of the first people to get sick with COVID in America, in February 2020. I had a flu with a lot of fatigue and fever, and from one second to the next I became deaf in one ear (the deafness lasted 6 months, and I had assumed it would be permanent). A few days after I was sick, I began to grasp just how serious the situation was. The hospitals in New York were overflowing. They were putting beds in parking lots and convention centers. Bodies were piling up. Outside the hospitals there were huge freezer trucks so they could keep them for later burial. There were so many unidentified bodies that they had to make thousands of graves on Heart Island to bury them. For a couple of weeks, more than 1,000 people died every day in New York. For a time, all news was bad. The mother of a good friend of my son's had died of COVID, as well as a couple of doctor friends.

Since I had gone suddenly deaf in one ear, I was given corticosteroids to see if my hearing would improve. Between the fever I had, the mental side effects of the corticosteroids, the insomnia, extreme tiredness, the anxiety of watching the world go down and not knowing if my disease was going to get worse, my life seemed like a nightmare. I lived those 14 days of isolation "one day at a time", and it felt like 14 years. I came back to this world feeling blessed and grateful, with a great desire to continue living, learning, loving, and giving. I confirmed that what gives strength and meaning to my life is love, art, science, and medicine. I wanted to connect deeply with people and be able to help the world survive. The more destruction there is, the more chance we have to create.

I returned to work just when the consortium was created that brought together all the pharmaceutical companies, academia, and regulatory agencies to look for solutions. The plan was short-term (drugs that already existed), medium-term (drugs in development and vaccines) and long-term (pan-coronavirus drugs for viruses that may come) solutions. The short-term plan involved making a list of drugs that were already on the market that could be used to treat COVID, and the company I work for had several in mind. It was an exciting time, which was short-lived as soon the scientific evidence proved that the first drug candidates we had did not work. At the time I am writing this chapter we have a vaccine, and some drugs are starting to come out that might help with the symptoms, but we still don't have a full-on treatment.

When I was cured of COVID, the pandemic had just arrived in the United States, and had not yet reached Latin America. But I had already been there, back, and around. I started to reconnect with the important people in my life, I joined the WhatsApp chat of my old schoolmates and reconnected with childhood friends. I also joined the WhatsApp chat of my friends from medical school. At the same time, I reactivated a Twitter account that I had never used. When my friends found out that I was a physician and epidemiologist, they started asking me hundreds of questions. Although I studied epidemiology, I had always focused on neuropsychiatry, and I saw epidemiology as a tool to do research. From one day to the next I started to be very proud of being an epidemiologist and being able to understand a little more than most what was going on. There was a lot of disinformation. As an epidemiologist and physician, I felt it was my duty to explain to family and friends important facts about the disease.

To keep myself updated, I read the articles published on COVID daily. I receive everything published in PubMed; on average I get 800 articles a day. I read the titles to see if there is anything relevant to my work, and I take the opportunity to post what I find most important and interesting on Twitter (@sandralopezleon), I focused on informing people how to prevent the disease. What has filled me the most and motivates me to keep posting on Twitter is that very often doctors, friends and specialists that I don't know contact me and thank me for putting a summary of the latest published articles, since they don't have time to be looking for literature because they are saturated with COVID patients. That makes me feel honored and happy since I know that, if I help one doctor, that can help hundreds of people as well.

Another interesting thing I did during the pandemic was to do research related to COVID. I have a group of 7 friends who are Ph.D. researchers. Incredibly bright women with a myriad of different backgrounds. Together we have the following specialties: immunology, neurology, psychiatry, oncology, genetics, internal medicine, epidemiology, infectious diseases, and science communication.

At the end of 2020 we began to worry because we started to hear that there were long term sequels of COVID, and we decided to do the first meta-analysis on Long-COVID. This article went viral because it opened the eyes of doctors, researchers, and the public that there were sequels of COVID. It was very impressive to see news in all the languages (Arabic, Chinese, Scandinavian, etc.) naming us. Our article was the most viewed on Publons for several weeks. We were very proud that our work accelerated a little bit the knowledge, research, and treatment of such a big problem. At the same time, I talked daily with friends working directly with patients and with friends doing research. It's very impressive to see when a friend's study resonates on a huge scale. It's amazing to be involved in research that impacts every human on earth. We had the world listening and depending on us.

What did I do in the pandemic? Enjoy every second of my family and the friends I gained throughout my life. In person and virtually. I treasured every breath and second of my existence, because it's in these types of moments that one realizes what a blessing health and life are. The pandemic made me grow emotionally, intellectually, and professionally. It was a time of great learning and love on every level imaginable. It was an opportunity to bond with childhood friends and colleagues around the world. I strengthened friendships and showed the people close to me how much I love them.

Sandra López-León (Continues on page 285)

Rafael G. Magaña

(ENGLAND, UNITED STATES)

I think these last few years I've had a difficult time finding a balance between my profession and other things that make me happy. On one occasion, my father was visiting us from Mexico and, after going to the doctor, he was diagnosed with type two diabetes. After discussing it with the whole family, we decided to join the gym.

In order to inspire my father to improve his fitness and mitigate his diabetes, I went to the gym almost daily and, in the process, my health improved as well. My father lost weight and now only needs one metformin pill a day. That to me is a small triumph that helped us both, and today I feel better than I have in ten years.

In August 2019, my brother convinced me to sign up for jiu–jitsu classes. I went for it and began a new stage that gave me personal balance, satisfaction, and happiness.

At the end of January 2020, while traveling to the Philippines to treat patients with cleft lip and palate, I saw on the news that in Wuhan City (Hubei province, China) they began to build a hospital to care for patients infected with a new virus.

Due to the scale of the project, I realized that this maneuver would have bigger implications. They were obviously very worried, but I never imagined that it would result in the global catastrophe we're currently facing.

Upon returning from that trip, on February 2nd, the first death had already been recorded outside of China, in the Philippines. We knew that, ultimately, it would spread to the airports. I was particularly concerned about airplanes, as they're favorable spaces for the transmission of the virus. In Japan —where I made a stopover on that trip— many were already wearing masks, including myself. When I got back home, a close friend and colleague told me very prophetically, "I think this has the potential to affect the world economy."

Returning to Connecticut, I continued to see my patients as usual, but the international outlook was getting more and more alarming. However, at that time, there was little government action to prepare us for the effects of the pandemic; in fact, it seemed they were aloof to the phenomenon.

As the weeks passed, the situation in other countries such as Italy and Spain became catastrophic, and the first cases began to be seen in New York.

Elective surgeries were suspended, as well as my medical practice, in a very justifiable and yet abrupt way. My family had traveled to Mexico and returned the same Friday the border between Mexico and the United States closed. I was worried about my family in the States; I was worried about my family in Mexico... I was a nervous wreck.

The feeling of uncertainty has definitely been the worst part. My father worried me, being at-risk population, but I also wondered if this would be the end of my private medical practice.

I started setting up an action plan. I spoke with the heads of the departments of the hospitals I work at and asked for on-call shifts every week, beginning in the middle of June 2020 until the end of the year.

I called my patients who were scheduled for cosmetic surgery and gave them the option to cancel or postpone the procedures, explaining that I had no clue when I could operate on them.

I braced myself for the worst but figured I could probably keep my practice afloat by taking emergency shifts; however, I was not sure if that was a viable option. February and March 2020 were the most uncertain times for me and, therefore, for my family.

Unexpectedly, at the beginning of June, when the hospitals were reopening, there were private patients who wanted to have cosmetic surgeries; and, with a strict preoperative protocol, I managed to continue operating.

Plastic surgery emergencies did not abate during those difficult months and the office remained stable. I couldn't explain how or why this was happening, but it was, and I felt extremely lucky, since other practices had to close.

I proceeded with great caution and good judgment, investing and taking as many emergency on-call shifts as I could to stay productive.

As I write this, we are still immersed in this horrible pandemic, and the first wave persists in the southern states of the U.S.; although it seems that the cases have decreased in Connecticut and New York, where I live.

There's a lot of speculation about the national and world economy, and we begin a decade with a new world order because of the current situation.

So, in my case, this year began with many aspirations, plans, hopes, and with a balanced life, both personally and professionally. Currently, I see an extremely uncertain and difficult outlook for the world, and that worries me a lot.

However, I think right now the Greek myth of Pandora is quite insightful. By opening the box and releasing all the evils of humanity, the last thing left inside it is hope.

Rafael G. Magaña (Continues on page 287)

Nissin Nahmias

(UNITED STATES)

The COVID-19 pandemic has changed everyone's lives and has made us face difficult times that require tenacity, intelligence, union, and our best efforts in almost every sense. I hope this is the last pandemic we'll endure, although I have my doubts.

During the pandemic, all non-emergency surgeries were cancelled. All members of the department volunteered to work in intensive care and in treating the thousands of COVID-19 patients who flooded the hospital. In New York City, the pandemic hit the Bronx the hardest and, unfortunately, my hospital was one of the centers with the most patients. At first, we thought this would pass quickly, that it was temporary, but weeks turned into months and things went downhill. The streets of the city were empty, the friendliness of the people disappeared, and, due to the social isolation, the usual health problems worsened.

The pandemic reminded me of my ethical and moral values, and the education I received: the importance of being altruistic and serving others. For months, we worked incredibly hard, putting our lives on the line, but we were satisfied when patients returned safely to their homes. However, we needed more and more time and resources for each patient. Some were intubated for days, others for months; but those who were more fragile, sadly passed away.

Among the losses was my dear business partner, Dr. Ronald Verrier. He was a lively and cheerful man with a great fighting spirit. He was the best partner I've ever had, and a source of inspiration for me. Personally, losing him was what hit me the most about the pandemic. Ronald immigrated to New York from his native Haiti; he specialized in trauma surgery and critical care. Several years ago, while on vacation in Bermuda, he had an accident, required a tracheostomy, and suffered a heart attack. However, thanks to his strength and determination, he overcame it all with dignity. Ronald was a leader among leaders; he had a very peculiar style and sense of humor, but the best thing about him was his humanity and humility. I had spoken to him on the phone on a Tuesday since I hadn't seen him at work. I called him and he told me he wasn't feeling very well, and that his whole body was hurting, but he said not to worry. After a few days, he was admitted with respiratory failure and died three days later from multiple complications. Sometimes, I can feel his presence in the operating room, and it comforts me to know that he's no longer suffering.

This pandemic affects you personally; it's difficult to deal with, it requires organization and collaboration from all parties, and, therefore, finding a solution to it is extremely complex.

After an intensive course on critical care, my life consisted of doing shifts and checking on patients for four months, until there were less and less, to the point that the hospital services were no longer saturated, and we began to think about how to restart our normal operations safely.

During those months, I stopped seeing my children, which was very difficult for me. However, I was happily surprised by their attitude; they were proud of me, and called me daily and at all hours, which they still do to this day.

We remain alert and prepared in case the virus strikes back but, as I mentioned at the beginning of the chapter, I hope this is the last time we have to do so.

Nissin Nahmias (Continues on page 289)

Susana Ramírez Romero
(SPAIN)

In February 2020, I traveled to the city of Los Angeles for the presentation of the book *Doctoras con Alas*. At that time, there were several cases of COVID-19 in Asia, but we still believed that its impact on the West wouldn't be as immense. By the end of the month, cases were skyrocketing in Italy and, by the beginning of March, the first cases started in Spain, leading to a national lock-down at the end of the month that took us all by surprise. Schools and all non-essential workplaces were closed, including my clinic. You could only leave the house to buy food or go to the pharmacy, and the queues were especially long as the capacity was limited. You could only leave home with a printed self-declaration that you had to present if you were stopped by the police.

The streets looked empty; every night at 8pm people went out to the balconies to applaud the healthcare workers, and while some took the opportunity to exchange words of anxiety and concern with other neighbors, others took the opportunity to sing. Those with children drew rainbows and signs of hope. Those who had dogs were allowed to walk them once a day. Those of us who loved sports had to find ways to exercise at home. I myself joined my youngest son's online taekwondo classes.

I went from working every day of the week to only working one day on-site and two days online. Being so passive led me to think about signing up as a volunteer to join the list of doctors to attend patients with COVID-19. "Aren't you afraid?" people asked me time and again. How could I be afraid of viruses being a doctor? I've dealt with tuberculosis, measles, and many other infectious diseases during my training. If I had the right equipment at my disposal, there was no question I wanted to be there. However, I am a mother, divorced, and an immigrant, three conditioning factors that made me reflect whether it was wise to put myself on the line. If I get sick, who will take care of my children? They were my only concern. These thoughts stopped me from signing up, but then I felt like I was betraying my calling. I felt a deep sadness for not following my medical vocation, but before long I found a position in the right trench.

After a quick training in video consultations, but without having the necessary tools, I dared to check on patients online, making a sort of triage between cases that could wait and those that needed immediate treatment. Pharmacies, exceptionally, filled prescriptions sent by email or WhatsApp. Many cases could be resolved this way, but others required taking care of things in person.

I had to become an expert in COVID-19 skin manifestations in record time, for which I had to read a lot and listen to multiple international lectures where doctors from China, Italy, and all around the world, shared their experiences and knowledge.

Dermatologists were facing the same problem everywhere while trying to determine whether skin lesions were related to the virus, to the medication or to the immune response. Multiple Zoom webinars organized by international dermatology associations allowed us to exchange the newest findings and approaches to managing COVID-19 in our field. We also had free access to multiple internationally recognized medical journals.

It was a great experience to feel accompanied by professionals from other parts of the world in this simultaneous learning.

My life during the pandemic was a time of locking myself up physically and opening myself up virtually to infinite scenarios.

Susana Ramírez Romero (Continues on page 289)

Luis Rodrigo Reynoso

(ETHIOPIA)

Aguascalientes, Mexico, 2020.

The pandemic has been an extreme period. Full of emotions: everything is bizarre, absurd, challenging, mystical and distressing. In my day to day, the scientific, the religious and the magical coexist.

I kept my mind with any possible project. I tried to get involved mostly in prevention. We joined forces with other people and, even without meeting or meeting physically, we managed to produce thousands of personal protective equipment. I became desperate when I saw how in the face of the pandemic, there were people who profited from medical supplies, the worst thing I have seen in my life.

I was able to identify and witness the hemispheres of ambition, service, love, hate, compassion. I want to understand, but when I finally find a justification for the reality I am living, a massive wave arrives that transforms everything in the blink of an eye. We have pressed the fast forward button and it seems that total destruction will be what will finally stop us.

We are experiencing changes by leaps and bounds in each and every area. Now we have a modus vivendum that goes straight ahead at the speed of light. For those of us who like to believe in energy portals, the portal we have just passed through is undoubtedly transcendental.

As a doctor, it has never ceased to amaze me how this pandemic has made us collaborate academically, technically, and technologically. As I write this, there are still few certainties about the virus: when one of the aspects is finally deciphered, a new symptom appears. And yes, I am still scared!

Today, almost all the time I wear face masks, a shield or goggles, and if I am not wearing them, I feel guilty, even if breathing is difficult. On my daily walk to work, I can no longer stop to smell the scent of flowers, and during the long hours in the office, I hardly dare to take a few sips of coffee. Also, the constant rubbing of the mask has filled my face with rashes.

During consultation I would like to be able to hug those patients who have become close friends. I do know the face of my new patients. I would like to ask them to uncover their face, but I do dare, so I dig into their Facebook or WhatsApp profiles in an attempt to get to know them. Greeting each other and say goodbye with the hand on the chest is the most cordial and humane thing I have found to show my appreciation and gratitude.

In the operating room the changes are radical and the processes more strenuous. We must use personal protection material that consists of a p100 mask, a three-layer mask, goggles, and a shielf. This makes breathing and vision difficult. In addition, you must be careful that no drops of sweat drip off. We have to pause to release the tension and weight from our heads. We have limited surgical procedures, selecting patients very well, who have to go through an exhaustive filter of imaging and laboratory studies.

I was in lockdown for 60 days. I only went out three times to take care of emergencies, and everything else I attended virtually. But I was able to enjoy my home, my marriage, and focus on our true needs, our essence. I learned to grow some legumes, fruits, and vegetables; and therefore, I learned to appreciate more the work of farmers, and the balance that we must have with our environment.

I am writing this on August 14, 2020, and at this point I have already overcome some fears. I already leave the house; I take off the mask several times a day so that my patients can see my face and I feel that things begin to flow.

I have no idea where this is going but ultimately it will not be as bad as I was speculating. In my mind the thought that this would be catastrophic was lurking. However, nothing is written. This has been a unique experience in our paths, and it has brought us many learnings.

- Today more than ever I think: Gumoni! We are alive!

Luis Rodrigo Reynoso (Continues on page 292)

Alejandra Rodríguez Romero
(UNITED STATES)

My story and experiences during the pandemic will be very different from those of my co-authors, as I am one of the only ones not currently working. I remember clearly when we started hearing daily, hourly almost, about this new virus that no one knew about, in March 2020. It was all over the news. After days of hearing terrible stories and with a bit of anguish, I set out to do our weekly grocery shopping, not imagining what awaited me. When I arrived at the store, the situation looked like a scene out of an apocalyptic movie: all the shelves were empty, there was no milk, eggs, fruits, vegetables, meat and, of course, no toilet paper. People were desperately grabbing what little was available, and you could see the panic on their eyes. At that moment, as I pushed the cart with my two children on top, I remember feeling a tear roll down my face; worry and uncertainty invaded my thoughts. I feared not having food, diapers, and basic necessities for my children. This concern was increased by the fact that my husband works for a construction company that always takes him to different states and cities, but always away from Tucson, away from us. Depending on the location and job, he sometimes comes home every two or three weeks. I went through several stores hoping to find one that still had food and diapers. Unfortunately, that was not the case. Luckily, however, there's always someone willing to help. Several friends informed me of grocery stores that still had the essentials, and one of my co-authors even sent me diapers online, as they were sold out. All these acts of kindness have remained engraved in my heart.

Those first few months of the pandemic were strange and difficult, both for me and for my daughter who, after spring break, did not see her friends in person again for a long time. I'm sure Jeffrey also noticed that something was going on, but, because he was only 18 months old, the impact was not as severe. Most of us parents became teachers this past year and, honestly, it wasn't my favorite part. Without going into too much detail as to why, I'll just say that I long for the day they go back to the classroom. I've always admired teachers and their work and now I definitely appreciate them much more.

Professionally speaking, because I'm not currently practicing medicine, I became a bystander to the pandemic. I saw colleagues, family, and friends work in their countries, some of them in direct contact with COVID-19. To this day, I'm not sure if I was happy or disappointed not to be working in these times of pandemic.

On a more personal note, I've missed my parents and friends in Mexico terribly, as the U.S. border has been closed to non-residents or citizens since March 2020. I went to Hermosillo in December of that same year, making sure I was in isolation 2 weeks before, and I only went to visit my parents. I decided not to see any of my friends so as not to put anyone's health at risk. I can't remember the last time I hugged my parents with such affection and excitement. The times of pandemic and quarantine have been difficult for everyone. For me, being home with the kids 24/7 is even tougher when they don't go to school, when there are no malls, no movie theaters, no parks, no friends to visit. It's a feeling of isolation that has made it necessary to modify routines at home in order to cope without losing your mind.

Regarding my son Jeffrey's health and his radiological studies, every 3 months we are presented with a challenge, as he has always been treated at the Phoenix Pediatric Hospital, two hours from home. Before the pandemic, my husband and my daughter tagged along to make the trip more pleasant and to cheer Jeffrey up after he woke up from anesthesia. Now, only he and I are allowed in, so I have to ask for help from family or friends to take care of my daughter for the day. Definitely, regardless of all the difficulties and losses we've experienced, every cloud has a silver lining. In my case, the pandemic has made me appreciate things that I used to take for granted, such as the freedom to leave the house without fear of getting infected, or the freedom of not wearing a mask. Another positive change was that my husband had to work from home for 4 months, which was something new, wonderful, and easy for me to get used to.

I'm writing these lines in July 2021, still in the midst of a pandemic that we never imagined we'd live through. Things change daily and we don't know for sure when we will be able to return to a somewhat normal life, but, when we do, I hope that COVID-19 made us reflect on our existence and helped us understand that life is fragile, and health is the only means we have to move forward.

Alejandra Rodríguez Romero (Continues on page 295)

Jack Rubinstein
(UNITED STATES)

> "I hope your children get coronavirus, Rubinstein."
> -Twitter comment

To be honest, I deserved this and worse comments I received on social media. I woke up one morning in the middle of the coronavirus crisis with a crystal-clear epiphany: young people are the least affected by the virus and, therefore, should be the first to be exposed to initiate a process of immunity. I admit that the idea was extreme, and I supported it with scientific data —firm and reliable— but I could not have imagined the international reaction to my short op-ed in a local newspaper. Within the next few days, I received invitations to expand my views in international magazines and media, and also countless invitations to go to hell with all my ideas.

The pandemic exposed weaknesses at every level from international organizations and governments to ourselves and our families. It forced us to question the ability of our elected officials that for years campaigned with poetry and slogans but were incapable of governing when decisions needed to be made. As individuals, it forced us to reevaluate our lives and our decisions when faced with the choice between bad and terrible.

And among the bad and the terrible, I decided to offer an option that resembled the "least awful" I could think of. The reaction online was swift, aggressive and almost entirely negative, but surprisingly positive, productive and frankly constructive in person. Where did the difference lie? Part of it had to do with the protection the internet offers to vent grudges and anger, and part of it had to do with the fact that I surround myself with like-minded people. However, there was also another factor that was made clear to me by a doctor friend: people were afraid. Really afraid. They feared uncertainty and the lack of consistent information (even from exceptional medical journals). They feared the unknown. And, in the face of fear, everyone reacted differently. For many, the first reaction was to protect the offspring at all costs, and rightly so: the survival of the species depends on our ability to keep the next generation alive. Others found solace in venting their frustrations online. Those that fell into these groups found a worthwhile target in me and my op-ed, and I can't really blame them, I can only explain that in the face of fear I attempted to find solutions; not necessarily good ones but having options and discussing ideas was how I tried to cope.

To have options is to have freedom. As the circle of activities becomes more restricted, we feel more secure but, at the same time, more and more imprisoned. There will be many who would gladly trade freedom for security but, as Benjamin Franklin said, "Those who would give up essential Liberty, to purchase a little temporary Safety, deserve neither Liberty nor Safety." During the peak of the pandemic we found ourselves sacrificing essential freedoms, which a few months ago we considered ordinary, in exchange for temporary security against the virus, but we were doing so without clear direction and in fear.

There's no doubt that the quarantine was necessary to reduce contagion and not to exceed the capacities of the medical system. In many places, the task was accomplished but, when the first crisis was over, we were filled with mistrust and false hopes due to the absence of planning and leadership. Mistrust is what drives the masses to demonstrate in public and demand a return to normalcy. During the pandemic it was impossible to engage in civil conversation, let alone reach a consensus in the absence of real leadership[6]. Sadly, this story played out around the world as leaders were incapable of stepping up to the historical moment and as always the rest of us were the ones left to suffer the repercussions. But this moment too shall pass and, as we will see in the next chapter, tomorrow is ours. We will hopefully learn from past mistakes and move forward by making decisions based on science and evidence, not fear and aggression. And maybe, just maybe, we may even be able to have productive conversations online.

Jack Rubinstein (Continues on page 296)

Alberto Saltiel

(Israel)

For years, we've heard time and again about the great pandemics that have severely affected humanity. Since we were little, we studied in school the Black Death, smallpox, cholera, the Spanish flu and, recently, HIV. We hear news from distant countries where viral outbreaks of zoonotic transmission have emerged such as SARS (severe acute respiratory syndrome) caused by the SARS-CoV virus; o MERS (Middle Eastern respiratory syndrome) caused by the MERS-CoV virus; however, we never imagined that we could experience a situation like the one we're currently facing.

It's curious to think that, even during the beginning of a pandemic, when it spreads to distant places and becomes endemic, we continue

---

[6]   Editor's Note: This text was written during Donald Trump's administration.

to believe that it will not spread abroad and affect us. I remember listening to the news at the end of 2019, and thinking that the situation in Wuhan, China, was terrible and, yet I didn't really give it much importance. I thought it was just a new outbreak that would be limited to one area, and it'd fade away pretty soon. In the same way, in early 2020, when COVID-19 (caused by SARS-CoV2) began to spread, arrogance blinded us, making us think, once more, that we wouldn't be impacted by it.

Infections increased rapidly, more and more countries were affected, people began to worry; masks, gloves and antibacterial gels became scarce in pharmacies, and I felt like it was 2009 all over again, when the swine flu (H1N1) hit my country. During the beginning of that pandemic, I was an undergraduate intern in Mexico City and, later, in Be'er Sheva, Israel. I remember the fear of the Mexican population, the people hoarding food and personal protection equipment in panic, and how anxious and careful everyone was. When I arrived in Israel, I heard the jokes about the Mexican who had imported the swine flu into that country over and over again, but they faded quickly. People forgot about the situation, cases were limited, panic subsided, and life returned to normal.

This new situation proved to be different. Entire countries in quarantine, curfews, and absolute uncertainty. On February 21st, 2020, the first case of COVID-19 was diagnosed in Israel. Were we prepared? Life as we knew it was about to change both professionally and individually. To paraphrase my father's wise words, "You have to be prepared for everything, because the patient needs answers." The country panicked, but, in the beginning, I couldn't help but feel a pinch of excitement and think, "Incredible! We're experiencing a historic moment, something that future generations will study just as we did with other pandemics." Little did I know how much my life would change in the next few weeks.

Immediately, the hospital where I worked took drastic measures. Four specific departments were set up for infected patients. One of them, the first, was a mobile department in the backyard of the hospital that began to function until the rest of the departments were ready. The intensive care unit (ICU) was renamed "intensive corona care unit," and ICU patients had to be transferred to the coronary care unit. Entire departments joined forces to free up beds and space in order to be able to hospitalize coronavirus patients; furthermore, most surgical departments were forced to reduce their number of beds to allow them to be designated as "corona" departments.

Working hours also changed: eight-hour shifts with a few night shifts scattered per week ceased to exist, and eternal thirty-hour shifts took their place. Eventually, they became twelve hours of work followed twenty-four hours of rest. Most of the elective surgeries were postponed and hospitals focused mainly on urgent procedures only, so most of my work as a vascular surgeon decreased. During this time, I missed surgical procedures greatly and reaffirmed my passion for them.

The country was not far behind with aggressive measures to reduce the number of infections. Shops, beauty salons, entertainment centers, public parks, bars, restaurants and, of course, schools were closed. This meant a drastic change in the style and quality of life in Israel and, particularly, in Tel Aviv, a place that's been referred to as "the city that never sleeps." Here, we're used to spending time outside the house, in the open air. The bars and coffee shops are constantly full, the markets always saturated with people doing their daily shopping, the parks full of families and friends enjoying the weather, the noisy streets full of life at all hours. Suddenly, overnight, the country became a ghost town, and everything got worse when the government decided to enforce a ban restricting residents to within 100 meters from their homes.

Drastic changes occurred during this time. From being a country that lives each day to the fullest and where internet sales were minimal, to a country that depended on them. From being a country of outgoing and warm people who talk to everyone and who get involved in other people's conversations, to becoming a country where people wouldn't even look at each other while crossing the street. The patients stopped going to the emergency room due to fear of infection and, therefore, put their lives in danger. However, people showed their resilience and, little by little, they went back to being more humane.

Life during the pandemic hasn't been easy. I've learned to value spaces, family time, freedom, and the right to live. I learned that, if we detect a pandemic early on, the benefits will outweigh all the time and energy we put into it. Imagine being able to prevent health crises, and not just treat them.

Alberto Saltiel (Continues on page 298)

Luana Sandoval Castillo
(SPAIN, DENMARK)

In mid-March 2020, I decided to separate from my family in order to protect them and I wrote a diary to my girls explaining the situation we were facing. Here's a little piece of it:

The day we separated, we drew a coronavirus on your hands, with the deal that if you managed to wash it off, you'd win a prize at the end of the day. You went straight to the gel and almost made the drawing disappear. Your little faces filled with joy.

- Look mom, it's almost gone!

You walked out the door, not imagining that many days would pass without all of us being together again.

When you were in the car, dad saw that one of you was holding tightly one hand with the other and asked:

– What are you doing?

– I am taking care of Denmark

That's what we were all doing, or at least that's what we were trying to do.

March 12th, 2020. Business shutdown: Mette Frederiksen gave a conference where she explained that, as of the 15th, we had to isolate at home for two weeks. Companies were invited to work from home and announced that, unfortunately, many would lose their jobs. Public transport would be reduced and there would be no schools, childcare would only be available for the children of staff who keep the basic services of society running, i.e.: police, firemen and doctors. Although we met the requirements, we decided that it would be much better not to expose you and to isolate you. In the last few days when we came in from the street, we went straight to bathe, and washed all the clothes we had on and our hands religiously. On the 11th, there was a *forældremøde* (parents' meeting) which was cancelled due to the intervention of some of us who realized the seriousness of the situation and, in addition, in places like the hospital it was forbidden to gather more than 10 people in the same physical space.

On Friday, March 13th, I went to work as I normally did. I was not in contact with patients, but I did spend the day around colleagues. I started sneezing a little, no big deal, but by the afternoon things were going from bad to worse. The next morning and with thermometer in hand, one of the measurements was tinged with yellow: borderline normal, but I clearly had a cold. That day, although without fever, I felt exhausted and spent many hours in bed hoping that it would not get worse.

A few hours later, they announced the closing of the borders, which took effect from March 14th at midnight. Many planes were left without entry or exit and only Danish residents or those with a clear justification to enter Denmark could do so. Many returned, and news reports showed that the government had gone in search of 130 Danes who were stranded in Morocco, an undertaking not implemented by all countries.

I made a video for my family in Mexico so I could explain the situation at home. We never imagined the impact that this and other videos would have. Social media and medical publication sites were blowing up, pharmaceuticals joined in, protocols were implemented. We all shared the same purpose: to find a vaccine.

On Monday, March 16th, I spoke to my boss to explain my symptoms and we decided it was best for me not to go to work. My shift was covered: we were all helping each other out through these tough times. I found it hard to get into a routine without my colleagues; today, I consider all those activities that involve working together a luxury. I looked for excuses to get out of bed, eat and even exercise, but I missed my people, I needed to hug them. I needed the hugs that, in those days, were considered a risk.

On Tuesday the 17th, Queen Margrethe II gave a speech at 8 p.m. where she asked us to be sensible and stay at home, to avoid contagion and take the suggested measures seriously (Https://nyheder.tv2.dk/ samfund/2020-03-17-dronningen-taler-til-nationen-klokken-20). The streets were empty for a few hours but, as the days went by, people started to roam the city again. Who would have thought that, after all, the safest places would not be homes, but outdoor spaces?

You and I invented a lot of different games, danced ballet and the Macarena together, played Elsa healing a little mermaid's injured tail, sang poems and nursery rhymes while daddy tickled you in your side of the screen. I gave it my all to make you feel like I was there. It was very hard being without you.

On March 18th, thanks to the contact from *Doctoras con alas*[7], I received a message from a Mexican journalist, inviting me to be interviewed live on Radio Mexico. I prepared myself, I thought about what I wanted to communicate to my country, I talked about the number of people affected in Denmark, the prevention measures, and current recommendations. I listened in the distance as I was introduced to Carlos Loret de Mola. Those 6 minutes of my life will go down in history. I feel fulfilled with my contributions to the world from home, a home that, without you, is simply empty.

You can listen to the interview here: https://play.wradio.com.mx/audio/111RD010000000095956/

On Thursday the 19th, I received my first visit. Aunt Anita took the risk of coming to greet me and brought me a few essentials to keep me going. We focused on maintaining social distance: we greeted each other with our elbows, I washed the surfaces of what she brought me with bleach and diluted vinegar, and I cleaned the whole house after she left. I don't know if it will seem like an exaggeration, but I washed everything she touched, including towels and handles. Aunt Anita has been a very special part of our lives since before you were born. She

---

[7]   https://www.amazon.com/-/es/Hazel-Ela/dp/8417772642

has taken care of you, changed you, taken you to school and today she offered to take care of you if someday Dad or I couldn't. She left me feeling calm and very grateful.

On March 20th, I started writing this diary trying not to burst into tears. I need you in my life, I long for your laughter in my ears, I miss your touch on my skin. Girls: you can't imagine how much I miss you. Today I talked to *Abu* and *Abue* and they are still in isolation -and they would be for almost 6 months-. Aunt Eme is at home and, although she is feeling fine for the moment, her and your grandparents are not hugging or touching each other, for fear that she might be infected but asymptomatic. They will wait for another 24 hours before they can sit together at the table. She's been working tirelessly from home. I hope she can develop a new routine. In the meantime, Uncle Marquito is still going out for his business. He and aunt Eme have decided that they will not see each other for a while and are thinking about what to do about the wedding. Hopefully, the situation will improve, and we'll be celebrating in 8 months.

On Saturday 21st, after analyzing pros and cons, I was able to visit you. You filled my life with colors and wonderful flavors. We spent a weekend full of dancing, drawing, going for little walks dodging people on the road, but we enjoyed as a family the rays of sunshine that welcome the Danish spring. Today, we slept under the same roof after so long, all four of us, and it was wonderful.

On the 22nd, my heart filled with tears for having to start the logistics of saying goodbye. We enjoyed our time together and, when we were giving thanks for three things that happened in the day one of you said:

- Thank you for letting mom come to see us.

And mom couldn't help (and still can't help) but tear up.

On Monday 23rd, EP was positive for COVID-19, and we agreed that I should take the test as well. I made an appointment and was scheduled an hour later at my hospital, but this time as a patient. It's always strange to arrive at the hospital as a patient, since you go unnoticed for not wearing white, but this time I stood out for wearing a green mask. I went through door 7A, normally enabled for acute patients, and traces of the days left by this pandemic were already visible: a makeshift canopy with chairs distributed at least one meter apart, brave professionals with a stunned look on their faces.

On Tuesday, there was neither a resident nor an attached physician on duty, both were suspected of contagion. Two other colleagues were isolated and the one who was on call that day was waiting to be tested. I worked the shift to fill the gap and, since that gave me two days off, we agreed I'd go visit you.

Two days full of you. I love to kiss your little faces and fell you waking up in my arms. Today I don't care that you get up at night and come looking for me. Today it doesn't matter that you call for me a thousand times and want my full attention, that you want to jump and dance the day away, that you want to sit on my lap for hours even though we haven't yet had breakfast. I miss you and I always want you close but, more importantly, I want you alive and healthy. What's vital is that, when I return from work tomorrow, you are back with your grandparents (*farmor* and *farfar*) so you're safe from me. You've been very brave lending mom to Denmark, but it makes me cry when you tell me:

– Mom, if I die, you can have another baby.

– My loves, you're in good hands. We are all taking care of you.

March 27th. Today was hard. I have seen eyes full of fear, trays of food covered with plastic, positive test results, sick colleagues, fear, pain, tiredness, uncertainty, anger.... and me, I come home to an empty house, and have a shift tomorrow. Extended on-call due to the opening of a new department for cohort isolation. All patients regardless of age, pathology, prognosis, or surgical need are admitted in the same place with colleagues from different specialties. A big part of the staff is sick, and emerging positions have been opened for final year medical students and foreigners (who work for free) and, meanwhile, the temporary canopy set up outside the hospital to receive suspicious patients is still full. Today, I have mixed feelings. Today, the world hurts. I have seen 4 ambulances pass by the window while writing this, and just thinking that tomorrow I have on-call duty makes me dizzy and anxious. I have no words.

Yesterday, March 28th, I worked a shift. 3 out of every 4 patients were tested positive and awaited admission. Two of the three ED units are packed with isolated patients, when only one had been set up for cohort isolation. The new unit has a 95% bed occupancy. Long sessions to discuss the current situation, clinical doubts about treatment, no clear protocols, doubts about isolation and material. Residents and several other staff members were suspected to have COVID-19 as well. The priorities are clear, and patients have been displaced to the last place in this war. It has been mentioned that we should intensively evaluate the need for ventilators, since their price is estimated at 7,000,000 kroner. In my opinion, this should not be a limiting factor, we should simply prioritize the therapeutic effort and individualize each case. These are the kind of things I simply don't understand.

While my people try to appease my heart with FaceTime calls, there are difficult times, decisions based on unclear guidelines and a bombardment of unsubstantiated evidence in the last month that makes us doubt any approach we've taken. Today, they announced that the UK leaders have tested positive.

The closing of the borders is extended to April 13th, but the news expects the peak of the curve to happen around the 19th. When will I see you again?

Dad does what he can to comfort me, but he also wants to give *farmor* and *farfar* some room to breathe. The idea of all of you going to the summer house doesn't quite convince me. I'm afraid of you getting out of Kommune, being even further away from me. I'm terrified they'll even close the borders between regions, but I understand you'll have more space and also need to enjoy a little vacation, even from coronavirus. I have to think about it. I'll sleep on it.

More than a year after I wrote this, we have seen fear, uncertainty, restrictions, distance, fatigue, and death, but it has also shortened distances, exploited the endless information available and, in my case, forged bonds with people who live miles away, both personally and professionally.

Denmark's first vaccination day was December 27th, 2020. It's been offered according to age and risk pathologies. Initially, its main target were people over 18 and later extended to people over 12. Nowadays you can get vaccinated without an appointment. While other countries are struggling with regulations and chaos, Denmark has a *Coronapas*, which is valid either by immunity acquired by vaccine or by contagion, or with a negative test that is valid for up to 96 hours. It's the only option to have some social life. At the moment, some countries are open and there are more tourists. We were able to go to my sister's wedding.

What worries us as of July 2021 are the side effects of each of the vaccines on the population, (some rare diseases secondary to them;

myocarditis and coagulation problems), the delta variant that threatens them despite being vaccinated, an imminent fear of a third wave of contagions, mostly due to the new variants of coronavirus and the re-vaccination that, for the moment, is recommended after 12 months of the last dose. But life goes on and we're here to live it and enjoy it. I sincerely believe that the best thing that this pandemic has left us with is to think about others. To think that there are consequences if you go to work sick, even if it's just a little cold. To think that it's not important that I get vaccinated first or with the "best" vaccine: the goal is to get vaccinated and encourage our neighbors to do so. It's important to think about fragile and at-risk people, but also about their caregivers. We learned to appreciate the importance of a hug and the necessity of a kiss. A year goes by in the blink of an eye, but the lessons this one has taught us are remarkable.

Luana Sandoval Castillo (Continues on page 299)

Ilan Shapiro
(United States)

I must say that, when I read what was going on in China in January 2020, it seemed to me that everything sounded very similar to what I had already experienced in Chicago, in 2009, during the H1N1 virus pandemic.

I had already seen it, lived it and understood the magnitude of the problem coming our way. It was like watching a car accident in slow motion. My first TV report on the subject was broadcast on January 21st and, by February, everything spiraled out of control. Below, I describe what happened and attach a couple of ideas for the future.

In 2009 in Chicago, I saw the evolution of the new H1N1 flu virus and how devastating it was for the community both medically and mentally.

I saw how families, fearing deportation or arrest, did not approach community medical services. That would not have been the case but, at the time, misinformation was spreading through the air.

In 2009, panic, fear and fake news were key to finding a solution: it was necessary to provide clear and reliable information to the community. Among the measures that were carried out, an alliance was created between different public and private actors, so that the message would be constant. Thanks to that, the truths and lies about the disease were clarified, and that experience served as a kind of training for the current COVID-19 pandemic.

Already in 2020, the first thing I felt was that no one had any control whatsoever. In a few days, "normality" was crumbling in front of me. Since February, the negative effects of the virus began to take their toll. The partial closure of activities, borders and even supermarkets was brutal. I still don't understand why toilet paper was suddenly so important, and how it became scarce. To be honest, I bought two industrial rolls myself that are locked "just in case."

Here are some specific areas that had positive and negative changes during the pandemic.

The only constant is change

Family: Unlike 2009, when it was just my wife and I, now there were four of us and the more people the scarier. Based on the experience in Florida, the first thing we did was check that we had the basics, our first-aid kit was complete and that everything was in order. Because we had no information to go on, it was important to make the wisest decisions possible. My wife stopped working and, in the blink of an eye, the children's classes were now online, and our routines, in every aspect, were turned upside down.

Funnily enough, the children adapted faster and much better than us. I openly talked to them about what was going on since the very beginning. I tried to explain the situation and, above all, the actions we were taking to protect ourselves as a family.

Since our family is spread all over the world, it was difficult to give the best advice based on information that was changing almost by the minute. Using technology to communicate with family and friends has been a fascinating experience. The rise of games and applications (some weren't supposed to come out for years) facilitated communication and we got closer, virtually, to convey a feeling of hope.

Partner: The first weeks were very difficult, and we always kept in mind that we had to take care of ourselves. Every time I left the house and kissed my family goodbye, I felt I was going off to war. I began to understand the physical and moral strength soldiers are known for; they have a mission and will sacrifice their own soul to fulfil it. Many times, I promised my wife that everything would be okay, but, secretly, I was filled with uncertainty. Naturally, I took care of myself, and continue to do so. I went to war with my rifle (my knowledge) and my ammunition (mask, antibacterial gel, social distance), while my family stayed at home. For me, the hours turned into weeks, but for them —because of the quarantine— the minutes turned into decades. After acknowledging the obvious —that no one in the world knew anything about this virus— we decided to enjoy our time together as a family, create spaces where we could exercise and, above all, talk a lot to share what we were experiencing. In fact, I had never exercised so much until COVID-19 came to my life.

Work: The first weeks involved drastic changes at work. We could not shake hands like we were used to. Physical contact is important for bonding with colleagues and was now limited to a minimum. But something that fascinated me was that, in that time of crisis, in meetings with my team, we were able to share many personal aspects. I am extremely grateful to them for their leadership and for taking care of the community. I also have to clarify that this would not have been possible without the help of my nuclear reactor aka: my love and partner.

A few tips for the next pandemic

Communicate clearly: This pandemic showed us the importance of communication, of being clear and truthful when exchanging ideas. At first, paternalism prevailed. But trying to hide or tamper with the information only hinders everything, incites fear, creates falsehoods, and shatters the community's trust in the health sector.

When we go through many changes, it's very important to learn to filter the information and convey what's useful at the moment. The changes in these messages have to be clear and must be exposed in a truthful way, so that the community receives them with trust.

Medical practice and balance: The hours turned into months. The pace of life accelerated, traffic and activities increased. In the blink of an eye, all feelings and sensations were amplified again. Being a wellness preacher, I really understood the importance of certain habits that protect us against diseases like COVID-19, but also prevent diabetes, depression, and other problems.

My wife reminded me of the importance of exercising, eating and sleeping well, and taking a few breaks during the week to recharge and keep moving forward. I won't lie, some days the pressure, fear and anguish were horrendous, but for each scar this period left me, I've gained a deeper understanding of how to help, and how I can continue on this path full of adventures, surprises and smiles.

Alongside two of my *compadres,* I created a group to send us jokes via text. So, we all take a moment to vent our frustrations and gather our strengths to continue fighting. We also keep our eyes open to see if a partner is in one of those dark vicious cycles; and thus, be able to cheer them up of at least comfort them so they won't feel alone.

Ilan Shapiro (Continues on page 300)

René Sotelo
(UNITED STATES)

Uncertainty, confusion, fake news due to a lack of knowledge of the real dimensions of the problem, all of it sums up what life has been like during the pandemic. The questions that don't escape my mind, and possibly nobody's, are: how long is this going to last? Will there be a truce between us and this virus that's hit the entire world without mercy or distinction?

Life during this rough time has been about trying to recognize how to deal with a difficult situation over which one has so little control.

Isolation is the other qualifier of the pandemic, not only the physical distancing from our friends and relatives, but also from our role as physicians.

At the beginning, we suspended all hospital operations for a week, isolating ourselves, and then we resumed them, with all that distancing from the patients implies: not being able to hug them or greet them in the way I always do, with affection.

I usually start the consultation by taking off my mask for a few seconds so that the patient can see my face, and then I immediately cover myself. I do this in an attempt not to feel masked, and in my desire to minimize the feeling of distance that I consider particularly unpleasant in the medical field, since I find it to be an activity in which generating closeness is fundamental. To reinforce their peace of mind and confidence regarding biosafety protocols, I confirm that I have washed my hands, in addition to wearing gloves.

On the other hand, the pandemic has meant opening the doors to the latest technological methods and solutions. Telemedicine is here to stay. New ways will have to be explored in which technology will continue to develop its role as a support, even to perform part of the physical examination from a distance, with devices that can record vital signs, heart rate and pulmonary auscultation remotely. A device will be sent to the patient with which these parameters will be taken. This will certainly be a determining factor in this new process that has already taken off.

René Sotelo (Continues on page 301)

Karla Uribe
(UNITED STATES)

It was the last months of 2019 when, for the first time, I heard the name of the virus that was causing an unprecedented situation in the world. At first, I wanted to think that it was a distant and alien situation. I was afraid to think about the future. I was terrified of getting sick and not being there for my children.

2020 started exceptionally well for my family. In January, we took a trip that we enjoyed very much. In February and March, I lived very special moments when we presented the predecessor of this book, *Doctoras con Alas*, first in Los Angeles and then in McAllen. Surrounding myself with this group of brave and courageous women and identifying with their stories had an impact on my life that is hard to describe. Let's just say that I finally found myself in a place where my professional life was once again becoming important.

Spring break was around the corner, so I decided to take a week off from work. I said goodbye to my colleagues the way I always do, with the certainty that we would see each other a few days later. Around that time, we were preparing my son's birthday party, as he was about to turn five. He asked to spend a few days at the beach as a gift, and some of his classmates were also going to come home to sing happy birthday and cut the cake. On the day of his party, the lock-down began and, one by one, the guests started to cancel a couple of hours before. I had a hard time explaining to him that his friends weren't coming. Fortunately, two girls showed up and that was enough to celebrate. The trip to the beach, unfortunately, had to be canceled as well. Even without wanting to accept it, the life we had known up to that moment had changed indefinitely, and we had to face a tremendous challenge as individuals, as a family, and as a society.

A few days later, we received the news that the schools were closed, so I didn't go back to work. My professional life was on pause again. The following nights were difficult, the uncertainty kept me awake and I felt hopeless. Being away from my parents and knowing that they were at risk frightened me. My father is seventy years old, and his commitment to his patients led him to continue working, and for me that was a great cause for concern. Seeing the seriousness of the situation made me feel very helpless. I felt the moral duty of a doctor as a burden, the impulse to go out and see my patients. But the reality was that we depended financially on my husband's job, and we agreed that the children would be safer at home. Once again, my place was at home. My way of contributing as a physician was to sign up for a volunteer network to see uncomplicated coronavirus patients remotely.

We gradually got used to our new lives. Learning to live in isolation has also been a struggle. This mandatory time-out has made me re-evaluate the important things in life. It has made me rearrange my priorities and understand that everything in life is a matter of attitude. If you have a good mindset and look for the positive side of things, any situation is easy to cope with.

During the pandemic, I had the privilege of joining my youngest son in his virtual classes and witnessing the sparkle in his eyes when he learned something new. I got to watch him learn to read, and that memory will live in my heart forever. We just graduated from kindergarten!

The pandemic forced me to do things I wouldn't have tried otherwise. Now, we make our own bread and yogurt at home. After the first month, my son was in dire need of a haircut, so I watched a tutorial on YouTube and, with a pair of Metzenbaum scissors that I have tucked away among my personal treasures, I dared to cut his hair. To be honest, my "hairstylist mode" is on and here to stay.

Now, except for my six-year-old son, all the members of my immediate family, here and in Mexico, are fully vaccinated. I am thankful that, now that the outlook is starting to improve, we are all healthy and not missing anyone.

Karla Uribe (Continues on page 303)

Jeannette Uribe
(UNITED STATES)

It wasn't like watching a movie, but rather like being part of it. We could breathe the fear, the uncertainty, the frustration, the pain of the people. The exhaustion was wearing us down physically and mentally. The pandemic in New York City caught us off guard, and the first few weeks we weren't prepared at all. We didn't have enough masks, gloves, protective clothing. Well, we didn't know what was considered "enough" but, looking back on it, it sounds a bit selfish to complain about lack of equipment knowing what our countrymen in Mexico and other countries suffered and continue to face. We went through too many changes in an incredibly short period of time. We tried to prioritize patient care. We canceled elective surgeries, office visits that were considered non-urgent, and implemented a COVID-19 schedule for residents that consisted of making smaller work teams to keep four residents out of the hospital for a week to reduce exposure. The first week of the pandemic was the worst. I worked most of the time because several of my colleagues were in quarantine, and the few of us who were left were on the verge of collapse. I remember that walking back home required a tremendous effort and it literally hurt to breathe.

The people on the subway had suffering and sorrow written all over their faces. I was starting to feel weaker by the day. However, there were people who took it upon themselves to lift our spirits, to shout or clap from their windows every evening at 7 o'clock. There were people who, with great effort, made donations of all kinds: food, masks, protective equipment, ice cream, posters, drawings, even dermatological products as a token of gratitude.

That's what the pandemic was like for me: I was a first year OB/GYN resident, without my family, not because of COVID-19, but because I had planned it that way. My husband and children were in Michigan, as were my brother, his wife and their children. I remember urging them to prepare and get ready because dark times were coming our way. The next day, the city came to a standstill.

I missed my children and my husband very much. Four months went by before I saw them again. On the other hand, I was sure they'd be better off far away from me. I didn't have to worry about infecting them, or getting groceries for all of us, or figuring out how to manage living locked up in a small place for who knows how long. My kids never worried. They experienced it as an extended vacation.

The pandemic, nonetheless, did leave good things in terms of medical care, allowing us to implement remote medicine, which is still used to this day when feasible. It taught us that, no matter how well developed a country considers itself to be, a pandemic is a pandemic, help is needed at all levels and should be directed to where the virus is headed.

My heart breaks when I think about all the lives lost and the suffering of the people who had to face the disease all alone in a hospital bed. For Mexicans, and perhaps for many other cultures, being surrounded by your loved ones is key to recover from an illness. That was my *abuelita*'s case. She went from agonizing in a hospital bed in Los Angeles to being almost completely recovered at home in Mexico with her family, thanks to the support of Rigo and his wife, her angels fallen from heaven.

Jeannette Uribe (Continues on page 304)

9

My vision for the future

Patricia Bautista Rivera
(**UNITED STATES**)

In my work, phone calls help me keep in touch with the community, allowing me to share prevention and health promotion measures. Furthermore, I've found an excellent way to put into practice and use what I've learned from studying medicine and public health through videos and radio programs. Being able to share information aimed at improving the community's health led me to discover a way of practicing medicine that differs from what I had planned. It's not exactly pediatrics or allergy, but it feeds from what I've learned, which in turn enriches me and challenges me to continue studying and learning: preventive medicine and health promotion.

The community I serve faces many disadvantages and barriers: language barriers, education barrier, culture barriers, resources barriers, and, consequently, health barriers. Although this has been known for a long time, the pandemic has brought to light the tough situation many

LCC families are going through. It's in this organization that I found the place where I can contribute and be of service to the community through my work. We aim to empower people with knowledge and promote access to services to improve their health and prevent disease. At the same time, my work has also allowed me to collaborate and contribute to what other organizations do to improve the disadvantaged conditions described above. I love what I do, and it fills me with deep satisfaction.

I would like a future of greater equity in access to health and education services, better working conditions, and fair wages for all. I believe that would improve the living and health conditions of all populations across the country.

As for myself, I intend to continue learning not only about medicine, but also about communication, to find the best ways to share what I've learned in order to contribute to everyone's health, that is, not only people in the community I serve, but as many communities possible.

One activity that started with the pandemic and that stuck to my routine is to virtually meet with my college friends several times a week to pray. All of them are incredibly successful doctors in each of their fields. We gather to unite in prayer for our families, friends, communities, and the world at large. These meetings have allowed me to confirm the importance of prayer and friendship, and they give me peace. We plan to continue to meet virtually as long as the pandemic continues. Amen, amen, amen, may the whole world stay safe!

I intend to continue to care for my family, the one here and the one in Mexico, supporting and accompanying them in whatever they need however I can. I'll keep growing vegetables and walking or running with my dog. I'd also like to restart the painting classes I began during the pandemic but, due to work, I've had to put aside.

Patricia Bautista Rivera (Continues on page 307)

Edmundo Erazo
(THE NETHERLANDS)

I think the future will be full of innovations in medicine. In my opinion, the profession will face a radical change in aspects such as the doctor-patient relationship, telemedicine, and the gathering of health data.

Collecting the data will potentially benefit the personalization of medicine. Still, it will also be a challenge that said data doesn't become the final product but improves medical care.

I want to believe that the future will bring positive changes; human beings constantly evolve in the face of the worst adversities. However, it's important to remember that many people will turn to their worst instincts when faced with frustration and complex situations such as discrimination and intolerance. Nonetheless, if we've learned something from history, it's that union, education, and the search for goodwill lead to a higher quality of life for all.

Edmundo Erazo (Continues on page 308)

Sandra López-León
(ISRAEL, THE NETHERLANDS, SPAIN, UNITED STATES)

In order to feel good and happy, I have learned that every day I must nurture my family, my intellect, my emotions, and my body. My vision for the future is to continue enjoying all of this and the new things that I will encounter along the way. I hope to enjoy good health and a long life.

Intellectually, I need to learn, do research, and teach. Emotionally, I need nature, good music, art, literature, and love. I also continue to write poetry, but that's not a goal or a project, it's a necessity. The urge to write comes at the most unexpected moment and, when inspiration strikes, I must stop everything and write. I feel good when I sleep 8 hours, exercise, and eat well. I really enjoy a good lunch or dinner along with a glass of red wine and a good conversation. Body-wise, my goal is to balance cardio, endurance, and flexibility exercise, eat right, and sleep well. One thing I love to do is travel, especially with my family. I am always planning a trip. I thoroughly relish planning and then traveling. Almost every time I come back from a trip, I start thinking about the next one.

As for my family, they are my number one priority. Daily, I show my husband how much I love him, allowing our relationship to grow even more; I want to give my children the necessary tools to be happy and fulfilled, I want them to learn to manage their emotions and teach them to nurture their spirit, their minds, their curiosity. I want them to learn to care for and listen to their bodies, to fly, to live, and to be as happy as they can be.

We must always have short-, medium-, and long-term goals. These goals are what keep us enthusiastic, excited, vital, fulfilled, and happy. Short-term goals are set at the beginning of the day, and you mustn't go to sleep until you finish them. As for my long-term goals, I don't like to talk about them until I've made them happen. I can tell you that my biggest goals have nothing to do with material possessions. They relate to my own achievements: always having slept eight hours a day, including when I was studying medicine and when my children were babies; being a mother of three, having a Ph.D., having lived in five countries, playing the piano, learning English and Dutch, and knowing a little Hebrew and Catalan; having written scientific articles, and having run the New York marathon.

We must keep in mind that goals are not desires. Fantasies and desires are what make us set goals for ourselves. Goals are what we work every day to achieve. We must always have pleasures that are not destructive and goals that fill us with long-term happiness. What we do now, day by day, reflects our happiness and satisfaction in the future. We must not let life carry us or take control of our destiny. We build our daily lives; we are the ones who craft our future. We must live in a way that, when death comes to take us, we can say that we gave everything and experienced it all.

Sandra López-León (Continues on page 309)

Rafael G. Magaña
(ENGLAND, UNITED STATES)

Amidst all these changes, remaining optimistic has been a challenge. But my philosophy is that, without adversity, there's no growth, and I like to think that the degree of difficulty is proportional to personal and professional development. The point is to visualize that success and not deviate from the path that'll lead you there. That's easier said than done but, for me, there's no alternative.

The pandemic began and, pertinently, healthcare centers suspended all non-emergency surgeries. That was terrible news for everyone, but especially for those of us who are in private practice, which had to close.

Unexpectedly, the health and safety of my family, as well as my practice, were in serious jeopardy. All this was accompanied by a general feeling of existential anguish, and great irritation to know there was no political leadership in the country to deal with the problem.

During these confusing and uncertain times, things happened that were completely unexpected and very welcome. Let me explain: when the pandemic started and I could no longer perform elective surgeries, I began taking all the plastic surgery trauma shifts I could in all the hospitals available.

I was constantly treating ER patients, which helped me a lot, because it kept me busy, involved with medicine, and seeing patients at the office. However, after a month and a half, when hospitals restarted elective surgeries, something completely unexpected happened: the office was filled with patients seeking cosmetic plastic surgery.

To this day, I still don't understand how the pandemic acted as a stimulus for patients to undergo a surgery so widely regarded as vain. I have several theories about it but, in the end, this allowed me to keep my practice afloat and growing.

I feel lucky, because many of the plastic surgery offices in New York just didn't make it. Thanks to that unexpected wave of patients, I am now cautiously expanding the practice because I know that 2021 will be difficult for the type of surgery that I offer. Nonetheless, unlike many other surgeons who only focus on cosmetic surgery, I never stopped seeing emergency patients for reconstructive surgery. I hope the economy allows my practice to continue growing.

As always, I keep moving forward, but now more than ever with a cautious optimism.

Rafael G. Magaña (Continues on page 311)

Nissin Nahmias
(United States)

Someday, I hope to see a friendlier, more harmonious world. In the nearby future, I see myself developing my academic work alongside the medical schools for which I direct the cycles of third-year students; I even consider teaching first- and second-years. I would like the bariatric surgery program to grow to the extent that I can work with two more partners.

I'm interested in taking a graduate degree in management or focused on minority leadership and healthcare equity. Eventually, I'd like to become head of the department of surgery and then take up an administrative position at the university. That would allow me to help a greater number of doctors in training, influence them, and put them on the right track. Another of my dreams is to create a scholarship to help underprivileged medical students (like I was) to do residency programs abroad and, thus, begin a new chapter in their lives. When it comes to my family, I see myself enjoying a beautiful relationship with my children and their families and spending more time with my grandchildren and my partner.

I've learned to live life intensely. I hope that, in the future, I can continue loving my fellow man, and enjoying my hobbies: playing the guitar, and riding motorcycles and bikes.

Nissin Nahmias (Continues on page 314)

Susana Ramírez Romero
(Spain)

Currently, my children are in elementary school. They are now more independent: they bathe themselves, brush their teeth, tie their shoelaces, know how to use a knife and fork. They don't wake up at night, or if they do, it's a rare occurrence. Not having to dress them or lull them to sleep at night has added a few hours to my day.

After so much hustle and bustle between adaptation, formalities, and paperwork, I suddenly find that I can sit down for a cup of coffee without interruptions; I can dedicate myself to writing a chapter of this book at some point in the evening without having a baby latched to my breast or snuggled in my arms. I enjoy these moments, just as I intensely enjoyed their baby stage to the point of exhaustion.

Ten years after arriving in this country, I look at my life and find myself a transformed woman, evolved by the clash of cultures, changed by motherhood, accustomed to living seasonally, and strengthened by all the experiences that have led me here.

I find myself in what's commonly known as the "mid-life crisis." It's said that this crisis can be caused by the worry of not having achieved certain goals or the thought that we are running out of time to fulfill our dreams. At this moment, with my wrinkles and my first gray hairs, I'm taking the time again to look to the future and set new goals. Brand-new projects on a professional level, on a family level and, most importantly, on a personal level. When children are young, they're your main concern; you must keep them alive, healthy, and happy. That means spending twenty-four hours a day with them. Even when you're at work, your thoughts are with them. If you go to the supermarket, shopping and food preparation are based on their tastes. When you manage money at home, they're your priority.

Now I realize that, every year, I will have more and more time for myself, and I can plan what to do with it, like when I was a teenager, only now I make a list of what I have already accomplished and another one of what I still want to achieve. To this last list, I add new things I never thought of in my twenties, while eliminating projects I didn't meet, but that I don't need any more. I started by buying a reflex camera; I felt it went well with this particular stage of my life. With photography, I'll learn to look with other lenses; to use new filters. I'll elaborate new compositions taking advantage of the temperatures and the different types of light. On a professional level, this year I will finish a master's degree that will allow me to charge more fairly for my work. In the near future, I want to improve my English and my French.

When it comes to my health, I want to continue to exercise in a more organized way. Since 2012, I have not stopped running. In 2018 and 2019, I participated in triathlons and the Boston Half Marathon is my next one. At the beginning, exercise was just fun, a time with myself; now, it's my way to meditate and to age healthily.

Later on, I'd like to take up my teenage dream of doing missionary work, maybe in Africa or in refugee camps, but I want to commit to it and do it wholeheartedly. Perhaps in a couple of years I'll seriously consider making that happen.

My purpose is also to continue the education and adaptation of my children to this ever-changing world. Motivating them to strive, to be constant, to be strong without losing tenderness; to be accepting and compassionate with others. To be brave, but also know how to cry and ask for help when they need it. To be happy with little.

Susana Ramírez Romero (Continues on page 316)

Luis Rodrigo Reynoso

(Ethiopia)

My medical practice in Ethiopia was conducted in an organized manner. I worked Monday through Friday from eight in the morning to eight at night, and until noon on Saturdays. On days dedicated to surgery, I performed between six or eight surgical procedures, and in the office, I saw up to 45 patients a day. Every day I took more control of the place: I oversaw the progress of the patients, of discharging them, of giving them pre and postoperative instructions. My knowledge of the language improved thanks to the six hours of class that my wife and I took with an Ethiopian soap opera actor. In the country there are still no structured courses to learn Amharic. A book that tries to explain grammar has just been published, but the literature on the subject is scarce; there are no dictionaries and therefore I have had to build my own. If something distinguishes me, it is my taste for languages and my passion for learning something new. I always try to break the ice and talk to my patients: "Tinish hamam, tinish yakatela" (it will burn a little, it will hurt a little); and they are surprised to hear a white man speak to them in their language.

I find it amazing to see how, for many of them, receiving an injection represents the greatest trauma, even as 45-year-old adults. They scream, cry and howl, since in most cases they had never received an injection. It has been difficult for me to assimilate it, but that has spiced my days.

And so, among these daily challenges, new cases of both reconstructive plastic surgery and aesthetic plastic surgery began to arrive. Evading government filters, I opened a profile on social networks, to make myself known in a city of three and a half million inhabitants: "There is a white man who does cosmetic surgeries in Adís." I also took advantage of the trips that my patients made abroad to order the necessary supplies from them: sutures, bandages, girdles, syringes, needles, medicines and even Botox, facial fillers, and implants.

That is right, implants ... Who would want to have implants in Ethiopia? In Ethiopia there are three socioeconomic classes: poor, rich, and diplomatsic. And the rich and diplomats might be interested. In a short time, I had two Ethiopian actresses interested in having a breast augmentation; and in less time than you might imagine, I was already putting Botox and fillers in diplomatic houses.

But not everything was honey on flakes, nor did everything flow perfectly. And understanding the language began to have consequences. One day I heard in the waiting room of the clinic: "I don't want the white man to touch me", "I want another doctor to treat me." Holy molly! I could not believe it ... Thus, little by little, I opened my eyes to another reality, one that I did not imagine.

Suddenly I began to notice other situations. I began to realize that the reconstructive surgeries that I did out of love and on a voluntary basis, actually did get charged. And that the director justified those payments as "recovery fees." I started to crunch the numbers and I could see that I was generating between two and five thousand dollars a day. Then I understood the reason for those delicious macchiatos that the director offered me before asking me: "Doctor, can you see a couple more patients?"

I had taken over the reins of the clinics, and the director now arrived at eleven in the morning and was busy painting and writing a book that he had not had time for before. Holy molly!

And that is when I finally realize it! So, I started to wonder: "Who am I? Where am I? Where am I going and what am I doing to achieve it?"

For her part, Anahí found me fatigued. Tiredness did not allow me to share with her details about the patients, and to that was added that I felt that my good intentions were becoming a gold mine for the director. He was frustrating my dream!

What was the cherry on top of the cake? I had two breast augmentation surgeries scheduled but had decided to take the days leading up to celebrate my wife's birthday with a Hakuna Matata-style surprise: a five-day safari to the Masai Mara reserve. When I returned 24 hours earlier than planned, I went to the clinic, and my surprise was greater when I found one of those two patients, in the post-surgical recovery area. She was very sore and distressed, and while I was examining her, I realized that the result was not related either anatomically or aesthetically: one breast pointed to Egypt and the other to South Sudan. Visibly worried, she asked me, "This is normal, doctor." I limited myself to answering him that I had not had the opportunity to be in his surgery, but that I would speak with the doctor in charge to see what had happened, and that it was still too early to judge the result.

But inside me, I felt like I was exploding. I could not believe what was happening. Why did he do it? He did not know how to place breast implants! He had even asked me to teach him. And when I questioned him about the result and the poor handling of the tissues (he mistakenly placed one implant below the mammary gland and the other below the muscle), he only replied: Well, I saw a video on YouTube. We are surgeons and we know anatomy. I really think you did not choose the implants well.

I was furious, I had to fight to control myself. I scheduled the second patient and asked the director to allow me to show him how I place the implants, and then he could decide for himself if he wanted to continue using his technique.

At the same time, I started looking for other opportunities. Offers began to come in from national and foreign investors who were planning to build a private hospital, and they wanted me to take care of the surgical area. Can you believe it? In a country with 109 million inhabitants, I would be the only doctor with surgical training in the aesthetic and reconstructive area. They promised a lot of money and I am sure I could have become a millionaire. But that was not my goal. In addition, my wife and I did not believe that there we could have the necessary conditions to start a family.

And then, after several conversations, we decided to undertake a long journey through the north of Ethiopia, to decide the next step in our lives. We weighed several things, including the warnings of an ambassador friend who alerted us of the legal implications that could present in the event of a complaint by an Ethiopian citizen. Unfortunately, in Ethiopia the issue of human rights is deficient, and there are macabre stories of missing persons.

Luis Rodrigo Reynoso (Continues on page 316)

Alejandra Rodríguez Romero
(United States)

What I want most, my short-, medium- and long-term goal, is to be able to see my son Jeffrey survive cancer. I have this vision and I hold on to it: that the cancer will not come back, and that I'll be able to see him healthy and happy for the rest of my life. In the future, I see myself healthy, fulfilled, content, nourishing my body, mind, and soul with positive things and people. I visualize myself teaching my children to be honest and generous, and providing them with a warm and loving home. I encourage them to take care of themselves first so they can love others, to live in the here and now, to enjoy every day, because time flies.

When my children are a little more independent and the time is right, I will focus on resuming my professional life. This goal is not very well defined at the moment, but what's clear to me is that it will be focused on healthcare, the field I'm most passionate about. In the future, I would like to get involved in charity and volunteer activities. I will join an organization where I can travel and, at the same time, provide my medical or humanitarian services to communities in need. There are still many goals to accomplish and many roads to take. I don't know what tomorrow will bring, but what I am sure of is that I am no longer afraid of change, and I will welcome whatever comes my way with open arms.

Alejandra Rodríguez Romero (Continues on page 319)

Jack Rubinstein
(United States)

> "We cannot predict the future, but we can invent it."
> —Nigel Calder

On November 8, 2016, India's prime minister surprisingly scrapped all 500- and 1,000-rupee notes in the country. Over the next few days, dozens of people died, thousands of businesses closed, and hundreds of millions of people had their lives disrupted. Behind the decision was a man named Anil Bokil, who conceived the idea in the late 1990s as a way to end his country's corruption. In an interview, Bokil described the instant he came up with the whole idea as a moment of divine inspiration. With the clarity and determination of a prophet fully convinced of his message, he devoted years of his life to developing the project until he finally got a nine-minute audience (which turned into a two-hour conversation) with the future prime minister. A few months later, his plan was implemented, and its repercussions resonate to this very day.

Not everyone succeeds in fixing current problems or seeks divine inspiration to do so. Many find their purpose through everyday actions, caring for their patients, their children, their pets, and creating a better future one day at a time. Those who find inspiration —or are found by it— describe that instant as a kind of divine enlightenment that elevates and guides them, but sooner or later it becomes a burden they need to shake off. The feeling is understandable and frustrating. In the biographies of scientists, there is no shortage of moments of ridicule at the hands of peers or disbelief from superiors. These patterns are so typical and common that they have even been described by philosopher Thomas Kuhn (originally from Cincinnati!) in his little book *The Structure of Scientific Revolutions*. I first read it in high school, and over the years, I've seen first in biographies of others and now in my own life, how difficult it can be to change a paradigm, be it political, religious, scientific, or medical.

Note that the paradigm shifts are not necessarily positive, on occasions they are frankly negative and more likely they have mixed repercussions (as in the case about India); but I believe the words of Martin Luther King (adopted from Theodore Parker) hold true: "The arc of the moral universe is long, but it bends toward justice." As long as we continue to work towards improving our lot in life, overcoming obstacles and staying focused on our goals I believe that the positive repercussions will usually outweigh the negatives.

Jack Rubinstein (Continues on page 321)

Alberto Saltiel

(Israel)

Since we were little, we've been asked where we see ourselves in the future. Although in elementary, middle, and high school the answer was always the same, today I find myself in that place I longed to be for years. Sure, there have been significant changes, particularly when it comes to the location, but, at the end of the road, the goal is the same. Today, talking about my vision for the future involves short-, medium-, and long-term projects.

In the immediate future, I see myself finishing my residency and becoming a vascular surgery specialist. Since I'm currently in the last year of a long residency working as chief resident, I'm planning ahead now more than ever. I want to apply for a fellowship in complex aortic surgery, which probably won't take place in Israel. Finishing these chapters, and with a future relocation already in mind, I sit down to analyze everything I've written and, with a smile on my face, I'm excited about what's to come. I know it won't be easy; there will be multiple challenges, difficulties, bureaucracy, achievements, and failures, but it will be a very interesting and rewarding path to travel.

In the medium term, I see myself living outside of Israel, possibly in the United States, Canada or even Mexico. I see myself working as a specialist, growing, and learning day by day. I think I'll remember the process of emigrating to Israel, and subsequently to the place where I'll reside, as the best decisions I've ever made. I see myself enjoying my family, becoming a better person alongside my children and my wife, enjoying our achievements, and celebrating our failures. I look back and remember what we went through and the changes during the

COVID-19 pandemic and I'm certain we can do everything we set our minds to.

Professionally, I'm excited to see the changes that will take place in medicine, and in vascular surgery in particular. I want to witness the implementation of new technologies and the modification of surgical and endovascular techniques for the benefit of patients.

My big dream for the future is being able to look back on my life, 30 or 40 years from now, and say that I achieved everything I set out to do, and that I'm where I wanted to be. I hope to grow both personally and professionally, to be recognized for my work and my personality, make my family proud and be admired by my children. I want to be able to say that I enjoyed every moment of the journey and that each stage taught me something I'll take with me forever.

The future is uncertain and much of it does not depend on us, but our job is to get to where we want. We must fight for our goals and aim for the stars. Thus, tomorrow, wherever I may be, I'll be exactly where I'm supposed to, because the right choices led me there.

Alberto Saltiel (Continues on page 322)

Luana Sandoval Castillo
(SPAIN, DENMARK)

It's a bit trivial to write about the future at a time when I have just experienced an unexpected loss, to see unfairly how life takes surprising turns. I think we should concentrate on the present, enjoy the good and the bad, fully experience what makes our life worthwhile.

I wish I could go back to my Mexico, but we are still thinking if that's a wise decision. Today, I am happy with what I am and what I do. I want to continue doing it and leave a little piece of me in this world and in my family's hearts.

Luana Sandoval Castillo (Continues on page 324)

Ilan Shapiro
(United States)

This chapter excites me. I believe that, without a compass, you cannot move forward. Here's my vision for the future:

Family must be considered before taking any decision, and every step we take must never hinder the quality time we spend with them. I've seen great people who have many family problems, so I try to provide my family and friends with a solid foundation so they can continue enjoying life and reach their goal of (metaphorically) retiring to Fiji.

Let me tell you the course I think my professional life will follow from now on. In recent years, I changed my focus: I left behind the idea of being the director-general of the WHO, and now I aspire to have a positive and real impact on people's lives. My current goal is to start an NGO, foundation or socially responsible company that will generate the necessary resources to support health projects for immigrants.

Another area I find fascinating, and I'd love to know more about is media. Reaching millions of people, thanks to traditional and now digital media, creates monumental opportunities to talk about health-related issues.

At first, I didn't know how I'd change the world by just helping 20 patients a day. But now, thanks to the media, I can answer the questions and address the concerns of millions of people in a matter of minutes.

I always say that my work, whether in an NGO, in medical practice or in the media, sort of resembles a waiter's. I provide a service; I show the menu so people can choose their own meal. That way, I can highlight the specials of the day and know if the "diner" has any allergies or preferences; that's why I'm their waiter. I have had great teachers and tutors who have opened doors for me and hundreds of reporters, producers and directors who gave me the opportunity to share my concerns, passions, and fears.

Among my goals, there's always the desire and wish for balance. For me, the best-case scenario is doing what I love without neglecting my family. And I believe that overseeing an NGO or a foundation would give me the possibility both of bringing health services to those in need, and of spending quality time with my family. That's my dream and I work for it every day. Ultimately, as the Dalai Lama puts it: "happiness is temporary, but joy is everlasting."

Ilan Shapiro (Continues on page 325)

René Sotelo
(United States)

What's clear for me, among my purposes for the future, is to continue focusing on education. That's a goal I strive to achieve: to continue to spread knowledge in Latin America, and in Spanish. Throughout all these years, I've trained 81 fellows from 17 countries, most of them from Latin America. I firmly believe that the opportunity for progress we have as Latin Americans should have study and work as its foundation, as well as dedication to increasing experience, academia, and knowledge. There's a lot of medical talent in our towns and villages and capitalizing on it will not only guarantee health in our societies but will also give us the tools to move forward.

For this to be possible, my efforts must also go hand in hand with the consolidation of my personal brand, through which I manage to project not only my essence, who I am, but also to generate awareness and shine a light on a purpose that must be widely shared to ensure that it reaches everyone effectively.

On this path, moving forward with discipline and taking care of my health through physical activity, proper nutrition, and strengthening my positive thoughts is essential. That's also something I focus on, so it goes hand in hand with my work. Mainly to advance successfully in this stage in which I estimate I still have about fifteen years of surgical activity, as it would already be the third stage of my professional life.

This chapter is an interesting one, as it's full of experiences to share. Added to this is the advantage provided by the robotic platform, which allows for the prolongation of the surgical activity, since you can work while sitting down. The handling of the robot's arms guarantees the firmness of your own hands; the three-dimensional, magnified vision, typical of the technology of the robot's lenses, supports and reinforces that of the physician, so I'm sure I still have some entertaining years ahead of me.

And that's without taking into account my plans for retirement. It's something to think about responsibly, not only in terms of the physical activity that will occupy me, but also financially. I have seen how many professionals don't prepare for the non-productive stage, and that's something we should all keep an eye on. The difficult situation in

Venezuela produced an important imbalance in my personal finances, and it's something that, little by little, I've been trying to get back on track.

I also plan to do an MBA in Health. I want to deepen my knowledge in administration and planning of health services, which, linked to my experience in the medical direction of the international department of USC, will be another way to continue supporting and guiding the patient towards adequate care.

Developing hotel services oriented to the care and recovery of patients is another idea that will occupy my life once I finish my stage as a surgeon. This, without a doubt, is something that I'll take on in the future, and that's tied to my current home in Margarita, #PiedrasBlancas, and the rehabilitation wing of the medical institute (#HospedajeClínico) that I started in Caracas. That's something that I'll continue to develop and in which my medical experience will be essential to make a difference.

René Sotelo (Continues on page 326)

Karla Uribe
(United States)

When I was a kid and I fantasized about the future, I always dreamed of being a doctor. I imagined myself in an office with big windows and lots of patients in the waiting room. Unlike other girls my age, I never dreamed of my wedding day, nor did I ever think of having a family. Over the years and since I left Mexico, I've had a hard time reinventing myself and finding myself in this new reality that, although it was not in my plans, has given me the happiest moments of my life. I have been trying for many years to go back to work, but when the time comes to take the last step and leave my children in the care of someone else,

I have not been able to do it. Perhaps that's why I've been having such a hard time writing this chapter. I've been learning to let go of the frustration that arises when things don't go according to plan, to enjoy and be grateful for every moment in the company of my family, to live in the present. I never want to lose the desire to move forward. I wish to continue learning. Above all else, I wish for health and inner peace. Professional development will come when I am ready.

Karla Uribe (Continues on page 329)

Jeannette Uribe
(United States)

After what we experienced in 2020, it's not easy to have an idea of what the future will hold. As the saying goes: Man proposes, but God disposes.

My family and I have one goal: to be happy. As simple as that. As parents, we strive for our children to be two things: kind and grateful. Higher education in this country is very expensive and, unfortunately, so are extracurricular activities. Our goal is for them to have the opportunity to develop their full potential without being limited financially but, at the same time, to realize that, for that to work, everyone has to chip in. My oldest son is eight years old, and he knows that, for him to be financially independent in the future, he needs to save a certain percentage of the money that comes into his hands in the present. He doesn't get much money, but the idea is that he learns things that are not necessarily taught at school.

I want to be a good wife and friend to my husband, who has been by my side during these sixteen years of marriage. His support and understanding during my days, weeks, months, and years of absence have been invaluable. For the way he loves and cares not only for me, but for our children, a monument should be erected in his honor.

My goal as a professional is to finish my residency and learn as much as I can. I want to learn something new every single day. I do not rule out the possibility of doing a subspecialty in minimally invasive robotic surgery but, right now, I want to spend as much time with my family as possible, and a specialty involves working and striving for years to be accepted into a program. Once I finish my residency, I have the possibility to choose any place to work. We haven't really decided our next destination but, as a typical Mexican family, we tend to return to our roots. My husband will have other suggestions, but, as soon as we make up our minds, we'll pack our bags and set course for another adventure.

Jeannette Uribe (Continues on page 330)

10

Advice to my younger self

Patricia Bautista Rivera

(**UNITED STATES**)

Staring at the title of this chapter, the image of my younger self that comes to mind is that of the hurried, giddy medical student, overwhelmed by the immensity of information she had to review, read, process, and learn. I imagine her, as well, burdened by heartaches of her own making that, looking back, could've been avoided. To that younger self, I'd say:

"My dear: persevere, don't lose your calm and hope. Persevere! In the end, after any storm comes the calm. Even if things don't seem to be going the way you have dreamed and planned for so long, it's important that you learn that, although it doesn't seem like it right now, you'll get there; you'll arrive where you belong. Keep working hard, don't give up, don't get distracted. But don't stop enjoying every day either. Listen to music. Dance.

Learn, learn, learn, and learn as much as you can! Read; read as you always have and more. Read everything: history, geography, philosophy,

307

a novel... everything! Enjoy and be grateful for learning to be a doctor and be present in every moment. Take advantage of each and every lesson that comes your way. Be attentive to the people around you and listen to them. Always express your gratitude. Tell your mom and siblings that you love them, with words and actions.

Study English, be persistent and constant in it, even if it's complicated or you don't have the time. English will make things easier for you in the future. Exercise, and enjoy it.

Treasure and be grateful for each day. Start by being grateful for the miracle of living one more day. Fill yourself with optimism. You are on the right track, keep it up..."

Edmundo Erazo

(THE NETHERLANDS)

Who wouldn't want to warn a younger version of themselves how to avoid every mistake and achieve great success? However, I once heard a colleague say, "An expert in a subject is someone who's made all the possible mistakes in that subject but remembers and learns from each one of them."

To my younger self, I'd advise the following:
–Be less afraid of making mistakes.
–Never underestimate new options on how to get to your true vocation and your true professional calling.
–Look for more challenges no matter what people say.
–Believe more in yourself.
Learn to be more patient and enjoy it even if the road is long.
–Remember, "Don't swim against the current; let it carry you."

Sandra López-León

(ISRAEL, THE NETHERLANDS, SPAIN, UNITED STATES)

Here are some useful tips that have helped me in life, which I would like to pass on to my children, grandchildren, great-grandchildren, and anyone who wants to hear them.

Other countries or cultures
- Travel.
- Move to another country, even if it's only for a few months.
- Learn to fly far away, knowing that you will have to land eventually.
- Surround yourself with interesting, creative, intelligent, and good people.
- Enjoy and appreciate your friends, your family and, above all, life.
- Be flexible and adapt, don't expect others to change for you.

Education
- Turn your defeats and failures into successes.
- Never stop growing, studying, and learning.
- Everything can be interesting if you take the time to understand it.
- Love what you do.
- Devote yourself to something you can work on in times of war or pandemic.

Love

- Love is the strongest energy and guidance there is. Use love as your engine to create, to grow, and to feel.
- Love is neither created nor destroyed, only transformed.
- Choose your partner with your neurons, heart, and hormones.

- Always have family as your top priority.
- Keep your family close, they're there to share the good and difficult things in life.

Health

- Have a balanced, connected, and healthy body, spiritually and intellectually.
- Sleep 8 hours a day, because if you do not sleep well, genes for diseases (organic and mental) to which you are predisposed are activated.
- Exercise (cardiovascular, weights and flexibility).
- Eat healthy, varied, and include fruit and vegetables of all colors of the rainbow every single day.
- Prevention is the best way to avoid suffering.
- Connect with your unconscious and your emotions, that's where the answers are.
- Health and life are the most sacred of treasures.

In general

- Finish the things you must do first, then the things you want to do. You will enjoy them more.
- Responsibility equals freedom.
- Before you do anything or say anything, think about whether it is constructive. If it is destructive, don't do it. Whatever you destroy, destroys you in return.
- Finish everything you start.
- To choose is to renounce, analyze well what you are willing to give up.
- Live intensely.
- Everything in moderation.
- Know yourself. Learn to identify what makes you feel good, at peace and happy.

- Do what you love and surround yourself with people you love.
- When the world seems to crumble around you, surround yourself with people who support you.
- Support the world.
- Write a book.

Rafael G. Magaña

(ENGLAND, UNITED STATES)

Everything I wrote in this chapter has no particular order. Fair warning: this is just me brainstorming ideas, so bear with me.

Start

The word *procrastination* comes to my mind a lot, because I think it's been one of my biggest obstacles. One of my main disadvantages is that I spent more time planning than doing.

Starting a project, task, or challenge right away would've given me a huge advantage. Planning is a good thing but getting started is just as important. It's like going to the gym: if you think about it too much, you end up staying home.

In retrospect, many of the tasks, paperwork, or challenges were so overwhelming that, metaphorically speaking, I was paralyzed, instead of taking advantage of every moment.

Have courage (yes, courage)

I once saw a YouTube video about art. In it, it was said that, for an artist, it's important to practice but, regardless of the final product, what's essential is finishing the project. I left so many things unfinished.

This reflection leads me to the advice I mentioned above: planning and getting started is wonderful, but finishing is key. Over the years, I remember enthusiastically starting many important projects, I could picture them clearly, but I didn't always see them through.

Whenever you read a tale or a novel, there is a preface, a beginning, the story unfolds, and then there's a climax and an end. A surgery also has several stages: you plan it, make the incision, do what you must, stitch it up, bandage it, and start postoperative care. There are really no other options; a surgery must be carried out religiously from start to finish, and as much as I had the discipline to do so, I couldn't apply that ability to other areas of my life.

My projects had stages as well. I started out very inspired; the beginning of the process was simple, the topic was interesting, and I felt motivated, but many times I didn't finish because I ran out of inspiration. You need to have grit, courage to complete these endeavors.

If I had more courage to carry out parallel projects such as publishing more articles, being part of more professional associations for academic purposes, advocacy associations for patients or minorities, etc., that would've enriched my professional and personal development.

However, even though I procrastinated, I did have other qualities that allowed me to move forward, such as tenacity. Thanks to that, I was able to meet other goals that allowed me to make progress and achieve some of the things that I'm proud of today.

Visualize

When I decided to go to medical school, I still had the dilemma of whether I should dedicate myself to the special effects industry, or if I should study something else. So, I promised myself that, if I could not pursue plastic surgery, I would drop out and seek a career that would make me feel fulfilled in the artistic scene. Over time, I matured and realized it would've been a personal mistake not to pursue a profession I now love so much. That leads me to give you another piece of advice: visualize. When I was about to finish high school, I didn't know anything about life, so I made a list of the goals I wanted to achieve. I must've been around 16 or 17 years old. I'm going to share it here. Please don't laugh, okay? This stays between you and me.

- Finish high school.
- Go to Hollywood and do special effects for well-known studios.
- Become a plastic surgeon in NYC.
- Make a movie and win an Oscar (or several).
- Invent and patent something and earn a billion dollars for it.
- Do all of the above before turning 40.

Yeah… that wasn't the case.

Of course, to this day that list still amuses me. But that was my plan, and I envisioned it with absolute clarity. It inspired me and, as you can see, my imagination had no limits.

The advice I would give myself in this circumstance is not to change plans, but to stick to them. I say this because, obviously, by not completing the list as I had imagined it, I did not have a plan B. I thought that, when I finished my studies, I would just open my office on Park Avenue, it would be packed with patients, and I would be famous.

Well, things don't happen that way; they require a vision that goes hand in hand with a plan, and to get to a successful private practice, I had to walk a difficult and tortuous road.

There are many tips that I'd give to my teenage self, my medical student self, or my resident, fellow, and specialist self, but out of all of them, the most valuable is not to stop visualizing the goal, even if it changes, and to set up a plan and a strategy to get there.

The good news is that, during this pandemic and subsequent lockdown, I've been forced to change my strategy and, to do that, at least in my case, I had to visualize what I wanted. And so, it was during this pandemic that my current strategy came to life.

Consistency

Right now, I have a different, less ambitious list, but I think it's more realistic. My last advice encompasses the others and makes them more valuable because it requires their simultaneous and continuous use: consistency.

To be consistent, you need to be constant in the pursuit of what you want and how you'll achieve it, and that's only possible through habits.

These are the tips I'd give to my younger self. If there were more, knowing me, I probably wouldn't have read them all.

Nissin Nahmias
(UNITED STATES)

Whenever I think of my younger self, there are many things that I'd love to tell him; so much advice, so many tips ...

I think that, currently, my life is very interesting: I live in another country and I'm fortunate to do new things every day. I think that, if I could talk to a younger version of myself, I'd first tell him that everything happens for a reason, that there's no sweetness without bitterness, that success depends on defeats.

I'd tell myself not to be afraid to dream and aspire to the highest, because everything is possible, and I shouldn't doubt that. Sometimes, life's opportunities only come when you're ready to receive them and the only constant in this continuous coming and going of people and things, is myself. I would say, "This is your life. You deserve it; it belongs to you, and you're its center, so love yourself more and spend time with yourself. Focus on one thing at a time: when you try to achieve many things at the same time, you're inevitably going to fail at some of them. Do not get distracted from your goals, complete them, and then move on. Remember, one thing at a time."

A few more things I would also say, would be, "If you want to make God laugh, tell him about your plans. It's important to plan, but you must realize that your plans will change as time goes by, and nothing will turn out exactly as you planned, so there's no point in stressing about it."

"Trust yourself and your instincts. Don't be afraid to be happy; it's not a crime. In fact, you deserve it."

"Your dreams will come true. Invest your time wisely in the people who deserve it."

"Don't take everything so seriously; don't get angry, because investing time and energy in negative emotions is unproductive and exhausting. Remember: it's okay to make mistakes once in a while, and it's also okay to forgive yourself and others."

"This life is precious, and the only non-renewable resource is time. Time never comes back; use it wisely, dear young man."

Susana Ramírez Romero
(SPAIN)

Here's a piece of advice I would've given myself:

-Persevere but learn to take a break from time to time.

-Finish what you set out to do or improve your goals.

-Do your best.

-Learn how to say no and don't allow others to hurt you.

-Don't give anyone the power to steal your happiness away. The ability to be happy is within you and belongs only to you.

-Treat each and every one of your patients as very important people.

-Follow your dreams and let them drive you to fight and move forward.

-Live in the present; remember that today is a great day and yet tomorrow can always be better.

-Always begin your day with a smile on your face.

-End the day giving thanks for everything you experienced.

Luis Rodrigo Reynoso
(ETHIOPIA)

This is the chapter I had hoped to write after all this journey. I lack words and I have plenty of feelings to express what happened there.

Looking at the past makes us reflect on the way we see life and it is interesting to analyse those areas of opportunity in you, that you had no idea that they were there. And Ethiopia was for me that place of great catharsis.

It first made me realize that when you really want something, you dream it and you believe it, you create it. And the universe conspires to make it happen. Consciously and unconsciously, you are weaving it together and if you focus your attention to achieve it, it will happen.

After the trip that my wife I took to the north, I came across other signs of greed and coldness, as well as more warnings for us to leave the project. I really felt that things would not change. So, we decided that it was best if I quit.

That has been one of the most bitter experiences, but at the same time the most liberating of my life. I had never left a project unfinished, and I still had many plans for Ethiopia; leaving them unfinished made me question my ability and hurt my ego.

I wrote my resignation letter, trying to focus on the positive, trying to show my appreciation. But I could predict that there would be no more macchiatos and no more smiles from the director.

We began to explore the possibilities of anticipating our return to Mexico, but the costs were very high, and it was better to keep the existing reservation and travel through Africa for a month and a half, before the end of the stipulated stay by the visa.

Scraping through our savings, looking for deals, accessible destinations, and hostels, we decided to go to Madagascar. And there the magic happened. We let ourselves be carried away by the beauty of the song of the whales, the huge baobabs, the palm trees, the rituals ... And today we are the happy parents of one of the most magical beings in the universe: Apsara.

Today I am deeply grateful to life for each and every one of the lessons learned. Making the decision to emigrate to Ethiopia was one of the most challenging experiences I have had to live as a person, as a couple and as a professional.

Below I recapture some of the lessons that this period left ingrained in me.

Let go of everything.

Get out there without fear.

Act with passion.

Do not expect anything from anyone.

The words "thank you" comes from the heart, gratitude is a habit learned at home.

Saying no and abandoning a project is also a way to complete a mission.

Allow yourself to explore other universes.

Welfare breaks the bond of love and generates parasitism.

Listen to your heart, follow where it leads you. The best experiences will derive from it.

Appreciate air, water, and life.

Not all social programs are real. There is much justified cruelty in poverty.

Love, kindness, and generosity move the world. But do not forget that there is hatred and greed.

Another recommendations to my younger self, is also to be grateful for the experiences lived in Ethiopia, which have helped me to value each step, each breath, and the relationships that we made there. We met magical beings that even now continue to contribute to our existence, they make us laugh, love, grow and value every moment of our lives.

Seek out experiences that keep you thinking about how extraordinary life is and dreaming about what you can achieve. Sure, sometimes our mind is so unnecessarily complicated. Let us not ruin the moment by thinking about the future: enjoy the present, feel that you are alive, touch your heart, connect with it.

Thanks to all of those who directly or indirectly made this book possible. Thank you for allowing us to remember what we have experienced and giving us the opportunity to share it.

We all know that place, deep within us, where we dialogue with ourselves. Do not forget what you came for. The connections are receptive, and it is up to us to generate the appropriate neurotransmitters to connect and generate a wonderful synergy.

I would like to wrap this up by inviting all those who are waiting for a signal to start the journey, to take these words as a message of encouragement to embark on the adventure.

Take into account the words of Mark Twain. "20 years from now, you will not regret what you did, but what you did not dare to do."

And if I can offer something to you, count on me.

—In lak ech.[8]

Alejandra Rodríguez Romero
(UNITED STATES)

Many times, I've let my imagination run wild, pretending that I can take a trip to the past and avoid some unpleasant situations. After imagining various scenarios, and at the risk of sounding trite, I always remind myself that I am here and I am me because of all those experiences. Honestly, I wouldn't want to be anywhere else or do anything different than what I do. Still, there are some recommendations that could have helped young Ale to make her life easier and happier:

1. Only you can make yourself happy. Don't look for happiness in anyone else or you will be disappointed. You have everything it takes.

---

[8] Editor's Note: Greeting in Mayan that means "I am another you."

2. Never assume anything or try to read people's minds. That will only cause you worry and most of the time you'll be wrong.

3. Stay healthy physically and emotionally. Never stop moving or doing what makes you feel good.

4. Be grateful for everything you have every day of your life. Gratitude makes us humble and attracts positive things.

5. Hug and tell your loved ones that you love them, don't just assume they know.

6. You will go through very painful moments, and you'll think they'll be the end of you. They won't. That too shall pass, and you'll win every fight. Life's not always fair, but you have to move on. Time heals or soothes all wounds, give it a chance to work its magic. Be patient.

7. Don't worry too much about controlling everything and don't be so demanding with yourself. Do your part and let life take its course.

8. Don't let anyone tell you that what you're doing is not important, keep doing it with all your strength and love.

9. Life goes by in the blink of an eye. Enjoy it. Your family and friends were, are and will be your greatest treasures, so spend every moment you can by their side.

Jack Rubinstein

(UNITED STATES)

"If I am not for myself, who will be for me? If I am only for myself, what am I?"
-Hillel the Ancient

Rastafarians have a tradition of not referring to the other as "you." When referring to another person, they use the phrase "I and I." This expression can be a bit confusing at first and, seen from the outside, it might seem unwise, or just a quirky tradition from an odd religious group. However, this is the most important concept I could recommend my younger self.

In my transition from youth to adulthood, I was fortunate enough to wait for hours on end while my then girlfriend, and current wife, got ready for us to go out. I was always on time, but rather than get annoyed or upset, I made the most of the time in the extraordinary library my in-laws had in their living room. Over the years, I read Albert Einstein's biography and, one day, I received one of the most important lessons of my life thanks to the book *I and Thou,* by the philosopher Martin Buber. The title of the book refers to the two ways one can see one's neighbor: as *It,* or as *Thou.* In the first meaning, we link ourselves to the other from experience; not in a necessarily negative way but separating our lives from the life of the other. In the second meaning, we bond from relationship, recognizing not only the humanity of the other, but the shared humanity between all of us. This conceptualization seems simple but, like meditation and exercise, it can only be understood and applied through years of practice and concentration. Personally, I'm still a long way from achieving the mental clarity required to observe the *Thou* or the "I and I" of the other but, occasionally, I come close to that feeling, and it inspires me to keep searching.

In Mexico, when I was young, this concept was the opposite of what I experienced on a daily basis: I saw the world and people as alien to me. It wasn't until years later that I had a revelation. One day, stuck in traffic, the ideas of Buber and the Rastafarians made sense. There, amidst the noise of the horns, I realized that I was not stuck in traffic, I was part of it. And then, almost like a scene out of a movie, the cars were silent for a few seconds, the juggler at the traffic light looked me in the eye and smiled, the sky was blue.

Nowadays, I have more chances to experience those moments of clarity. Sometimes they come to me when I connect with a patient; others, when I suffer along my children during a difficult time in their lives and, occasionally, with my wife, when we understand each other without having to utter a single word. To my younger self, I would say: there is no "you."

Alberto Saltiel
(ISRAEL)

I'd love to get the chance to chat with my younger self, to be able to meet that first-grader who decided to become a doctor and thank him for making the best decision of his life. Without scaring him, I'd warn him he's got a long road ahead with many difficulties, but that, in the end, it will all be worthwhile.

If I came across teenage Alberto, I'd tell him how important it is to learn to study, concentrate, and know how to prioritize. I'd tell him to keep fighting for his dreams even when people don't believe in him; and that only he can show others that where there's a will, there's a way. I'd assure him than nothing and no one could ever stop him.

If I ran into myself in college, I'd say it won't be easy. I'd tell college Alberto he must strive and fight for his dreams, despite the many obstacles he'll encounter along the way. I'd also tell him that he should not plan so much, because life takes its own course, and it'll set the tone for us. I'd advise myself to be open to new opportunities and different experiences, to enjoy every moment and learn from it. I would assure myself that the road is long and winding, but it's beginning to take shape and now is the time to start defining details.

If I had the opportunity to send a letter to my past self, it'd go a bit like this:

> *Dear me,*
>
> *You are about to enter a life full of passion and learning. You chose the most beautiful profession in the world, one that will allow you to connect with people in a very special way. They will put all their trust in your hands. Don't lose it because you'll never gain it back. You will be a member of a select group of people with an immense and priceless tradition. You will protect life and help your neighbor unconditionally.*
>
> *Be patient. Don't bite off more than you can chew. Move slowly but surely. Learn to listen and analyze every advice you're given. Smile, even when the days are tough. Be persistent. Treat your mistakes like building blocks and use them to add steps to the ladder that'll take you to the top. Open the doors to new experiences. Remember that poor performance is usually due to poor preparation, not lack of talent. Remember there's always a helping hand nearby. Celebrate your triumphs, but also your failures.*

Concentrate: understand the problem before trying to fix it. Be curious. Be resilient. Worry about the people around you. Take care of your patients, but do not neglect yourself. There are no limits; follow your dreams. Treat others with the same respect you deserve. Sleep, rest. Don't punish yourself. While self-criticism is important, don't be so harsh on yourself. Enjoy the road. Doubt, question and don't accept things blindly. Your opinion is as valuable as any other. Have no regrets. If you make a decision, trust in it and believe it's the right one. If there's something that you cannot change, don't let it affect you, but if you can change it, do it, and don't let it stress you.

Learn to read between the lines because not everything is written. Be sensitive. Let your hunches warn you. Pay attention to your heart. Listen to your parents, "there is no substitute for experience".

Dear me, thank you for this trip, thank you for bringing me here. I'm proud of you!

Luana Sandoval Castillo
(SPAIN, DENMARK)

10- Advice to my younger self

- Choose happiness.
- Study. Be up to date about everything that surrounds you.
- Do yourself a favor, learn to be on time
- Prioritize.
- Be curious, allow yourself to be surprised by life, if something doesn't add up, follow through on your doubts and your different assessments

- Keep dedicating time to yourself. Breathe, travel and savor.
- Sometimes, mum's the word. Shhh!
- Continue to cultivate your network of friends. You'll need it in the future.
- Strive to take care of your body, you only have one and it will thank you for the care over the years. Don't go down the easy road.
- If your heart tells you to, don't be afraid to let your voice be heard.
- Set new challenges and fight for them.
- To quote a good friend: Always start with what you don't want to do.
- Make your voice heard, you will not regret doing the right thing.
- Don't let yourself be left with the feeling of "what if".
- Don't worry about love, it will come. The pain will pass, and the scars will heal.
- Enjoy. Squeeze joy from every second invested in the things that make you happy and use sadness as a learning tool.

Ilan Shapiro
(UNITED STATES)

Hi Ilan,

Technology has come a long way and I want to send us this message with a list of actions that we need to keep doing.

Make your voice heard. All my life, you've been wrongly neutral. For fear of confrontation, you're not assertive nor protect your opinions. You must have more confidence in your own voice.

You're a sensitive being, you appreciate the delicacy and subtlety of change. When you notice it, give that new adventure all you got, because we don't know what the world has in store for us, but you will feel better betting on what you want. Mistakes are medals of maturity and are necessary to travel to the place where you want to be.

Scars are trophies that inspire you to move forward. The key in life is getting back up after falling many times. Don't stop moving.

Remember to be kind. Many times, you've thought that turning the other cheek is a sign of weakness. It's actually the opposite. Being able to hit back and deciding not to do will exhaust your attacker, and the pain will make you wiser and resilient.

Continue to care for the community. Reach out to the most vulnerable people and be there for them. It is not just about helping but showing a little empathy. There's no way you're ever giving this up.

Don't take things so seriously. Worry about what's important and put aside the relationships and activities that do not bring you anything.

Keep opening doors and keep loving with passion. Don't let small potholes stop you; you will reach your goal happier.

Remember that the only constant in life is change.

René Sotelo
(United States)

In short, experience is the best companion to achieve progress and make the best decisions along the way. Everything gained through experience, the lessons learned, are part of what I would tell my young self to continue to develop with even more strength and passion.

To that René Sotelo about to graduate from medical school, I'd say:

1. Learn more than two languages; communicating in different languages will open doors for you with greater ease. Master English as your mother tongue.

2. Be proficient in epidemiology and statistics. These are tools that will allow you, on the one hand, to interpret scientific studies with mastery; and on the other, to manage collecting scientific data in an optimal way. This will be the basis for writing articles, book chapters and scientific papers. Don't forget, this is a discipline perfected through practice.

3. Become an expert in the use of new technologies, hardware, and software, which are increasingly becoming an extension of medicine. I started writing and developing medical records in physical format, now I work digitally.

4. Don't let it be enough for you to communicate adequately and make yourself understood by patients. Worry about comprehending and getting to know more cultures that will impact your view on health and the way you'll help the patients you'll meet around the world.

5. You can't possibly be acquainted with all there is to know about medicine or be up to date in everything. Identify and choose a very specific area in which you want to be an expert, that you want to deepen by conducting research, documenting yourself and leaving contributions. Developing and advancing in the academic expansion of an area will allow you to leave

a legacy, something humanity can profit from. Recognize a field in which others, because it's complicated or infrequent, do not want to venture, and learn how to approach it, how to study it. Those cases will later be sent to you, turning you into a reference in that pathology and, over the years, into an expert.

6. No one's born knowing everything. Arriving implies walking the path, making the journey. And on that journey, mistakes are made. We're only human, it can happen, but if it does, it should not be because you have not studied enough or paid attention to every single detail. Think and review the whole process, evaluate the possible scenarios and complications so that, if something inopportune happens, it'll only take place a few times. If you do that, you'll come out stronger than ever. Always keep in mind that medical judgment comes with age. Focus on cultivating it.

7. Develop a relationship with your patients, listen to them, ask them questions, talk to them beyond their ailments. Get to know the human being behind them, their families. That'll contribute to your focus and effort to cure their disease, but it will also nurture your soul.

8. The ethics and honesty which characterize the way you practice medicine is learned at home, it stems from your family, and those same principles will guide your life. I wish you success in this wonderful profession and life career, which goes by faster than you could ever imagine.

Karla Uribe

(UNITED STATES)

I once heard someone say: "If I were twenty years old again and knew what I know now". That phrase left an imprint on me. I believe that, had I known what I know now, I would have done some things differently. Today, I am grateful to have the opportunity to address my version of the past and share with you my experiences of the past 43 years.

Dear Karla:

- I am proud of that little human being who, against all odds, clung to life. If you survived the circumstances that surrounded your birth, you can overcome anything. Don't forget that.

- People give only as much as they're able to give. So, take things from whom they come from, don't take anything personally, and surround yourself only with people who bring you good things. Life will teach you little by little to choose your friends well. Take care of them.

- Trust yourself, follow your heart, and trust your instincts. You are brave, resilient, and very capable. Don't let anyone else's opinion define who you are. The decisions you make should respond only to your principles, convictions, and priorities. Be true to yourself. Live for you.

- Nothing lasts forever, so enjoy the good times to the fullest and, when you are going through a rough patch, think that this too shall pass.

- You have the right to be wrong. When you make a mistake, reflect on it, and learn the lesson. Then, forgive yourself and move on. Guilt is a heavy burden to carry, so don't. Set yourself free.

- "Mom" is your most important title. Nowhere is your time worth more than with your children, and they are your greatest contribution to the world. Enjoy them and be proud of the work you have done with them.

- Don't give up on your dreams, it's never too late to start over and it's not over until it's over.

A loving hug,

Karla Uribe

Jeannette Uribe
(UNITED STATES)

Despite being where I want to be, fulfilling my dream, the road has not been easy, and some decisions I've made have added extra complications. However, they left me with great teachings, life lessons, and valuable experiences. Every single one of them have made me who I am today. It's illogical to think that my children, or you who are reading this, will not make mistakes, because it's part of life. However, with the help of my story, at least you can avoid the ones I made. And, even if you do, you can be certain that tomorrow will be another day.

The adaptation process for us immigrants is tough. We must endure cultural shocks, the feeling of separation, the financial struggles. I would advise that, if you have the option to choose where to migrate to, go somewhere with a robust Hispanic community, somewhere with childhood or family friends so the first few years are not such an uphill battle. For most Hispanics, family is our sanctuary and, even though we may fly off to pursue our dreams, we always return to where we belong.

If you're fortunate enough to have a supportive partner, half of your problems are already solved. Treasure that because that's where you'll find strength and comfort. My only advice is to keep each other in mind when making plans. If a problem arises, don't argue right then, or in front of your children, but don't go to bed or to work without fixing things, because you never know if you'll see each other again.

Nowadays, it's essential to know the basics about how money works. If you live in the States, it's important to have good credit, a retirement account, invest in the stock market, do your own taxes. Educating children on how to manage their money and how to save for a rainy day is absolutely necessary. If you have a credit card and know how to keep it with a zero balance at the end of the month, you can add your child as an authorized user without them knowing (it's up to you) and, when they're of age, they'll have already established some credit history.

When it comes to book-keeping and investing, there are many guides, websites, and podcasts whose sole objective is to guide you so you make the wisest choice possible. Regardless of our salary, what we have to do is basically spend less than we earn and get rid of the idea of wanting to impress someone by the way we dress or the car we drive. For example, here's a mistake we made: We had a humble salary, but we had been able to save enough to buy a decent car. Our minivan was quite old, it had more than 100K miles and a second engine that had cost us a little more than 1000 dollars, but it worked very well even in the snow. We went to a dealership, saw a truck we liked and, just like that, we kissed our savings goodbye. We also signed a five-year contract to pay for it with an interest rate of 2.4%, which we thought wasn't too bad. At that time, I saw things another way. We had never bought a new car, and everything seemed great: its smell, how clean it was, the color, everything was perfect. My husband still believes that nothing compares to a new car because you can be sure it won't break down and leave you stranded in the middle of the highway. I have a different point of view. If I still had the money I gave as a down payment, I could've bought a decent used car, and I would have invested all those payments of more than 500 dollars a month for 5 years with a possible annual growth of at least 5% (maybe even 8%). However, at the time I had no idea that something like that could be done and, to be honest, buying a new car felt wonderful.

Professionally speaking, my main advice for foreign medical students is this: if you want to practice medicine in the United States, start preparing now. Register with the ECFMG, take the exams (USMLE), and look for rotations during your free time. The best thing is to take the exams while you're in school, because they're about the core subjects. Be careful about doing residency in your home country. While it provided me with an invaluable experience that I would not trade for anything, it automatically excluded me from many programs because more than five years had passed since I was out of medical school. If you are already in residency or you finished it, like I did, the process isn't impossible either. Do what you have to do, so you won't be left wondering what could've been. Try it!

Biography

Book Coordinators

Sandra López-León (Israel, the Netherlands, Spain, United States) @sandralopezleon

Sandra López León has lived in Mexico, Israel, the Netherlands, and Spain. She currently lives in New York, USA, where she works in genetic and neuropsychiatric drug development. She is also Adjunct faculty at Rutgers University in New Jersey. She studied medicine at the Universidad Anáhuac México Norte, in Mexico City. She completed the rotating medical internship at Hadassah Hospital in Jerusalem, and she has a DSc and PhD in epidemiology and genetics, awarded by the Erasmus University of Rotterdam, in the Netherlands. In 2014, the U.S. government recognized her as an outstanding researcher for her work focused on identifying genes associated with neuropsychiatric diseases. She has published more than 60 scientific papers and wrote the book *Toma mi mano y vuela conmigo* (Take my hand and fly with me). Sandra is also the coordinator and author of the books *Doctoras con alas* and *Doctores con alas* a compilation of Mexican doctors living in different countries around the world.

Ilan Shapiro (United States) @Dr_Shaps

Ilan Shapiro studied medicine at the Anahuac University (Mexico), followed by a specialty in Pediatrics at Mount Sinai Hospital in Chicago (United States). He has an MBA with a specialty in Health from UA. He has lived in Mexico, Israel, and the United States, where he currently resides. He began as an advisor to the Secretariat of Health assigned to the World Health Organization and has done community service as a physician in Chicago and Fort Myers, Florida. As part of his professional career, he has been involved in mass media to translate specialized medical language into an understandable source of information that the community can use to make decisions about their health. His passion for creating binational bridges to improve the quality of life using technology and social media has led to the creation of multiple start-ups. He can be reached through his website: DrShaps.com and

Talia Wegman (United States) @taliawegman

Talia Wegman was born and raised in Mexico City. She studied medicine at UNAM, she has a PhD in genetics and is board certified as a clinical geneticist. She was a postdoctoral fellow at the National Cancer Institute in Maryland, USA. Now, she is a researcher and works with families with hereditary cancer.

Authors

Patricia Bautista Rivera (United States)

Patricia Bautista was born in Mexico City. She studied at the Faculty of Medicine of the Ciudad Universitaria (UNAM). She specialized in medical pediatrics at the National Institute of Pediatrics, where she also studied pediatric allergy. She emigrated to Kentucky, accompanying her husband, who pursued medical specialization studies. In the United States, she became a mother and dedicated herself to caring for her children. In 2018, she obtained a master's degree in Public Health with concentration in Health Promotion from the University of Louisville. She worked on the evaluation team for the Compassionate Schools Project at the Curry School of Education, at the University of Virginia. Patricia currently works as the Health Empowerment program Coordinator for La Casita Center, a Latino-led non-profit organization serving the socially disadvantaged Spanish-speaking migrant population of Louisville, Kentucky.

Edmundo Erazo (the Netherlands)

Edmundo Erazo lived most of his life in Mexico City; however, in 2017, he moved to Rotterdam and then to the city of Maastricht. He is a surgeon who graduated from the Mexican School of Medicine of the La Salle University and is a specialist in internal medicine. He completed his master's degree in clinical research at the Netherlands Institute for Health Sciences at the Erasmus University in Rotterdam. He is currently working in diabetes and metabolism at the University of Maastricht. Music, reading, travelling, and his family are his greatest inspiration.

Rafael G. Magaña (England, United States) @Maganaplasticsurgery

Rafael Magaña is a plastic surgeon. He currently practices privately in the states of New York and Connecticut. He began his career as a special effects' artist for the film industry. His interest in the plastic arts and his love for medicine led him to specialize in various areas of reconstructive and cosmetic surgery. After completing two residencies and three specialties, he focused primarily on breast reconstruction and reconstructive craniofacial surgery. Much of his practice is devoted to cosmetic surgery. In his spare time, he works as part of a surgical team to treat patients with cleft lip and palate in Southeast Asia. He is part of the clinical teaching faculty for medical students and surgical residents at three hospitals. His love for cinema has led him to be a consultant for film projects and to be in contact with artists and special effects in Hollywood, California.

Nissin Nahmias (United States) http://www.sbhny.org/blog/sbh-to-offer-bariatric-surgery/

Nissin Nahmias is the director in charge of bariatric and minimally invasive surgery of the Department of Surgery at Saint Barnabas Health System Hospital (SBH) in New York. He is an associate professor of surgery at the City University of New York (CUNY) medical school and director of the surgery rotation of CUNY and NYIT. Born in Mexico City, he attended the Anáhuac University School of Medicine, where he graduated with honors. He completed his training after finishing a general surgery residency at the Albert Einstein Healthcare Network in Philadelphia and is a subspecialist in advanced laparoscopic and bariatric surgery at Virginia Commonwealth University/Medical

College of Virginia. He holds a diploma from the American Board of Surgery and is a member of the American College of Surgeons and the American Society for Metabolic and Bariatric Surgery. His scientific work includes five publications, two book chapters, and more than fifteen talks in national and international conferences.

Susana Ramírez Romero (Spain)

Susana Ramírez was born on August 20th, in Puebla, Mexico. In 2000, she obtained her medical degree as a medical surgeon from the Universidad Popular Autónoma del Estado de Puebla. In 2001, she entered the specialty of Pediatrics at the CMNSXXI Hospital. Subsequently, she specialized in Pediatric Dermatology at the HIM Federico Gómez. In 2009, she obtained the degree with honorable mention of Master in Clinical Research from the Universidad Autónoma del Estado de México (UAEM). In 2011 she moved to Barcelona, where she currently lives and works.

Luis Rodrigo Reynoso (Ethiopia) @doctorreynoso

He is originally from Aguascalientes and develops his professional practice in Tulum, Quintana Roo. He is a doctor graduated from the Autonomous University of Aguascalientes, general surgeon and laparoscospist from the Christus Muguerza Hospital; and aesthetic and reconstructive plastic surgeon graduated from the Jalisco Institute of Reconstructive Surgery.

Alejandra Rodríguez Romero (United States) @schatzeale9

Alejandra Rodríguez Romero was born in Hermosillo, Sonora (Mexico) on May 11, 1984. She's the daughter of two doctors, which led her to develop a passion for medicine that made her begin her studies at the Faculty of Medicine of the Autonomous University of Guadalajara in 2002, getting her degree as a surgeon in 2008. She emigrated to the United States in 2009 and began the process for the revalidation of her degree. In 2012, she obtained her certificate by passing the exams required by the ECFMG (Educational Commission For Foreign Medical Graduates). She currently lives in Tucson, Arizona, where she is a full-time mother and wife with plans to resume her professional life in the future.

Jack Rubinstein (United States) @theperfectdose

Jack Rubinstein studied medicine at the Universidad Anáhuac. In 2002, he emigrated to train in Pennsylvania and Michigan, United States. He is a specialist in internal medicine and cardiovascular diseases, an associate professor at the University of Cincinnati, a researcher, and an inventor. He's married and has three children. He speaks four languages and is a mediocre polo player.

Alberto Saltiel (Israel) @VascularQx

Alberto Saltiel was born in Mexico City in 1986. He studied at the American School Foundation from which he graduated in 2004. He received his medical degree from the Anáhuac University México Norte and, in 2013, he moved to Israel where he applied for residency in vascular surgery. He was appointed chief resident during his final year.

He now lives in Tel Aviv, Israel, with his partner and children. He is currently in his last year of residency at the Tel Aviv Sourasky Medical Centre Hospital. Besides medicine, he is passionate about baseball, American football, cycling, music, boxing, whiskey, and wine.

Luana Sandoval Castillo (Spain, Denmark)

Luana Sandoval Castillo was born in Mexico, where she lived until she was twenty-five years old. She moved to Barcelona to do her specialty in cardiology. After graduating from UNAM, she received a scholarship to pursue a master's degree in Medical Sciences. In 2010, she did her specialty in geriatrics, where she was a resident representative with the Catalan Society. In 2015, she moved to Copenhagen. After a course in medical Danish, she started working in the area of orthopedic surgery at Bispebjerg Hospital. Ten months later, she moved up to the position of attached physician. She is a member of the Nal. Quality team for the optimization of hip fractures.

René Sotelo (United States) @doctorsotelo www.doctorsotelo.com

Dr. Rene Sotelo is a pioneer and international leader in robotic and laparoscopic surgery, with more than 20 years of experience using these techniques to treat both urologic cancers and benign conditions. He joined the USC Institute of Urology in 2015, and was recently appointed to the position of Medical Director of the International Medicine Department of USC, to lead initiatives both regionally and internationally. He is a distinguished researcher, having published more than 60 journal articles, 28 book chapters, and 3 text books. For his outstanding work, Dr. Sotelo has received 18 international awards from scientific and governmental associations.

Karla Uribe (United States) @karlauribem

Karla Uribe was born in the city of Guadalajara (Mexico) in 1978. Two years later, her family moved to Mexico City, where she lived since she was a child. She completed her professional studies at the Faculty of Medicine of the National Autonomous University of Mexico in Ciudad Universitaria, receiving the degree of Medical Surgeon in 2002. Subsequently, she completed her residency in otolaryngology and was certified by the Mexican Board of Otolaryngology in 2007. That same year she married, moved to South Texas, and settled with her new family in McAllen. She has been a full-time mom since 2008.

Jeannette Uribe (United States) @jeannettemd_boysmom

 Jeannette Uribe is originally from the state of Hidalgo. At 22 years old, she graduated as a surgeon from the Universidad Autónoma del Estado de Hidalgo. Passionate about Obstetrics and Gynecology, she completed her specialty at the University of Guanajuato-IMSS UMAE 48, in León. She emigrated to Michigan, USA, where she worked as a phlebotomist at Bronson Hospital in Battle Creek. Currently, she's in her third year of residency in the specialty of OB/GYN at BronxCare Hospital in New York City. Jeannette has been happily married for 16 years and is a mother of two. She enjoys spending her free time with her family, and is passionate about music, dancing, soccer, running, boxing, reading, cloudy afternoons and the smell of coffee.

CPSIA information can be obtained
at www.ICGtesting.com
Printed in the USA
LVHW051326050422
715338LV00002B/72

9 781506 539874